AUDITING
& EDP

AUDITING & EDP

BY GORDON B. DAVIS, CPA, PhD

PUBLISHED BY THE AMERICAN INSTITUTE OF CERTIFIED PUBLIC ACCOUNTANTS NEW YORK

TABLE OF CONTENTS

3. DOCUMENTATION OF THE DATA PROCESSING SYSTEM

4. HARDWARE FEATURES FOR CONTROL OVER EQUIPMENT MALFUNCTIONS

5. CONTROL OVER INPUT AND OUTPUT

6. PROGRAMMED CONTROL OVER PROCESSING

10. AUDITING A COMPUTER SYSTEM WITHOUT USING THE COMPUTER

11. USING THE COMPUTER TO TEST THE DATA PROCESSING SYSTEM

12. USING THE COMPUTER TO TEST THE RECORDS PRODUCED BY A COMPUTER SYSTEM

13. AUDITING ADVANCED DATA PROCESSING SYSTEMS

14. AUDITING DATA PROCESSING PERFORMED BY COMPUTER SERVICE CENTERS

15. THE TRAINING OF THE CPA FOR AUDITING EDP

APPENDIX A—AN OVERVIEW OF COMPUTER DATA PROCESSING

APPENDIX A (continued)

APPENDIX B—AN EXAMPLE OF DOCUMENTATION

APPENDIX C—STANDARD FLOWCHART SYMBOLS FOR INFORMATION PROCESSING

APPENDIX D—GLOSSARY

APPENDIX E—QUESTIONNAIRE FOR EVALUATION OF INTERNAL CONTROL IN ELECTRONIC DATA PROCESSING

TABLES AND FIGURES

CHAPTER 4

CHAPTER 5

CHAPTER 6

CHAPTER 7

CHAPTER 8

CHAPTER 9

CHAPTER 10

CHAPTER 11

CHAPTER 12

CHAPTER 13

CHAPTER 15

APPENDIX A

APPENDIX C

APPENDIX E

PREFACE

THIS PUBLICATION is the result of the efforts of a special Auditing EDP Task Force of Institute members with broad experience in auditing EDP, appointed by former AICPA President Robert M. Trueblood in March of 1966. The members of the task force were:

Donald L. Adams
Kenneth G. Cadematori
Gordon B. Davis
Donald R. Marvin
John J. O'Donnell
W. Thomas Porter, Jr.
Kenneth W. Stringer
H. George Trentin

Professor Gordon B. Davis, on leave from the University of Minnesota as computer consultant to the AICPA, acted as chairman of the task force and had primary responsibility for directing the work of the group, drafting material and editing and revising the text.

The book has the following purposes:

1. To guide CPAs in auditing business enterprises which use computers for record keeping

2. To provide a starting point for building a consensus of expert opinion on auditing practices for examining such companies

3. To suggest the utility and applicability of different auditing methods where experience is still lacking

4. To provide source materials for training and informational purposes

Each member of the task force prepared drafts of selected chapters assigned to him. These drafts were revised after review and discussion of their contents by the entire task force. When the task force had reached general agreement on the overall text, exposure copies of the proposed publication were provided to selected individuals for review. A final revision was prepared, taking into consideration the comments and recommendations received from this selected group. The text therefore reflects the work of Professor Davis and the special task force of eight CPAs, as well as the review and comments of almost 100 individuals in public practice and industry.

The book, after an introductory chapter, is organized into three major sections, with appendices at the end.

The first section, Chapters 2 through 7, discusses typical procedures and preferred practices utilized in the organization, administration and control of data processing. It is designed to assist the CPA in his review of the operation and management of the data processing system. This section describes the practices and procedures a company should follow to provide proper management and control of its computer operations. It provides some of the background which is ordinarily required by the independent auditor to enable him to competently judge the adequacy of a data processing system and to understand and utilize an EDP system review questionnaire, as illustrated in Appendix E.

The second section, Chapters 8 through 12, discusses specific audit procedures—evaluating internal control, evaluating the audit trail, performing audit tests without using the computer, using the computer to test the system, and using the computer to test the records. It describes the criteria which aid in deciding which auditing approach is appropriate in the circumstances and provides information for evaluating the usefulness of various methods.

The third section, Chapters 13 through 15, deals with problems arising from integrated systems, service centers and time sharing and discusses the training requirements for the CPA who audits business entities using EDP.

The appendices provide supplementary material. Appendix A, "An Overview of Computer Data Processing," is included as a review of the basic elements, concepts and terminology of computer data processing. It is intended to assist the auditor who needs a "referesher" review. Appendix B, "Standard Flowchart Symbols for Information Processing," describes the recommended ANSI standard flowchart symbols and their use. Appendix C, "An Example of Documentation," serves as an illustration of the principles covered in Appendix A and as a simple example of preferred practices in documentation, as described in Chapter 3. Appendix D, "Glossary of EDP Terms," includes definitions of all the computer data processing terms used in the book. Appendix E, "Questionnaire for Evaluation of Internal Control in Electronic Data Processing," is a sample of an internal review questionnaire. It is arranged for ease in referring to the chapter material which provides background for the questions.

It is suggested that the CPA who plans to use this report as a guide in auditing EDP should carefully read the entire text before concentrating on any one section. This procedure will provide him with an overall background for conducting an examination and will prevent him from taking information out of context.

The publication of this book completes one aspect of the study of auditing and EDP. There will be continuing investigation of the impact on auditing of new developments in hardware, software and systems.

This book is not intended to represent the establishment of auditing standards and procedures for EDP. However, it does contain the best current thinking of experienced members of the profession as to the most appropriate practices in this area.

JOE R. FRITZEMEYER, *Director, Technical Services Division*

CHAPTER 1

THE AUDITOR AND THE COMPUTER

THE CERTIFIED PUBLIC ACCOUNTANT may perform many functions related to data processing—design of data processing systems, furnishing of data processing services, consultation on system design and auditing. This report is directed solely at his function as independent auditor of organizations with computer-based data processing systems.

The impact of the computer on data processing

The computer is one of the most important technological developments of the twentieth century. Its uses and capabilities have been described in both popular and technical publications, so that it is not necessary to document the importance of computers in this report. The impact of computers on public accounting can be appreciated by noting the dramatic growth in numbers of computer installations for the period 1956-1967 (Figure 1-1, page 2). Computer installation estimates from different sources vary by about 20%, depending on the treatment of small computer-like equipment, but the figures show a clear trend in the use of computers. The impact of computers has been predicted for several years; the major effects have been in the last few years. Although the first commercially available computer was installed in 1951 and the first business installation was in 1954, the popular business-oriented computers can be dated from the early 1960's. Over half of the computers in place in mid-1967 had been installed in the preceding three years. The outlook was for the number of computer installations to double in the succeeding 3 to 4 years. The decreasing cost of computer equipment plus the development, now in embryonic stages, of computer sharing arrangements clearly portend computer use by an increasing number of organizations and an involvement with computer-based records by more and more CPA firms.

The computer has caused significant changes in business information systems, expanding both scope and operation. The first computer data processing systems tended merely to computerize existing clerical functions. Soon, however, systems embracing larger areas of the business and incorporating decision-oriented analytical techniques not practicable in clerical systems began to be implemented. Thus, although many computer data processing systems merely automate the prior manual processes, the trend is plainly toward higher level information systems. The auditor, therefore, frequently faces not only a computer but new system concepts as well.

An overview of auditing for EDP systems

The impact that computers have had on the audit process varies among clients and is dependent to a great extent on the level of complexity of the computer data processing system. A simple system may so resemble the predecessor card or manual system that the auditor has very little difficulty in adapting his audit procedure to the computerized system. A more complex computer-based system may require considerable computer expertise on the part of the auditor for understanding the system he is evaluating and planning his audit tests.

It is logical to suppose that auditing standards, which have been established in the light of the primary objective of auditing, are independent of the personnel or machines used to process and maintain the accounting and financial records. The auditing standards must be broadly based in order to have applicability to a wide range of audit situations. However, they still relate specifically to each audit examination since they refer to an acceptable level of quality which must be maintained by the

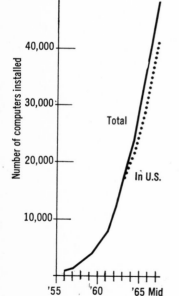

FIGURE 1-1. Number of computers installed by U.S.-based companies from 1956 to 1967

auditor in the selection and application of appropriate auditing procedures. Hence, auditing standards are also guides to procedures.

Auditing procedures are affected by the presence of a computer, especially when the system is complex. In describing these effects it will be useful to structure the discussion in terms of the major phases of an audit examination: (1) the evaluation of the system of internal control and (2) the evaluation of the records produced by the data processing system.

If he is to deal effectively with the computer, the auditor should have computer knowledge and capability at two levels: (1) a knowledge of computers and computer-based data processing sufficient to review adequately the internal control of the system he is auditing, to conduct proper tests of the system and to evaluate the quality of the records, and (2) an ability to use the computer itself in the tests, if necessary or desirable. Whether or not the computer should be used in performing audit tests depends on the applicability, effectiveness and cost of the alternatives for each particular situation.

EDP does not lessen in any way the need for an evaluation of the system of internal control. On the contrary, it appears that increased emphasis must be given in the review of internal control to ascertain that it is effective. The need for this emphasis has been brought about by the centralization and the concentration of data processing in an EDP system and the appearance of new controls that must be evaluated.

The evaluation of internal control rests on a review of the system to obtain a knowledge of how it is purported to operate and on an accumulation of evidence which demonstrates how it actually does operate. The manner in which the auditor seeks the necessary information and records it in his working papers is largely a matter of individual preference. Techniques used for this purpose include questionnaires, checklists, flowcharts and narrative memoranda.

Having obtained information on the system, the auditor must next obtain evidence to determine the existence and effectiveness of the client's processing procedures and controls. This is done by making tests of the performance of specific control procedures. The nature and availability of evidence and the types of tests to be performed depend somewhat upon the complexity of the system design and upon the audit trail found in the electronic system being audited. In some cases, the evaluation of the operation of the data processing system may emphasize direct testing of the processing programs; in other cases, the evaluation may rely largely on tests using printed output from the computer processing runs.

Evaluating Records Produced by the System

In addition to evaluating the system of data processing and control, the auditor must evaluate the reasonableness of those records produced by the system which relate to the existence and proper valuation of assets, liabilities, equities and transactions. Historically, the records evaluated have consisted of printed reports, listings, documents and business papers—all of which were readable by the auditor. To the extent that such records are available in electronic systems, the auditor may use traditional auditing techniques. However, part of the output from EDP systems is very frequently in machine-readable forms such as cards, tapes and disks. Although output in this form can always be converted to readable printout, it presents the auditor with an opportunity to use the computer to analyze the records.

Computer audit programs can assist in the performance of auditing procedures such as: (1) selection of exceptional transactions and accounts for examination, (2) comparison of data for correctness and consistency, (3) checking of information obtained directly by the auditor with company records, (4) performance of arithmetic and clerical functions, and (5) preparation of confirmations. In using the computer to analyze machine-readable records, the auditor may either design and develop specific computer programs for each client and application or use generalized audit routines.

The effect of the computer on data processing controls

It is incorrect, from an audit standpoint, to view the computer as a giant calculator. The installation of a computer introduces new control elements and causes changes in the form of traditional control procedures in the data processing system. These changes in controls may be classified as:

1. New controls necessary with the automation of processing.

2. Controls which substitute for those controls in manual systems that were based on human judgment and division of duties.

The auditor needs to understand the nature of these controls in order to properly evaluate and test the computer data processing system. The changes in data processing controls due to the computer are an important reason why the auditor cannot ignore the computer in his evaluation of internal control.

New controls are necessary because of mechanization. Their purpose is to detect and control errors arising from the use of EDP equipment and EDP processing methods. If these controls are absent, the system may be exposed to undue risk of error. If the omissions are deemed serious, the scope of audit procedures is influenced.

In a manual system, internal control relies upon such factors as human alertness, care, acceptance of responsibility and division of duties. Computer processing reduces the number of persons involved in data processing. Since the data processing activity is concentrated, many controls based on human judgment or division of duties are no longer available. However, for many checks, the computer program provides an alternative which substitutes for the judgment of humans engaged in processing. In most instances, the computer checks can be more extensive than those performed manually. The presence or absence in a computer-based system of controls such as these which substitute for human judgment or division of duties should influence the nature and extent of auditing procedures used in the circumstances.

The determination of the extent to which controls are embodied in the computer programs and the testing to determine if they are operative may utilize different techniques depending on the circumstances. One common method makes inferences about the program and the controls in it from an examination of inputs and outputs; the other method relies on a rather complete understanding and testing of the program itself.

It has been a common practice for an organization making changes in data processing methods to seek the help of its auditing firm in designing the changes or in reviewing proposed changes for adequacy of controls. This practice has also been followed by many organizations when implementing computer applications. The pre-implementation control review is recommended because of both the probable value of an outside review of control features and the contribution of such a review to the planning of future audit procedures.

In his review of the control features in a proposed application, the auditor can point out probable weaknesses in the controls and in provisions for audit trail and safeguarding files. Making these suggestions at the time the system is being designed will help prevent undetected errors, loss of data, loss of files and other serious conditions which affect not only the client's processing but also the ability of the auditor to conduct the audit.

A note on emphasis

It has been common in the recent literature of auditing to refer to two approaches to auditing computer-based systems—"auditing around the computer" and "auditing through the computer." These terms have been avoided in this report because they tend to be misleading. "Auditing around the computer" may imply to some that the auditor can ignore the computer and work around it. This is not true. The auditor should always consider the control framework in which the computer processing is carried out. In his tests of the operation of the system, he may choose to use computer printouts as the basis for audit tests rather than to test the computer program directly. For a test of the records produced by the computer system, the auditor may have the records printed out for manual review or he may make use of a computer routine to test them in their machine-readable form. In other words, he may use computer printouts in much the same way as he would use manually prepared records, or he may utilize the computer itself in performing audit steps. Consequently, this report distinguishes between auditing a computer system without using the computer and auditing a computer system using the computer.

The question of whether or not to use the computer in audit tests usually depends on the effectiveness and cost of the computer procedure versus the effectiveness and cost of the manual alternatives. This report does not favor one method over the other. The auditor should be capable of using the computer for audit tests when its use is advisable, just as he should be capable of testing without using the computer when its use is not advisable. Generally, it is not necessary or economical to use the computer to test simple data processing systems or to test files with small numbers of records. Audit tests of advanced systems or of files with large numbers of machine-readable records are more likely to require the use of the computer.

Meeting the challenge

Perhaps the major difficulty faced by auditing firms relative to audits of computer-based records is the staffing of audits with personnel adequately trained in computer methods. Relatively few auditors have received instruction in computer methods as part of their formal training, so the profession must provide substantial training for existing personnel in order to ensure an adequate number of auditors competent to conduct audits in an EDP environment.

If an audit involves a computer, the CPA must have sufficient competence in the methods and techniques of auditing EDP systems to enable him to conduct the audit properly. The proficiency requirement implied by this statement varies depending on the complexity of the system being audited. An audit of a company having a small, batch-oriented data processing installation requires less proficiency than an audit involving a complex, integrated computer system. Not all members of the audit team need be equally competent. In general, the audit of a computer-based system requires the auditor to possess a good basic understanding of computers and computer data processing methods. A specific understanding on the part of the auditor of computer facility organization, documentation, controls, safeguards and computer system audit techniques is also important. The approach followed by many firms is to have one or more members of the staff specialize in computer audit problems. Chapter 15 discusses the problem of training and suggests possible approaches.

Summary

Computers have been commercially available for over fifteen years, yet the recency of the major impact can be appreciated by noting that at mid-1967 over half of all computers had been installed in the preceding three years. The number was expected to double again in the succeeding three years. Although much has been written about the impact of computers on the auditor, many CPAs were just beginning to be affected.

This chapter provides an overview of the auditing of an organization using a computer for record-keeping. The auditor may not properly ignore the computer in the audit—first, because the computer requires its own set of controls related to automated procedures and, second, because many controls normally resulting from division of duties and human review and judgment are now concentrated in the computer programs. The auditor may use the computer in carrying out audit procedures but this is frequently optional, depending on the characteristics of the system and the cost and effectiveness of this alternative. The auditor should be capable of choosing and implementing the best method for each data processing application and each particular audit test.

CHAPTER 2

PREFERRED PRACTICES IN ORGANIZATION AND MANAGEMENT OF THE EDP FUNCTION

A DATA PROCESSING installation should be organized and managed by the same methods that have proved effective in other segments of the organization. There should be a plan of organization and clear assignments of responsibilities. This plan should, when feasible, include separation of duties to provide internal control. For management of operations there should be written procedures and standards of performance against which accomplishment may be measured. This chapter assumes a general knowledge of management principles so that the discussion can concentrate primarily on organizational features and operating procedures that are more or less unique to computer data processing. The explanation is divided into three major sections: plan of organization, typical organization charts and management of a computer installation.

Plan of organization

In data processing, as in other business operations, it is necessary to define individual responsibilities for all functions. To establish responsibility, job descriptions should be prepared for all data processing personnel. These descriptions should identify all job titles and clearly describe all job functions. Each employee

Assignment of
Responsibilities

9

should be given a copy of his job description and instructed in all factors related to his work assignment. Although titles vary among installations, the following abbreviated job descriptions cover the most common data processing positions:

TITLE	DESCRIPTION
Systems Analyst	Analyzes the requirements for information. Evaluates the existing system and designs new or improved data processing procedures. Outlines the system and prepares specifications which guide the programmer.
Programmer	Flowcharts the logic of the computer programs required by the overall system designed by the systems analyst. Codes the logic in the computer program language. Debugs the resulting program. Prepares documentation. (See Chapter 3 for documentation requirements.)
Computer Operator	Also called a console operator. Operates the computer according to the operating procedures for the installation and the detailed procedures for each program found in the Computer Operator Instructions. (See Chapter 3 for description of this manual.)
Unit Record Equipment Operator	Also called a tabulating equipment operator. Operates punched card equipment such as sorter, collator, reproducer, accounting machine, etc.
Keypunch Operator	Prepares data for machine processing by keypunching cards. Operates a card punch (also called a keypunch).

As will be seen from the sample organization charts, the functions of these positions may be combined or divided. In general, the systems analyst position requires the broadest background and highest qualifications. The programmer follows next in this hierarchy of qualifications with the computer operator requiring still less training and experience. The position of unit record equipment operator requires roughly the same level of training as that of computer operator in a relatively uncomplicated computer installation.

Separation of Duties

When a company establishes a data processing organization, proper recognition should be given to internal control. This section deals with that element of internal control obtained through the separation of duties. The same principle that calls for a separation of the functions of record keeping, operations or asset custody and internal auditing also applies to the separation of basic data processing functions.

DATA PROCESSING FUNCTION	POSITION
System analysis and design	Systems analyst
Programming	Programmer
Machine operation	Computer operator
Control	Control clerk or control group, internal auditor, etc.

Internal control is strengthened if these four functions are separate and distinct. This separation may also result in operational efficiencies because the four functions require differing levels of training and skill. It is usually satisfactory to combine the development activities of systems analysis and programming. These may be kept as separate jobs but combined organizationally under a single supervisor, or, in small installations, a single job may include both activities. In most cases it is not desirable to overlap development activities with machine operation, although this does occur in the very small installations.

A suitable plan of organization and the resulting division of duties is important because of the concentration of the data processing activity in a smaller number of people than would be required for a manual system. The small number of people and the high degree of mechanization expose the system to manipulation and fraud if a single person has both operational knowledge and easy access to procedures and programs at all levels. In one instance, for example, a former timekeeper was involved in both programming and machine operation. He was able to draw on his varied skills to manipulate payroll data in his favor without affecting the payroll control totals.

Another recent example of possible dangers from lack of division of duties occurred when a programmer for a company servicing a bank sometimes acted as an operator. One of the applications he had programmed was a listing of accounts which were overdrawn. While serving as computer operator he inserted a "patch" in the program to cause it to ignore overdrafts in his account when printing the overdraft report. He then proceeded to overdraw his account at the bank. The fraud was discovered when, because of a computer breakdown, the report was prepared manually.

The plan of organization and operating procedures should provide for a control function. The control function is divided into two types:

1. Processing control internal to data processing

2. Outside control

Internal processing control (data control, quality control, etc.) is a function of the data processing department and is concerned with monitoring the accuracy of processing and with ensuring that no data is lost or mishandled within the department during processing. For instance, if a detail transaction file is processed with a master file to produce an updated master file, the sum of the transaction file and the master should equal the total of the updated master. The person charged with the processing control is responsible for making or reviewing such a comparison. Control at the processing level is usually the responsibility of the data processing manager. A subordinate may be assigned control activities as a part-time or full-time assignment, depending on the volume of activity. If the assignment is not full-time, it is desirable to preserve a separation of duties and to avoid using a person who has systems, programming, or operator responsibilities (especially the latter).

Outside control can take several forms, but is basically concerned with an independent check of the functioning of the data processing department. This independent check can be performed by a user department. If the general ledger, for instance, is maintained through the computer, the accounting department may keep a control total of the debits and credits to be posted by the computer to the general ledger. The updated general ledger from the computer should show a total change equal to the accounting department debit and credit posting totals. Another form of outside control is an independent quality control evaluation of data processing's production. A separate group may be established for this purpose in a user department where the volume of data to be controlled is large. For example, one large corporation has a payroll processing control group responsible for evaluating the payroll data produced by the computer. This is done by performing various tests on the data totals and by using control amounts (explained in Chapter 5). The outside control function, as typified by the evaluation group, should be under the direction of accounting, finance, or some other function in a position to perform an independent and critical review of performance.

Typical organization charts

Three organization charts are presented here as illustrations of typical organization charts for small, medium and large computer installations. This classification corresponds roughly to the following monthly rental figures:

CLASSIFICATION	MONTHLY RENTAL
Small	Less than $5,000
Medium	$5,000 to $15,000
Large	Over $15,000

These organization charts do not show the location of computer data processing in the overall organization plan. Data processing can be under the control of one of several sections of a company, depending on the company. In most smaller organizations, data processing is the responsibility of the chief financial or accounting officer, such as the financial vice-president, the treasurer, or the controller. In many large organizations, the data processing system has been separated from the financial or accounting responsibility and the manager given a title such as Vice-President of Corporate Information Systems. The trend is to have a computer-based information system organized as a service center for the data processing needs of the entire organization. Acting in this service capacity and maintaining files used by many departments, data processing makes decisions which cross existing divisional or departmental lines of authority. Data processing personnel should, in such case, report to an executive who has authority to resolve conflicts that may arise among these divisions. This means that the executive in charge of data processing should be of the same rank as the heads of departments being served.

Figure 2-1 (page 14) shows an organization chart for a small

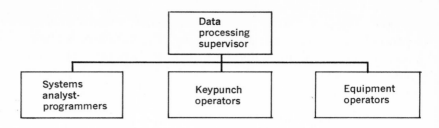

FIGURE 2-1. Organization chart for a small data processing installation (equipment rental less than $5,000 per month)

installation. Note that the systems analysis and programming functions have been combined. Whether or not the installation will require separate unit record equipment operators will depend on the type of configuration. There is a tendency in smaller installations to combine many card processing functions with the operation of the computer equipment.

Figure 2-2 (below) illustrates a medium-scale installation. Of interest is the separation of systems analysis from programming and the addition of an internal control clerk. In the expanded organization, there may also be opportunities for a hierarchy of supervision; for example, senior programmer and programmer.

Figure 2-3 (page 15) shows an organization chart for a fairly large installation, with a monthly equipment rental of over

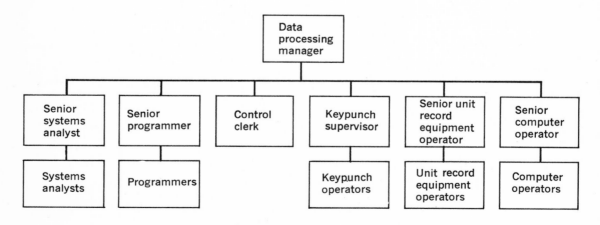

FIGURE 2-2. Organization chart for a medium-sized data processing installation (equipment rental between $5,000 and $15,000 per month)

$25,000. There is further specialization with systems analysts separated completely from programming. Programming includes a separate documentation librarian; there are separate data communications specialists; and operations has a separate position for a tape librarian responsible for custody of the magnetic tapes.

Management of a computer installation

The same management principles that apply to general business management also apply to data processing. However, since data processing is a relatively new discipline, the techniques for effective management control are still being developed. As so often happens in new fields, the personnel tend to feel that their work is creative and cannot be subjected to measurement or evaluation. For many years this feeling has prevailed in data processing, and management, not generally knowledgeable about EDP, has frequently failed to exercise adequate supervision.

As management and the other members of the business com-

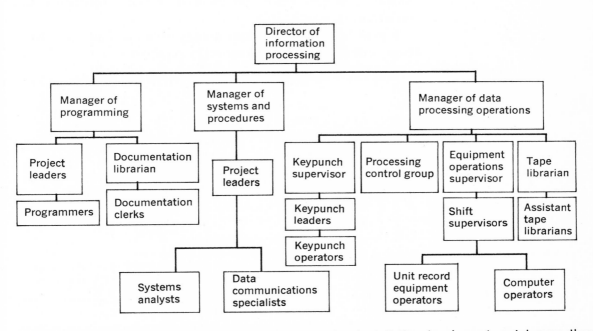

FIGURE 2-3. Organization chart for a large data processing installation (equipment rental more than $25,000 per month)

munity have become more knowledgeable in the computer field, effective control techniques have gradually begun to evolve. Various quantitative techniques have been used in performance evaluation of data processing activities. By using historical rating techniques, for example, yardsticks have been applied to the performances of analysts, programmers, operators and keypunchers.

The application of management principles to computer data processing operations typically results in the preparation and use of a systems and procedures manual which describes standard operating procedures. The contents of this manual cover the following topics:

1. Standard programming conventions and procedures

2. Standard operating procedures

3. Control procedures

4. Organization and personnel

As with systems and procedures manuals used in other areas, the manual is useful in training, supervision and evaluation of performance. The multitude of differing conventions in programming, documentation, operating, etc., leads to considerable confusion. The use of a manual setting forth standard procedures and conventions for the particular installation has proved to be an extremely valuable aid to management.

Standard Programming Conventions and Procedures

The major purpose of this section of a computer installation systems and procedures manual is to establish standard vocabulary, standard programming conventions, standard debugging procedures and standard documentation methods. The following brief summary of possible topics suggests the scope and purpose of the section:

TOPIC	EXPLANATION
Flowcharting conventions	These are the forms, symbols and conventions to be used in flowcharting. Generally, it is desirable for these conventions to agree with the standards defined by the American National Standards Institute (see Appendix B).
Decision table conventions	These conventions are used when preparing decision tables. This topic should include standard abbreviations for allowable condition entries.

TOPIC	EXPLANATION
Coding conventions	Standard names used by the installation, standard abbreviations and such conventions as the method to use in differentiating letters from look-alike numbers are included in this topic.
Standard glossary and standard abbreviations	Abbreviations are especially valuable for flowcharting. A standard list should be prepared and the use of non-standard alternatives should be prohibited. Any word without a standard abbreviation should be spelled out in full. The glossary should specify the meaning of special terms commonly used in the installation. Where there is confusion in the industry with respect to a term, the definition to be used by the installation should be included.
Standard programming techniques	Within an installation, it is a normal practice to develop standard techniques for performing particular computer operations common to many computer programs. For example, routines to clear storage, to print standard headings, or to calculate square roots may be used in hundreds of different programs. These routines can be inserted in a program as an independent package, thus avoiding the need to rewrite the same set of instructions every time they are required for a new program. These routines should be fully documented and subject to rigid rules in regard to their use within a program. The installation may set up special macro-instructions which are to be used for common operations such as accessing a record on a disk file. The "macro" is used to avoid the need for each programmer to rewrite the few program steps each time the operation is called for.
Debugging	The procedures to be followed in debugging include specifications for desk checking, program assembly, patching and approval procedures to be followed before a program is released. Desk checking (the process of reviewing the documentation and manually tracing the path of data through the program to see if the logic is sound) is a good practice before program assembly is attempted. Patching conventions specify the method of using and documenting patches (minor changes made directly in machine language and inserted in the machine language program). Since it is difficult for one programmer to understand patches made by another, an installation may specify that after a certain number of patches (say 3) the program must be re-assembled from a corrected symbolic deck.
Documentation	Documentation standards should be specified in full detail to avoid any possible misunder-

TOPIC	EXPLANATION
	standing. These standards are discussed in detail in Chapter 3.
Program changes	Every time a program is changed, the revised program should be tested and the revision should be reviewed. The procedures to be followed and the review and test functions to be performed should be clearly described. A change log should be maintained for each program. An entry should be made to record the nature, effective date and supervisory approval of the change.

Standard Operating Procedures

This section of the systems and procedures manual describes practices and procedures to be followed in the running of the processing equipment. The topics include specifications for machine operation, machine performance, scheduling, file retention, housekeeping, record keeping and emergency procedures.

TOPIC	EXPLANATION
Machine operation	Standard operating procedures for all computer and tabulating equipment are used to ensure that uniform techniques are employed. Such standards help to eliminate the poor operating techniques which individuals often develop on their own.
Machine performance	Timing standards for all computer and tabulating equipment should be specified. These standards are often based upon the equipment manufacturers' recommended allowances but modified to fit unusual circumstances or conditions within a particular installation or application. Operating procedural standards such as tape drive cleaning methods, program loading and other common operations should be outlined as operating instructions for personnel.
Scheduling	All computer operations should be scheduled on the basis of rules approved by management. Schedules should provide time required for reruns, assembly runs, program debugging and preventive maintenance.
File retention	File control and retention techniques as outlined in Chapter 7 are included here.
Housekeeping	This topic includes handling of files, use of supplies, storage of programs and procedures to keep the center neat and avoid loss or destruction of programs or data.

TOPIC	EXPLANATION
Record keeping	This involves procedures for recording utilization of equipment and personnel. Personnel should be required to record time on and time off the equipment for each job. These records should, if possible, be reconciled with elapsed-time clocks on the machine. The information provided by utilization records assists in evaluating personnel and equipment performance. An example of a simple time and record form is given in Figure 2-4, this page.
Emergency procedures	The manual should spell out plans and procedures for emergencies such as flood, fire, power failure, failure of communications, etc.

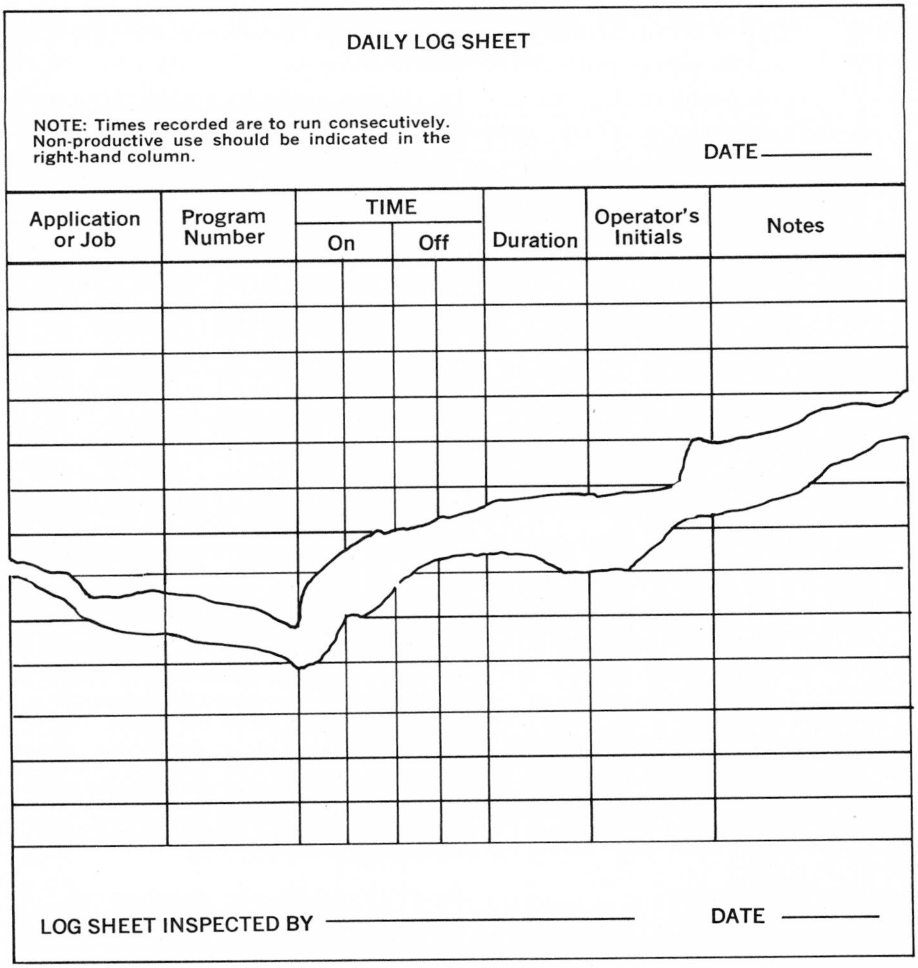

DAILY LOG SHEET

NOTE: Times recorded are to run consecutively. Non-productive use should be indicated in the right-hand column.

DATE _____

Application or Job	Program Number	TIME		Duration	Operator's Initials	Notes
		On	Off			

LOG SHEET INSPECTED BY _____ DATE _____

FIGURE 2-4. Daily computer log sheet

Control Procedures The activities of the control clerk or control group are specified through both the systems and procedures manual and the description of control activities found in the documentation of each computer application. In general, the control function will include the following duties:

1. Logging of input data and recording of control information

2. Recording of progress of work through the department

3. Reconciliation of computer controls with other control information

4. Supervision of distribution of output

5. Scrutiny of console logs and printed control information in accordance with control instructions

6. Liaison with users regarding errors and logging of correction requests and recording of corrections made

7. Scrutiny of error listings and maintenance of error log or error report

The work of the control section is evidenced by the maintenance of the logs, the signing or initialing of control documents and control reports.

Organization and Personnel The quality of the data processing is usually directly related to the quality of the personnel. Several of the equipment manufacturers as well as independent organizations have developed standard aptitude tests which can be used to evaluate prospective employees. Some companies ask programming and systems analysis candidates to solve a practice problem or write a short program. This can be a very effective and positive form of evaluation.

Personnel practices and methods of evaluation should be formalized and spelled out in detail in the systems and procedures manual. Every employee should know what is expected of him, what his own role is in the overall data processing function and how his performance will be measured.

Data processing operations are generally based on separate jobs or tasks. Personnel should be scheduled in all phases of their work. Programmers and analysts should be assigned to specific jobs, given job budgets and required to render periodic progress reports. Operators should be assigned to specific runs with specific equipment and required to report reasons for schedule deviation or slippage to the shift supervisor. Of course, the procedures will vary depending on the size and structure of the organization but the concept of scheduling is applicable for even a small organization. The scheduling of personnel should include accepted practices such as the rotation of operator duties so that responsibility for running a program is not continuously in the hands of one person and the requirement that personnel take vacations.

CHAPTER 3

DOCUMENTATION OF THE DATA PROCESSING SYSTEM

DOCUMENTATION CONSISTS of documents and records which describe the system and procedures for performing a data processing task. It is a means of communicating both the essential elements of the data processing system and the logic followed by the computer programs. Preparing documentation is a necessary, though frequently neglected, phase of computer data processing. Documentation can serve the following purposes:

1. Provide explanatory material necessary for a supervisory review of proposed systems and computer programs

2. Simplify program revision by providing full detail in support of each program

3. Provide the data necessary for answering inquiries regarding the operation of a computer program

4. Aid in instructing new personnel by providing background on previous programs and serving as a guideline for new programs

5. Provide operator with current operating instructions

6. Serve as one basis for an evaluation of internal control

In cases where documentation has not been maintained, some users have been involved in considerable extra expense when it has become necessary to modify a program. A change in withholding rates or the addition of a city income tax has, in some cases, necessitated a substantial amount of rewriting for payroll programs because documentation did not contain the information needed to make the required modification. An example of the danger inherent in faulty documentation occurred when an insurance company which had employed a very competent programmer did not enforce program documentation. Shortly after the programmer had left the company, the state insurance authority requested copies of all formulas used in computing agents' commissions. The commissions had been processed by the computer for several years and no one in the company knew the formulas which had been built into the program. To recreate the documentation, the company had to hire a consultant who worked for three months to build up the data by working backwards from a machine-language object deck.

This chapter describes a plan of documentation and briefly reviews the importance and usefulness of documentation to the auditor. While an individual installation may deviate in many details from it, the plan described provides a guide against which the auditor may measure the documentation performance of his client. A simple example of documentation is contained in Appendix B.

Summary of documentation

A data processing application, such as payroll, may include several separate processing tasks which are the basis for individual computer runs. Although separated to meet the requirements of the data processing system, the runs may be interconnected in that the output from one run may be the input for another run. For example, a payroll application described in Chapter 10 consists of 11 computer runs. The five which are used to prepare the payroll checks are listed here.

1. Card-to-tape for payroll detail

2. Sort payroll detail into employee number sequence

3. Validate data

4. Calculate payroll and update master file

5. Print payroll checks

The computer run is the basic unit on which documentation is based, but because of the interrelationship of computer runs an application overview which shows how the different runs are used is necessary for complete understanding of the runs. This application or system design specification describes the overall system. It may be prepared as a separate report or may be included in the different run documentations to which it applies.

Run documentation can take many different acceptable forms. This chapter will present a detailed outline of two common documentation manuals which fulfill basic requirements. These are the run manual and the computer operator instructions for the run.

The run manual is prepared by the systems analysts and/or the programmers. It contains a complete description of the program which is used for a data processing run. The sections of the run manual are generally the following:

1. Problem definition

2. System description

3. Program description

4. Operating instructions

5. Listing of controls

6. Acceptance record

Each of these sections will be described in this chapter.

The computer operator instructions, a reproduction of one section of the run manual, provide operating instructions for the machine room personnel. They may be filed separately or assembled in notebooks which contain the instructions for all runs. The relationship of the run manual to the computer operator instructions is shown in Figure 3-1 (this page). The computer operator instructions may also be known as the console run book.

The run manual is an important corporate record and should be safeguarded accordingly. For example, the manual should be given fireproof storage and should be returned to the files each night. For added protection against destruction or unauthorized changes, a control copy may be stored outside the data processing center. Ideally, access to copies of the manual should be restricted to systems and programming personnel. Machine operators do not require access to the run manual since all the information needed for proper machine operation is contained in the

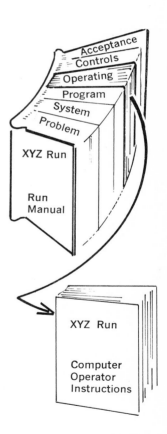

FIGURE 3-1. Relationship of computer operator instructions to run manual

25

computer operator instructions. Knowledgeable operators who have access to run manuals have an increased opportunity to make unauthorized changes in programs.

Run manual

The six basic sections of the run manual are discussed in detail. These cover the basic elements for adequate documentation. However, the auditor should recognize that individual differences can account for many variations in documentation.

Problem Definition
Section

The problem definition section is intended to provide a clear, logical and formal record of the problem to be solved. The individual elements in this section might be:

1. Title page

2. Table of contents

3. Project background

4. Project request

5. Problem statement

6. Minutes of meetings and copies of policy decisions relating to the job

The project background is a description of the reasons why the program was prepared and its role in the overall data processing system. This serves to place the program in perspective as it relates to other programs.

Those programs which are prepared in response to requests by user departments should be approved in advance by the data processing manager and the systems analyst. The approved request becomes a part of the documentation in case there is a discrepancy between the resulting program and the desired result. In some instances, a programmer may finish a program in accordance with a user's request only to find that the user has not defined the problem correctly.

A problem statement should be prepared in support of all new programs. This form is usually prepared by the systems analyst (if this function is separated from programming) and is the basic source of information concerning the purpose of the program.

The system description section supplements the problem statement by indicating the general outline of the new program and the related environment or system in which it operates. Although it may be brief, this description is valuable in explaining the program. This section contains the system flowcharts, the record layouts, the activity codes, and, if a control function is involved, the way it is to be handled.

A system flowchart indicates (1) the source and nature of all input, (2) machine, computer and manual operations and (3) the nature and disposition of all outputs. This chart assists in developing detailed operating and control instructions.

Record layouts which specify the placement of data items are used to describe records maintained on cards, magnetic tapes, paper tape, magnetic disks, magnetic drums, or printed reports. For example, a card layout contains the names of all fields, field locations, field sizes, a description of control punches and a description of file identification codes (see Figure 3-2, page 28). Tape layouts contain additional information on record size, blocking factors and the layout and content of all internal labels (see Figure 3-3, page 29). There should be a description of the codes used to identify the various types of transactions affecting the files being processed and of the codes in the files which denote type of account, type of customer, etc.

The control function for the computer run is described in this section. If this function involves a control group or control clerk, each man's duties are defined.

Whereas the system description section described the entire process, computer and non-computer, for accomplishing the data processing task, the program description section covers the details which document the computer program portion of the system. Typical topics in this section are:

1. Program flowcharts (also termed block or logic diagrams)

2. Decision tables

3. Table descriptions

Company _____

Application _____ by _____ Date _____ Job No. _____ Sheet No. _____

BILLING CARD	CUSTOMER ACCOUNT NUMBER	AREA CODE	SALESMAN	CREDIT CODE	Not USED	BALANCE FORWARD	CURRENT PURCHASES	PAYMENTS	ADJUSTMENTS	BALANCE DUE	NOT USED
	9 9 9 9 9 9 9 9	9 9	9	9 9	9 9 9 9 9 9	9 9 9 9 9 9 9 9 9 9	9 9 9 9 9 9 9 9 9 9	9 9 9 9 9 9 9 9 9 9	9 9 9 9 9 9 9 9 9 9	9 9 9 9 9 9 9 9 9	9 9 9 9 9 9 9 9 9 9
	1 2 3 4 5 6 7 8	9 10 11	12	13 14	15 16 17 18 19 20	21 22 23 24 25 26 27 28 29 30	31 32 33 34 35 36 37 38 39 40	41 42 43 44 45 46 47 48 49 50	51 52 53 54 55 56 57 58 59 60	61 62 63 64 65 66 67 68 69 70	71 72 73 74 75 76 77 78 79 80

ADDRESS CARD	CUSTOMER ACCOUNT NUMBER	AREA CODE	SIZE	TITLE	FIRST NAME	LAST NAME	STREET ADDRESS	CITY NAME OR ABBREVIATION	STATE	ZIP
	9 9 9 9 9 9 9 9	9 9	9	9	9 9 9 9 9 9 9 9 9 9 9 9	9 9 9 9 9 9 9 9 9 9 9 9 9 9	9 9 9 9 9 9 9 9 9 9 9 9 9 9 9	9 9 9 9 9 9 9 9 9 9 9 9 9	9 9 9 9 9	9 9 9 9 9
	1 2 3 4 5 6 7 8	9 10 11	12	13 14 15 16 17 18 19 20 21 22 23 24 25	26 27 28 29 30 31 32 33 34 35 36 37 38 39 40	41 42 43 44 45 46 47 48 49 50 51 52 53 54 55 56 57	58 59 60 61 62 63 64 65 66 67 68 69 70	71 72 73 74 75	76 77 78 79 80

FIGURE 3-2.   Punched card layout

4. Working storage and memory layout

5. Sense switches

6. Program modification

7. Program listing

The extent to which these topics are covered by a run manual depends on the size and complexity of the program. The program flowcharts and program listing are typically included in even fairly condensed documentation.

Program flowcharts form a pictorial representation of the logic of a computer program. As such, they are one of the most important records in the run manual. See Appendix C for a description of standard flowcharting symbols.

Decision tables are a documentation and programming aid used as a supplement to or in place of program flowcharts. They are especially useful in determining that all possible decision combinations have been provided for within the program. The decision table is a useful tool in the preparation of comprehensive test data for testing a new program. Although they are not in common use, these tables can be a very valuable aid to programming and documentation.

Whenever a list of values such as a tax withholding table is to be used in a computer program, a full description of the table should be included in the program documentation. The description should be sufficiently complete so that the table could be reconstructed easily if it were accidentally destroyed. A diagram of the table is often used to illustrate its particular layout.

A listing of all working storage areas is helpful. Working

RECORD FORMAT

Application __AGING ACCOUNTS RECEIVABLE__ Record Name __CUSTOMER HISTORY__ By __JBA__ Date __12-8-67__ Page __1__ of __1__

FIELD NAME	ACCOUNT NUMBER	ACCOUNT TYPE	CREDIT RATING	HIGHEST AGE	6 MONTHS AGE HISTORY							DATE LAST ACTIVITY MO. YR.	CURRENT MONTH							
					CURR. MO.	1ST PREV.	2ND PREV.	3RD PREV.	4TH PREV.	5TH PREV.	6TH PREV.		CHARGES	DEBIT ADJ.	SERVICE CHARGES	PAYMENTS & CREDITS	OTHER ADJ.	BALANCE	AMOUNT PAST DUE	TOTAL AMOUNT DUE
CHARACTERISTICS*																				
RELATIVE POSITION	1-8	9-11	12-14	15-16	17-18	19-20	21-22	23-24	25-26	27-28	29	30-1	32-37	38-43	44-46	47-52	53-57	58-63	64-69	70-75

1ST PREVIOUS MONTH			2ND PREVIOUS MONTH			3RD PREVIOUS MONTH			4TH PREVIOUS MONTH			5TH PREVIOUS MONTH			6TH PREVIOUS MONTH		
CHARGES	PAYMENTS	BALANCE	CHARGES	PAYMENTS	BALANCE	CHARGES	PAYMENTS	BALANCE	CHARGES	PAYMENTS	BALANCE	CHARGES	PAYMENTS	BALANCE	CHARGES	PAYMENTS	BALANCE
76-81	82-87	88-93	94-99	100-105	106-111	112-117	118-123	124-129	130-135	136-141	142-147	148-153	154-159	160-165	166-171	172-177	178-182

7TH PREV. MO. BALANCE	8TH PREV. MO. BALANCE	9TH PREV. MO. BALANCE	10TH PREV. MO. BALANCE	11TH PREV. MO. BALANCE	12TH PREV. MO. BALANCE	13TH PREV. MO. BALANCE	THIS YEAR			PRIOR to 13TH PREV.
							TOTAL PURCHASES	TOTAL PAYMENTS	HIGHEST BALANCE	
184-189	190-195	196-201	202-207	208-213	214-219	220-225	226-231	232-238	239-245	246-252

LAST YEAR			CUSTOMER NAME	1ST LINE ADDRESS	2ND LINE ADDRESS	3RD LINE ADDRESS
TOTAL PURCHASES	TOTAL PAYMENTS	HIGHEST BALANCE				
253-259	260-266	267-273	274-300	301-336	337-372	373-408

ZIP CODE
409-505

SORTING FIELDS — Major 1, 2, 3, 4, 5, 6, 7, 8, 9, 10, 11, 12, 13, 14, 15, 16 Minor

FOOTNOTES

File Description ____
Recording Mode ____
Records per Block ____
Characters per Record ____
Label Records are ____
File Identification ____
File Serial Number ____
Reel Sequence Number ____
Creation Date ____
Retention Cycle ____

Remarks ____

* Characteristics
Alphabetic or Blank ___ A
Alphanumeric ___ X
Numeric ___ 9
Assumed Decimal Point _ V
Examples of Signed Fields
X9999   9999V
X999V99 9999V9X

REVISIONS

Date	By

FIGURE 3-3. Magnetic tape record layout

storage is memory assigned for storing intermediate results during the processing steps. For each item this list might show:

1. Symbolic name assigned

2. Size (in number of characters)

3. Function within the program

4. Initial state (zero, blank or other)

5. Where cleared (i.e., on minor totals, on intermediate totals, on major totals or on final totals)

A layout of memory is not required in most cases since assignment of memory is regulated by the assembler program or by the operating system. However, in special cases where the programmer has specifically assigned memory to facilitate instruction modification or where there are tables used within a program, a memory layout may become necessary or desirable.

A copy of the most recent program listing (produced by the program assembler) should be part of the documentation. This listing, together with the program flowchart, allows a reader to follow the detailed coding flow and logic. The list also serves as back-up in case the source deck is lost or destroyed. Each listing should be dated and only the latest listing should be retained in current documentation. Minor machine language changes (patches) are usually posted directly on the program listing. These changes should also be authorized and documented by a program change and approval sheet.

In some situations, a printout of memory after the program has been loaded can be valuable in diagnosing program errors. This is particularly true when an error is detected after a program has been patched or modified. Memory dumps may be included as part of the documentation for such cases.

In a number of computers, sense switches on the computer console are used to alter the program flow. The program tests the condition of the switch and changes the program path depending on the switch setting. For example, a program written to print out account balances may, by a switch setting, be altered to bypass printing of credit balances. The documentation should identify each sense switch and describe the conditions or functions which will result from each setting.

The programmer can use instructions to modify or change other instructions. This modification process is an extremely powerful and flexible program technique but it does make programs extremely difficult to follow. For this reason, the purpose and result of all the program modifications should be fully documented.

This section of the run manual contains the information required by the computer operator to run the program. Some information which appears elsewhere in the run manual is repeated in this section because it is reproduced and furnished to the operator for use as the computer operator instructions. Any subsequent changes made in the run manual should, of course, be reflected in the separate computer operator instructions. This section of the run manual will be explained in connection with these instructions.

Operating Instructions Section

The purpose of this section is to summarize the controls associated with the run. Such a listing is valuable not only for internal use but also for the independent auditor's review. The section contains a brief write-up describing:

Listing of Controls

1. Controls outside the data processing department which check the accuracy of input data

2. Processing control procedures within the data processing department—such as checks of batch controls and reconciliation of run-to-run control figures

3. Programmed error detection and control procedures

4. Controls and checks of the accuracy of output performed by users or others outside the data processing department.

This section documents the steps taken to test the program for errors before acceptance for use. The information contained in this section covers the test data used in the testing process, the documentation review approval and the program change record.

Acceptance Record Section

Copies of input and output test data should be preserved as part of the program documentation. In the case of punched card data, the run manual should contain a listing of the input/output; the cards themselves should be retained elsewhere. Each time a program is changed, the test input data should be reprocessed and the new output compared with the original test output. This procedure helps to eliminate program errors which sometimes unexpectedly affect programs that have been changed.

When a program is first prepared, the documentation should be reviewed and approved by a responsible authority such as the program manager or the data processing manager. This review and approval should be recorded in the run manual. There should also be a record of all changes made in a program since its original implementation. This record (Figure 3-4, page 33) should show:

1. Date of change

2. Reason for change

3. Approval of change initiation

4. Approval of change method

The program change record is useful in keeping documentation current. It is very time consuming to correct all documentation, including flowcharts, each time a program change is made. Instead, a change record is included with the documentation and, unless there is a rather substantial rewrite of the program, the flowcharts are not redrawn. The original documentation plus the change records form the current documentation.

The audit impact of adequate change documentation has been illustrated by a client whose payroll registers, prepared on the computer, did not crossfoot. The auditor insisted that crossfooting be part of the computer program. On the next audit review, the first payroll tested did not crossfoot. However, the client's documentation was good, and the auditors were able to satisfy themselves that the requested change had become effective, though not until after the production date of the payroll in question. In the absence of such documentation, the audit tests might have had to be extended.

Computer operator instructions

As previously mentioned,, the set of computer operator instructions (also called the console run book) is a reproduction of one section of the run manual. The run manual is the complete

DATA PROCESSING PROGRAM CHANGE RECORD	
Program name or description	Change number_____
	Date change effective_____
Program No.	

Change initiated by_____ Date_____

Change request approved by_____ Date_____

Description of purpose or reason for change

Description of changes made (and effect on this and other programs)

Change made by_____ Date_____

Change tested by_____ Date_____

Change posted to run manual by_____ Date_____

Change posted to operator instructions by_____ Date_____

Review of changes by_____ Date_____

FIGURE 3-4.   Notice of program change

documentation; the computer operator instructions are those instructions necessary for the computer operator. The concept of separation of duties in data processing implies that the computer operator does not have access to the complete documentation. Without the complete documentation of the run manual, it would be difficult for the computer operator to alter the program for any unauthorized purposes. Therefore, the computer operator is often restricted to the operating instructions since they provide all information necessary for the running of the program. The extent of coverage is approximately the following:

TOPIC	EXPLANATION
Identification and description of program	The machine operator should have a basic understanding of the purpose of the computer program. This allows him to operate the program and helps to prevent him from committing gross errors. The description of the program should be brief and stated in as simple and straightforward a manner as possible.
Card layouts and keypunch instructions	The card layouts are sometimes included. In case cards are mangled during processing, the operator may need copies of the layouts and keypunch instructions to guide him in punching replacement cards. Such punching should be carefully controlled to avoid introduction of errors.
System set-up and take-down instructions	The operator should be given detailed instructions on how to set up all the equipment to be used during the computer run. These instructions should also prescribe the sequence in which the operations are to be performed. Careful sequencing of set-up and take-down instructions can usually reduce total job time (e.g., readying printer while program cards are being loaded; unloading the punch, reader and printer while tapes are rewinding).
Deck set-up (for card input)	The deck set-up is a diagram showing the arrangement of the program, subroutines, date card, data and sentinel cards which are normally processed during a computer run. (A sentinel card is usually a card containing special punching to indicate the end of a file.) Such a diagram helps to eliminate the errors and lost time which are often caused by improper arrangement of the deck.
Sense switch settings	Sense switches are external switches found on some computers and can be tested by the program. They are used to allow the operator to specify certain program options when the program is to be run. The function and proper use of each external switch should be fully explained. Instructions to the operator should describe exactly how the switches are to be set for the run.
Operator duties	These instructions should define the operator's duties in starting, running and terminating the program. Ideally, nothing should be left to the operator's memory.

TOPIC	EXPLANATION
Console messages and halts	The operator should be given a list of all messages and programmed halts contained in the program. He should also be given instructions as to what action he must take in response to each of them. Instructions may include the persons to contact in the case of unusual stoppages.
End-of-job instructions	These describe the disposition of cards, tape and printout, specify external labelling to be performed, and so on.

Minimum documentation

The explanations in this chapter are based on a rather complete documentation plan. Presumably there is a minimum acceptable set of documentation. While difficult to specify as a general rule, it would probably include the following:

1. Problem statement

2. System flowchart

3. Operator instructions

4. Record layouts

5. Program flowcharts

6. Program listing

7. Test data

8. Approval and change sheet

Importance of documentation for audits

The auditor may find it necessary to use client data processing system documentation in several ways. Two of these involve the review of internal control and the planning of audit steps using the computer.

It is normal audit practice to review and evaluate existing controls. Program documentation is frequently the best source of information on control features in the computer program and, accordingly, review of control may depend in part on adequate documentation of programs. Even if it is not necessary for review of program controls, the absence of adequate documentation probably indicates a lack of administrative controls which may influence the auditor's evaluation of internal control.

When review of internal control and methods of testing indicates that the auditor should use computer-based tests (such as test data, routines to audit records, etc.), proper documentation can be invaluable. Details of record formats, layouts, code structures and other basic data contained in the standard documentation eliminate much of the groundwork usually associated with writing a program or developing test data and reduce the time an auditor needs to devote to the development of his audit approach.

CHAPTER 4

HARDWARE FEATURES FOR CONTROL OVER EQUIPMENT MALFUNCTIONS

MODERN COMPUTER EQUIPMENT has a high degree of reliability and the auditor can usually assume that the equipment will perform reliably and will detect machine-based errors if they occur. Except where difficulties in processing are found to be a result of machine errors, the auditor can usually rely on the efficacy of these controls. Some of these are operable, however, only if program instructions test the equipment indicators. In order to understand the working of the equipment, to understand why it is reliable, and to evaluate the effectiveness of machine checks in cases where there are problems, it is desirable for the auditor to have a general understanding of built-in hardware control features. This chapter describes the general reasons for equipment malfunctions, the general types of equipment controls and the controls associated with the major equipment items.

How the equipment can malfunction

A computer system consists of both electronic elements and mechanical parts. The central processing unit, for example, consists almost entirely of electronic elements such as transistors, resistors and diodes, whereas most input/output equipment and file storage devices contain both electronic components and parts which move mechanically. Failure in the system, therefore, can result from the malfunction of either a mechanical part or an electronic element.

A computer system operates with electrical pulses that are created, counted, delayed, transmitted, etc. Communication between units of the system is by a controlled transmission of electrical pulses, and the electronic circuitry of the computer is designed to control the timing, shape, strength and frequency of these pulses. Failure of an electronic element such as a transistor, resistor, diode, etc., may cause a change in the timing, shape, strength or frequency of the pulses and lead to an error. Some of the reasons for deterioration of an electronic element are extremes of heat or humidity, power disturbances, mishandling and normal wear.

Quality control in manufacture, built-in equipment checks and programs of periodic preventive maintenance have made the electronic portion of the computer system very reliable. Preventive maintenance procedures usually detect elements which are getting out of adjustment or are close to failure and allow adjustments or replacements to be made. The preventive maintenance is performed daily on complex computer systems and less frequently on simple configurations.

Mechanical operation is required in almost all input/output and file storage equipment. Two mechanisms with mechanical actions are usually used:

1. A transport mechanism to move the media (input, output or file storage) past the reading or writing mechanism

2. Mechanism to read or write

These actions occur at high speeds. For example, a card reader must transport up to 1100 cards a minute past the read mechanisms (brushes or photoelectric cells) at a precise speed and in a precise position. A printer that prints 1000 lines of 136 characters per minute requires as many as 136,000 individual print mechanism movements each minute.

A machine error can be caused by a failure in the timing, speed or movement of a transport mechanism or by a malfunction of the read/write units. Such failures may result when devices get out of adjustment, are mishandled by operators, become worn, and so on. Failures may also be traced to bad media such as warped cards, magnetic tape with surface defects, or poor quality paper stock.

Equipment controls

Equipment controls are usually based on the concept of redundancy. This concept has received much attention in communication theory but is also applicable elsewhere as a general basis for error control. With respect to error control, redundancy involves the addition of an element to a process or to the code for an item for the sole purpose of detecting any error which may occur. If there is no possibility of error, the redundancy is usually eliminated.

Equipment controls can be divided into five types: redundant character check, duplicate process check, echo check, validity check and equipment check. Each of these involves a separate operation which provides a check on the results of the main operation. The general types of controls are described in this section; their application to specific equipment is described in the remaining sections of the chapter.

A redundant character is a character attached to a data item for the purpose of providing for error detection. The redundant character is developed from the characteristics of the data item to which it is attached. After an operation such as the moving of a data item in the system, the computation used to obtain the redundant character is repeated to derive a second character. The two redundant characters are compared, and, if they are the same, it is assumed that there has been no malfunction affecting the data during the transfer or some other operation.

Redundant Character Check

Another type of equipment control involves having the same process performed twice and the results of the two operations compared. Any difference between the first operation and the second signals an error. The duplicate process may be a complementary action such as reading after writing to check what was written.

Duplicate Process Check

Echo Check | In an echo check the central processor sends a command to an input or output device to perform an operation. The device returns a signal that verifies that the proper mechanisms for performing the actions have been activated. This check verifies that the equipment was activated without testing the actual results obtained.

Validity Check | Since, on many operations, only certain results can be considered correct, one method of checking is to compare a result obtained against all valid results. Any result not fitting into this set of valid results is considered incorrect.

Equipment Check | In this control, the computer checks the equipment to see if it is functioning properly instead of checking the results from the operation. It is not a positive check, since the equipment may be working properly while defective media or other factors are causing improper results.

Central processor hardware controls

The central processor has two equipment error-control problems. The first is that of ensuring that all data elements transmitted through the internal circuitry of the central processor are transmitted correctly and that no problem with the timing or pulses has destroyed or altered the data being moved. The second is that of avoiding the performance of an operation that is invalid. The typical central processor hardware controls are the parity bit, the operation validity check and interlocks. In some of the very early computers there were duplicate circuitry and double arithmetic in order to ensure correct functioning of the central processing unit, but these precautions are no longer considered necessary or desirable.

Parity Bit | The computer represents data and instructions internally using devices which have two recognizable states. A magnetic core, for example, is polarized in one of two directions. Each of these two states is used to represent a binary digit (abbreviated as bit) —one state represents a 1-bit and the other a 0-bit in the binary system. Decimal numbers and alphabetic characters are converted to binary representation for internal processing or for storage on magnetic media such as magnetic tape and are converted back to decimal numbers and alphabetic characters when printed on reports. There are various different approaches to coding of data for internal representation in binary form. In all of these approaches, the computer works with groups of storage devices, each of which can hold either a 1-bit or a 0-bit.

A redundant character, called a parity bit or check bit, is associated with each group of bits separately identified and moved as a separate unit through the computer. This unit may be a large, fixed set of bits called a computer word, a smaller set which can encode a single alphanumeric character, or a separately identified part, called a byte, of a larger fixed word. The parity of the binary word, character set or byte is made even or odd when the data is first converted to binary form from input items or when data is formed from a computation or other manipulation. The number of bits is summed and a 1-bit or a 0-bit is placed in the parity bit position to make the total number of bits odd if an odd parity check is used or even if an even parity check is used. Figure 4-1 (this page) illustrates the parity bit in a 6-bit binary-coded character bit set. Each time this basic group of bits is moved in the computer, the parity of the group is checked. If the parity bit as newly computed is different than the parity bit as previously computed, a bit has been destroyed. This test is not infallible since the destruction of two bits will leave the parity bit unchanged, but the probability of this happening is very low.

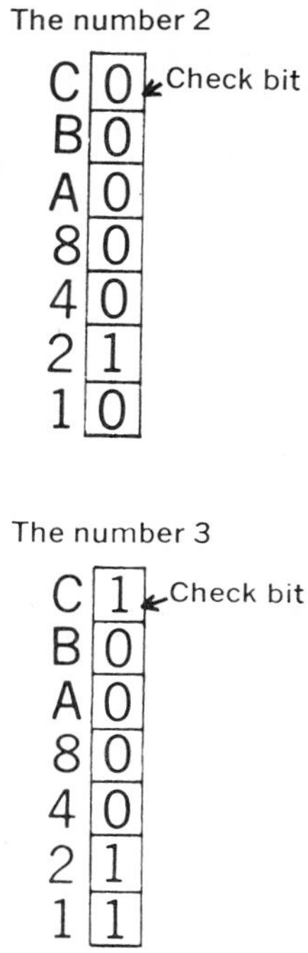

There are a few computers (usually equipment with a scientific processing orientation) which do not use a built-in parity bit control. Other reliability features including programming checks usually compensate for this omission. Parity errors in the central processor are seldom encountered and many of the errors which are registered are due to the checking circuitry itself rather than to an underlying error. The auditor should be aware of the parity check, but the lack of this check does not usually affect his assessment of the system or the extent of the audit tests.

The number 2

```
C  0  ← Check bit
B  0
A  0
8  0
4  0
2  1
1  0
```

The number 3

```
C  1  ← Check bit
B  0
A  0
8  0
4  0
2  1
1  1
```

FIGURE 4-1. Odd parity bit for a computer that uses a 6-bit binary-coded character bit set.

Validity Check

In the central processor there are only certain operation codes which are valid and which the computer can execute and there is only a certain range of numbers which the computer can access as memory addresses. Before attempting to execute an operation code or access a memory location, the computer usually performs a validity check to determine that it is a valid operation code or a valid address. Validity checks are used in some computers with character coding to check the movement of data. Each bit set can encode one character, but not all combinations are valid. An invalid combination indicates an error.

Interlocks

The computer system has automatic controls to prevent the equipment from attempting certain operations at the wrong time. For example, there is an input/output interlock which prevents the computer from signalling an input or output device to perform an action while it is already performing another operation. Thus, a card reader cannot be signalled to read a card while it is already performing a card-reading operation. A storage protection interlock is a hardware control used with fairly advanced computer systems that process several programs concurrently. It prevents the computer from using a block of memory locations that are not assigned to the particular program.

Card reader hardware controls

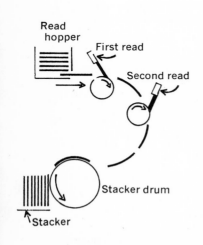

Read hopper

First read

Second read

Stacker drum

Stacker

FIGURE 4-2. **Path of card in card reader**

The card transport mechanism in a reader must pull a card from the input hopper and move it past the read stations (reading brushes or photoelectric cells) at a precise speed and in a precise position. (See Figure 4-2, this page). Malfunction of the card reader may therefore occur because the cards move past the reading stations at incorrect intervals of time, because the card is positioned incorrectly, or because the reading mechanism fails to sense properly. Card reading speeds vary from 200 to over 1,000 cards per minute, so that a slight delay or slight skewing can result in an incorrect sensing. The types of controls commonly used in card readers are dual-read and hole-count controls (both duplicate process), validity checks and photocell (circuit) checks. Another check, the double-punch blank-column check, has been used in some older equipment. These checks are summarized in Table 4.1 (page 43).

When an error is detected by the card reader, an internal switch is set. The typical error procedure is for the card which was misread to be routed to a different output bin (stacker) from those without errors. Depending on the application, the computer may halt processing for the error to be handled or it may continue processing with the error noted for later attention. If it halts, the reader will usually reject all cards then in motion. A corrected card and the other cards in process when the error was detected are re-inserted. Since the more a card is handled, the greater the chance of error, many installations prefer to complete the run with errors noted but without card re-entry during the run.

Card punch hardware controls

The problems of card punching are similar to the problems of card reading but there are some differences in controls. These

Hardware controls for card readers		TABLE 4.1
TYPE OF CONTROL	DESCRIPTION	USE AND EFFECTIVENESS
Dual read	The card is read by two separate read stations. Results of the two reading operations are compared.	Very effective at detecting errors in reading of cards.
Hole count	The card is read by the first read station and a count is made of the holes in each column or row (depending on which way the card is read). A second hole count is made by a second read station and the two hole counts are compared.	Effective at detecting errors. A small probability exists that a reading could be in error even though its two hole counts are identical.
Validity	Although there are 4096 possible hole combinations for a column on a punched card, only a few (64 is common) are valid. The validity check compares the punches read against the valid combinations. The check can usually be suppressed by programming in order to read non-standard punch combinations if this is necessary.	An error in reading which, for example, missed a punch might still result in a valid combination of punches. Sometimes used in combination with a hole count, dual read, or photocell check.
Proper photocell functioning	After a card is read, the photocell reader is tested to see that it is functioning. A check for mispositioning of cards is included. Not applicable to read heads using wire brushes.	Less foolproof than other methods, but apparently quite satisfactory.
Double-punch blank-column	The card is checked for double punch or blank column for those columns having numeric data (which should have only one punch). A wired panel is used for programming the test.	Very seldom used except in old computer systems, but a common test in unit record equipment.

are summarized in Table 4.2 (below). In one approach, the results of the punching operation are checked. There is a separate read station following the punch station. Cards are read after they have been punched in order to develop information for either a hole count or a full comparison. A second approach to punch checking is an echo check in which a signal is sent from the punch dies verifying that they have been activated. Both approaches are widely used.

Printer controls

The first step in printing a line is to assemble the characters in storage. These characters are then loaded into a print buffer where they are decoded into signals which will select the characters to be printed at each print position. There are usually from 100 to 160 print positions on a line, the most common numbers being 120 and 132. A hammer located behind the paper presses the paper and a ribbon in front of the paper against the type face at the exact moment the selected character is in position (Figure 4-3, page 45). After a line is printed the paper and the print ribbon are advanced and the hammer recoils.

There are two basic types of printers—impact and non-impact. Almost all are of the impact type which uses a mechanically driven type face pressed against the paper and ribbon. Non-

TABLE 4.2	Hardware controls for card punches	
CONTROL	DESCRIPTION	USE AND EFFECTIVENESS
Read compare	After a card is punched, it passes under a read station. The card contents as read in this station are compared with the data which was to be punched.	Most effective.
Hole count	A read station reads the card after it is punched but makes only a hole count (row or column) which is compared to a hole count for the characters which were to be punched.	Probability of undetected error very slight.
Echo check	The computer sends signals to punch dies to activate them to punch the required holes. A signal is sent back from the punch dies verifying that they were activated.	Probability of undetected error still slight, though the activation of the punch dies, rather than what they punched, is being checked.

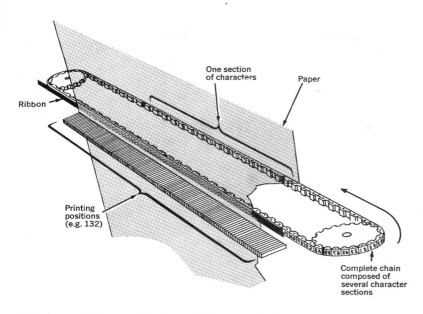

FIGURE 4-3. Diagram showing printing mechanism

Labels in figure: One section of characters — Paper — Ribbon — Printing positions (e.g. 132) — Complete chain composed of several character sections

impact printers form an image by electrical charges. This discussion deals only with impact printers. The major methods of impact printing are type bar, drum, chain and type slugs.

TYPE ELEMENT	EXPLANATION
Type bar	A horizontal type bar contains all the characters. The bar moves horizontally and the hammers are activated when the correct character on the bar moves past.
Drum	This consists of a rotating cylinder with raised characters arranged in bands around the drum. As the drum revolves, all the characters in the print set rotate past each position. At the instant the selected character is in front of a position, the hammer for that position is activated and presses the paper and inked ribbon against the type face.
Chain	This involves the same concept as the drum except that a chain containing the type faces moves horizontally past the print positions.
Type slugs	This method involves the same concept as a type chain except that there is a train of type slugs moving through a horizontal channel.

The hardware error controls for printing, as detailed in Table

FIGURE 4-4. Magnetic tape unit

4.3 (below) are echo, print synchronization and validity. Note that these controls test in various ways the mechanisms performing the printing but none of them is a positive test of what was actually printed. In practice, however, these controls have proved to be satisfactory.

Magnetic tape hardware controls

A magnetic tape drive consists of a feed reel, a takeup reel, read/ write heads, a mechanism to drive the tape past the heads and a mechanism to dampen the effect of rapid stopping and starting.

The device used to drive the tape past the read/write heads is a pinch roller, a vacuum capstan or a clutch operated capstan. Vacuum columns, mechanical storage arms or storage bins are used alone or in combination to provide several feet of slack tape for immediate movement before the reels start their independent motion. The most widely used tape units use pinch-roller drives and vacuum column buffers (Figure 4-4, this page).

Data is recorded by magnetizing small areas on the tape. A set of bits, encoding either one character or part of a computer word, is arranged as a vertical row of six or eight bits on the tape. A parity bit position is added to each row making the total number of bit positions equal to seven or nine (Figure 4-5, page 47).

TABLE 4.3   Hardware controls for printers

CONTROL	DESCRIPTION	USE AND EFFECTIVENESS
Echo	The central processor sends signals to the printer to activate the print mechanism for each character. When the print mechanism is positioned, just before printing, a signal is sent back from the print mechanism verifying that the proper print position has been activated.	Most common method
Validity	This type of control tests the signals transmitted to the printer against the set of valid signals.	Sometimes used in addition to an echo check
Print synchronization (timing)	This control checks the timing of the printer to determine that the print hammers are activated at the moments when the appropriate characters are in the correct position.	Next most common method

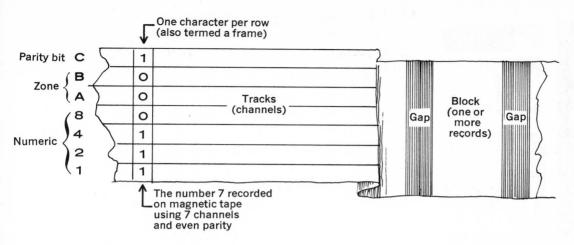

FIGURE 4-5.   Recording of data on magnetic tape

The positions are called channels. At the end of each record there is a blank space (usually ¾ inch) called an interrecord gap (or, more precisely, an interblock gap) to separate the blocks on the tape, each of which contains one or more records.

Problems with magnetic tape may result from difficulties with the magnetic tape itself (the primary reason), from malfunction of the read/write heads, or from malfunctions in the tape drive mechanism. The typical magnetic computer tape consists of a half-inch wide strip of polyester (plastic) film 2,400 feet long with a thin iron oxide coating. As the tape passes over the read/write head, any imperfection in the coating may lift the tape from the head and cause a signal drop. These defects can stem from manufacturing defects or from dust particles, but the most frequent source of difficulty comes from imbedded particles of oxide. Flakes of oxide break away from the coating and are redeposited on the tape surface by the tape heads and guides. These can be removed by a special cleaning process. Over a period of time, parts of a tape become worn. These worn sections must be removed or skipped over and not used for recording.

The proper operation of the read/write mechanism in the tape unit depends upon correct signals from the central processor and correct speeds and positioning as the tape moves past the read/write heads. If the tape moves at an improper speed the recording or reading mechanism will not operate properly. A malfunction of the write head may cause a recording to be made at less than an acceptable signal level. The drive mechanism has a device, usually a photoelectric sensing device, to sense the beginning and end of the tape. If this is not operating properly, the read/write heads may attempt to write or read on the leader at the beginning or end of the tape. Incorrect processing or loss of data will result.

The hardware controls for magnetic tape consist of a parity check for reading of data and a read-after-write comparison for writing on tape.

Parity Check for Magnetic Tape

The basic parity check for magnetic tape is a row check, often called a lateral or frame check, in which each character (coded one character per frame) is given a parity bit when the data is put on the tape. When the data is read from the tape the parity bit is checked. An improved parity check is the addition of longitudinal or track parity bits to give a two-dimensional check. Each record encoded on the tape is given a track parity bit in addition to the row parity bit associated with each frame. This serves as an added check over the single dimensional row parity. In addition, the intersection of a missing row bit and a missing longitudinal bit will, if only one bit is in error, define the exact bit position causing the error and will allow for automatic error recovery (Figure 4-6, this page).

A cyclic or diagonal check is used in a few magnetic tape units. This is a check character formed by taking a parity check diagonally instead of down or across. This provides additional capabilities for pinpointing any bit positions that happen to be in error.

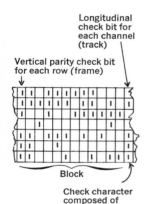

Longitudinal check bit for each channel (track)

Vertical parity check bit for each row (frame)

Block

Check character composed of check bits for each channel

FIGURE 4-6.   Parity bit check for magnetic tape.

Read After Write Check

The read/write heads on a magnetic tape drive may take two forms: the single-gap head which acts as both a read mechanism and a write mechanism (only one operation being performed at a time) and a two-gap head which has both a read head and a write head. The two-gap head (Figure 4-7, page 49) allows for a read immediately after a write comparison in which case the data just written is read and compared. The data is tested to see if it was recorded at a proper signal level and parity is checked. The automatic write/read comparison depends upon having the two-gap head. It is preferable from an error control standpoint because recording errors are detected and corrected when they occur rather than when the file is next processed. In the latter case, reconstruction is usually more costly and it is also time consuming.

A control used with some magnetic tape is that of counting the number of characters recorded and writing this count on the tape. When the tape is read, the character count is again computed and compared. An infrequently used method involves a dual recording of the information so that there is a back-up recording of information in case of any problem with the major recording.

Since most tape errors are caused by surface defects on the magnetic tape, an error in reading or writing is usually handled by backspacing the tape one record and repeating the operation. If the error persists, the operation is repeated again. Dust or oxide particles will usually be dislodged in this way. If the error is still uncorrected, the record is noted on the error listing for subsequent correction and processing is continued. A bad spot on the tape can be skipped by marking the beginning and end of the tape portion which is not to be used.

Hardware controls for direct access storage devices

A direct access storage device (drum, disk or strip file) consists of (1) a transport mechanism to move the recording media, (2) read/write heads and (3) recording material. The direct access devices can read or write directly on any section of the recording medium and for this reason they are also referred to as random access devices. Either the recording medium or the read/write head, or both, move until they are in correct position.

A magnetic drum storage involves a revolving drum with a magnetizable surface. The data is arranged in tracks and read/write heads record or read data as the surface revolves beneath them. Magnetic disk storage consists of metal disks mounted on a shaft. As the disk revolves, data which is recorded on concentric tracks passes beneath a read/write head mounted on an arm. There is often a separate access arm for each disk, but the arm must usually move in and out in order to be positioned

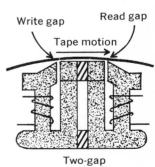

FIGURE 4-7. **Two-gap read/write head**

above the track to be used. The read/write head must be positioned and held a few ten-thousandths of an inch above the surface. A common approach is to have the arm float on a layer of air. In the event of power failure, a safety device retracts the heads to prevent them from damaging the disk. Strip file storage consists of cartridges loaded with plastic strips coated with a recording material. For a read/write operation, the selected strip is dropped from the cartridge onto a positioning drum which moves it past a read/write head. Errors may occur in this type of equipment because of incorrect positioning or because of improper reading or writing by the read/write mechanism. The major error control methods are the parity check, check character and read-after-write check (Table 4.4, page 52).

A major error can occur in a disk storage device if information which is sent to be recorded at one location is recorded instead at another. The recording at the incorrect location not only puts the information where it should not be, but also destroys information at the location improperly used. In order to avoid the possibility of such an error's happening through an improper movement of the read/write head, it is considered good practice, either through hardware controls or through programming, to compare the address of the location at which data is to be written with the address called for by the instructions.

Hardware controls for data communications

Errors occur in data communications primarily as a result of (1) the inherent characteristics of the communication links and (2) equipment malfunctions. The most common causes of data transmission errors are noise, fading, amplitude and phase distortion, and multipath distortion. A full discussion of these sources of error is beyond the scope of this review. In general, a switched or dial-up connection will have a higher error rate than a leased line and the error rate tends to increase with the distance over which the data is transmitted and the transmission speed.

Methods of
Error Control

Errors will occur in every data communications system. Therefore, the facts to be noted with respect to errors are these: degree of freedom from errors, probability of detecting errors which occur and efficiency in handling these errors. The methods of error control are code validity and data redundancy. The redundancy controls involve either a constant ratio code or parity bits. These controls are summarized in Table 4.5 (page 53). Where data is transmitted directly into a computer, the program accepting the data may perform additional error control procedures.

It is more difficult to correct errors than to detect them. There are codes which are designed for efficient correction of data transmission errors but they require a relatively large number of redundant checking bits and are expensive to implement.

Handling of Hardware-Based Communication Errors

The most common approach to error handling is retransmission of erroneously received messages or segments of messages. The retransmission may require operator intervention or it may be handled automatically. In one method, the receiving terminal checks each segment (character, block or message) as received and transmits an instruction back to the sending terminal either to repeat the transmission because there is an error or to continue with the next segment.

Other input/output devices

Readers for magnetic ink character recognition (MICR), used extensively in banking, have validity and timing checks built into the equipment. The timing check tests that the documents are moving past the scanning heads at the proper speed. As with other validity checks, the patterns read by the scanning heads are compared with the set of valid symbols. In addition, the circuitry may perform other checks. It may count the characters in the field to determine that the size of the field being read is correct or automatically compute a check digit and compare it with a check digit in the field being read.

Magnetic Ink
Character Readers

An optical scanner reads characters or marks by scanning with a beam of light. A character is read by recognizing a particular pattern of light and dark areas. There are several different methods for performing this task.

Optical Scanning
Equipment

There are two rates to consider in optical reading—the reject

TABLE 4.4   Hardware controls for direct access storage devices

CONTROL	DESCRIPTION	USE AND EFFECTIVENESS
Parity	A parity bit is generated and recorded for each character, word or record.	Detects a recording error only when the record is subsequently read.
Character	This is an extension of the **parity check.** A set of parity bits is generated based on parity for each of the bit positions in a group of bits. For example, there is a parity bit based on the first bit of each set of bits in the record. If the bit set contains eight bits, the checking set contains eight bits. The concept is similar to that of the tape record longitudinal check bits.	Detects a recording error only when the record is subsequently read. Some capability for correcting errors.
Read-after-write	This is a check to detect an error in recording. It consists of reading the record just written and testing for correct recording or correct parity.	The most positive check. Permits detection of most recording errors at the time of occurrence. Can also be programmed. When programmed, special "write check" instructions are usually available.

rate and the error rate. The reject rate is the percentage of documents rejected because the equipment is unable to recognize the character. At present, reject rates range from 2-20%. The error rate is the percentage of documents which were read but which contained one or more characters incorrectly identified. The error rate typically ranges from less than 1% of documents up to 2%.

The reject rate is significant in terms of handling time and reprocessing. The seriousness of errors undetected because of misreading depends on the type of application. A 1% error rate may be quite acceptable for one application but totally unacceptable for another. Programmed tests discussed in Chapter 6 can be used to detect many of the errors that are not found at the time of reading.

Hardware controls and the audit

There will be errors in data processing equipment. There are, however, satisfactory methods for detecting such errors and in some cases automatically correcting them. The auditor can usually put considerable reliance on the equipment and the hardware controls for detecting errors. The auditor is interested, for background purposes, in knowing the major types of equipment controls and in having an assurance that they are operating properly. This information is helpful for understanding the error procedures established by the client. The lack of a particular type of equipment control should probably not alter the scope of the audit unless the system does not seem to be operating within a tolerable rate of errors. In some cases, the hardware controls are not automatic but must be tested by programmed instructions. The fact that a client does not implement hardware controls requiring programmed tests may indicate a lack of administrative controls.

The auditor should be able to obtain general information on the reliability of the equipment from operating reports and from computer logs which record periods of machine breakdown (downtime) and the reasons for it.

In most cases the hardware error detection methods are satisfactory and do not require special audit attention. However, procedures for handling detected errors are themselves sources of possible errors that may go undetected. For example, a card reader with a validity check will reject a card with invalid punch combinations or a card which was sensed incorrectly so that it

Hardware controls for data communications		*TABLE 4.5*
CONTROL	DESCRIPTION	USE AND EFFECTIVENESS
Validity	This check determines that a received character is one of a number of permissible bit configurations.	This check has limited value in detecting errors and no value in correcting errors automatically.
Constant ratio code	The code is structured so that every character is represented by the same number of 0 and 1 bits. The receiving terminal counts the number of 1 bits. If there is not a constant number, an error has occurred.	The code is simple to generate and check but requires the transmission of extra bits per character. It has high value in detecting errors but does not permit automatic error correction because it does not allow for identification of an erroneous bit.
Parity (simple one dimensional)	A parity bit is added to each group of data bits to make the total number of bits odd in an odd parity check or even in an even parity check.	This check detects single-bit errors but not errors involving an even number of bits because parity is unchanged. It does not permit error correction.
Parity (two dimensional)	A parity bit is added to each character code and longitudinal parity bits are developed for each block. A separate bit is formed for each level of the transmitted code. This check is similar in concept to that of the longitudinal parity for magnetic tape and that of the character code for direct access storage.	This check ensures detection of up to three errors in a block. It has limited capability for error correction.

appeared to be invalid. If the procedures for handling this error are not followed properly, the result may be a double reading of the card or a skipping of the card. In reviewing processing procedures, therefore, the auditor should usually devote more attention to the procedures for handling errors than to the hardware controls which detect them.

CHAPTER 5

CONTROL OVER INPUT AND OUTPUT

INPUT DATA is the weakest link in the chain of computer data processing events. The reliability of equipment is very high and a computer program can usually be successfully debugged over a short interval of time, but the problem of the input data is a continuing one which affects all persons and machines creating or transmitting input data. A study of 100 computer installations showed input errors to be the major operating problem. Good systems design should include provisions for ensuring accurate and complete input into the system. The auditor in turn should be well acquainted with the sources of errors and with the range of techniques for prevention or detection.

Output should be controlled in the sense that it should be distributed to those who need it and should not be given out to those not authorized to receive it. This is termed "distribution control." Those receiving the output can frequently spot errors not otherwise detected. Thus, a procedure whereby recipients can report errors can form a feedback mechanism for error control.

How input data errors can occur

The input data for a program may be in error for one of four general reasons: it may be incorrectly recorded at the point of inception; it may be incorrectly converted to machine-readable form; it may be lost in handling; or it may be incorrectly processed when read by the computer equipment. The necessity for data controls of the type commonly used is demonstrated by the prevalent types of input errors.

Error in Creating Data

The data may be recorded incorrectly at the point of inception or the transaction may not be recorded. For example, a salesman may write down an incorrect stock number, the shipping department may record improperly the number of units shipped, or an incoming shipment may be put into inventory without the preparation of a receiving document.

Error in Converting to Machine-Readable Form

If the original document has been prepared by hand or in a manner which is not machine-readable, it is necessary to convert the information into machine-readable form. This generally involves punching the data into punched cards or preparing other input media such as punched paper tape. Errors may occur if the keypunch operator makes a mistake or, if the data is illegible, makes an incorrect judgment as to its meaning. Both the arrangement of the data to be punched and the legibility of source documents affect productivity and error rate. A study of keypunching error rates for experienced operators has indicated an average ranging from one error in every 1,600 keystrokes to one error in every 4,300 keystrokes.[1]

Loss of Document or Record in Handling

During the data processing cycle a record may be lost. Two paper documents may stick together, a record may be overlooked by the keypunch operator, or a record or document may be lost or dropped or may otherwise disappear in transit or in handling by the data processing personnel.

Errors in Processing by the Computer

A correctly recorded transaction which is correctly encoded into machine-readable form may still be processed incorrectly. There are several possible reasons for this:

1. Error in reading by the input device

---

[1] E. T. Hemmer and G. R. Lockhead, "Productivity and Errors in Two Keying Tasks: A Field Study," *Journal of Applied Psychology*, Vol. 46, No. 6, 1962, pp. 401-408.

2. Error in transmission of direct input data

3. Non-processing

4. Processing of data using wrong program or wrong master file

The conversion of the machine-readable media into the internal coding required for computer processing involves an input/output unit which must operate mechanically. The machine controls to ensure proper conversion have been described in Chapter 4. It is also possible, if necessary, to include additional programmed controls in the data processing system to ensure the proper conversion of data into internal form.

Where direct input devices are used there may be an error in the creation of the data as it is keyed in by the employee operating the device or there may be an error in the transmission of the data. Equipment malfunctions in the transmission equipment should be detected by the equipment controls. The keying-in of erroneous input data should ordinarily be detected by procedural or programmed input controls.

During data processing it sometimes happens that a record is not processed. This error may be due to a malfunction of the equipment, in which case the equipment controls should catch the error, or it may be due to some previously latent programming defects, in which case programmed error control procedures are necessary to detect the error.

In the normal course of events it is probable that sooner or later one of the data processing employees will pick up the wrong data file or the wrong transaction data when performing a data processing run. Accounts receivable data may be put into the program for accounts payable processing, for example. In an updating run, a data processing employee may use an old file being stored as back-up instead of the current file.

Input control in the design of a data processing system

Input controls can be placed at three different points in the data processing system:

1. At the point where data is created and converted to machine-readable form

2. At the point where the data enters the computer

3. At points where the data is handled, moved or transmitted in the organization

Table 5.1 (below) summarizes the most common methods for input data error control. These represent an inventory of methods from which the system designer selects in order to achieve the level of input error control required for an application. The individual methods are discussed later in this chapter.

In data processing system design, a special input editing run is usually performed with the data before it is used for updating files or for other processing. This procedure is especially common if data is batched and transferred to some file medium, such as magnetic tape, before processing. Generally this transcription computer run is also used to perform tests on the data, to prove the control totals to that point and to prepare any controls required in further processing. If a special input run is not used, each data item read is usually subjected, before being used, to the input validation appropriate for the application. Typical output from an input validation run is shown in Figure 5-1 (page 60).

If controls such as those described are built into the system, how should an input error which reaches the computer be handled? In a small data processing installation it may be both feasible and desirable to halt processing while the error is corrected. However, this is usually not desirable. As the equipment

TABLE 5.1.   Methods for input data error control.

At point data is created and converted to machine-readable form	At point data is first put into the computer	At points data is handled, moved or transmitted
Procedural controls Data review Verification Check digit	File label (internal) Tests for validity: — Code — Character — Field — Transaction — Combination of fields — Missing data — Check digit — Sequence — Limit or reasonableness test Control total	Transmittal controls Route slip Control total External file labels

becomes larger and the systems more complicated it is not economically advisable to halt the computer processing to make a correction. Instead, the transaction is shunted aside. It may be written on a suspense file to be examined at a later time, and information may be written on the console typewriter explaining the reason for the item's rejection. There should thus be a file of rejects and an error listing indicating why the data was rejected. This error listing provides valuable information to the auditor on problems in the system.

Items which are rejected by the input editing run should be carefully controlled to make sure they are not lost and are returned if sent outside the data processing center for correction. When items are rejected the control totals must be revised to account for the difference.

In the design of a data processing application, consideration should be given to techniques which eliminate all or part of the input preparation. Some examples of such techniques are:

TECHNIQUE	EXAMPLE
Prepunched data cards with only variable data added	Hourly payroll cards reproduced from master payroll cards (only hours worked need be keypunched)
Exception input	Salaried payroll in which no input is required unless there is an exception

The number and type of controls used in a particular application will depend upon the errors which can occur, the feasibility of the various error control methods and the importance of the consequences of errors compared to the cost of using the controls.

Control over creation and conversion of input data

Standard practices and well-designed forms impose procedural controls on the creation of data. For example, a part number to be written on a document may have to be written in a special position which contains the exact number of spaces required for the part number. The spaces can be marked in such a way that

Procedural Controls
and Data Review

```
BG  // JOB BETTY
BG  00.00.06
BG  BEGIN UNEARNED INCOME REPORT
BG  ALLSTORES CORP.
BG  OP111   I   DATA CHECK SYS001=181
           CCSW=02100031680E000000 SNS=085203C00000 CCB=003128
BG  NO MATCH CARD 021602R3
BG  NON NUMERIC FIELD   02980452
BG  DUP 03110004
BG  TERMS NOT EQUAL ACCOUNT 03200024 TB 48 CARD 36
BG  NON NUMERIC FIELD   03910053
BG  DUP 03910087
BG  TERMS NOT EQUAL ACCOUNT   04610200   TB 08   CARD 36
BG  TERM NOT GREATER THAN ZERO OR REMAINING PAYMENTS IS NEGATIVE 04610200
BG  NON NUMERIC FIELD   04660002
BG  DUP 06510011
BG  TRIAL-BALANCE READ ERRORS 000001
BG  END UNEARNED INCOME REPORT
BG  EOJ BETTY
BG  00.07.25
```

FIGURE 5-1.   Typical output from an input validation run

a part number containing less than or more than the required number of characters will be detected by the writer of the part number. Where direct input devices are used, templates over the keys, identification cards and other procedural aids serve to reduce input errors.

Review procedures require examination of input data before it is converted to machine-readable form. The person charged with this task may be assigned the responsibility of checking all coding of documents. This may be connected with the addition of information or it may be an entirely separate checking step.

Verification of
Conversion to
Machine-Readable
Form

When data is converted to machine-readable form (punched cards, for example), the accuracy of conversion can be tested by mechanically verifying the keypunching operation. Two separate keydriven machines are used—a card punch and a verifier. The data is first punched by a keypunch operator. The punched cards and the original data are then given to a verifier operator who inserts the punched card in the verifier and re-keys the information from the original source documents. The verifier does not punch but instead compares the data keyed into the verifier with the punches already in the card. If they are the same the punched card is presumed to be correct. A common indication that this check has been performed is a notch put at the right end of a correct card by the verifier (see Figure 5-2, page 64). An incorrect card is notched over the column containing the difference. The incorrect cards are returned for repunching and reverification.

A recent development is the use of a magnetic tape encoder as an alternative to keypunching of cards. Data is recorded directly on magnetic tape. The device can be used both to record data and to verify it. An advantage is the fact that the data is not written on tape until an entire record has been keyed in. Any error the operator notices may be corrected immediately. The verification process includes the correction of errors.

Verification is a duplicate operation and therefore doubles the cost of data conversion. Various methods are used to reduce the amount of verifying. One method is to verify only part of the data. Some data fields are not critical and an error will not affect further processing. Examples are descriptive fields containing vendor name, part description, etc., which, under most circumstances, are not critical. The use of prepunched cards and prepunched stubs and the duplication of constant data during keypunching may allow verification to be restricted to the variable information added by the card punch. The use of turn-around documents illustrates a technique for reducing the need for keypunching and related verification. In a billing operation, for example, a punched card is used as the billing document. The customer is asked to return the punched card (or a punched stub) with his payment. If the customer makes a full payment, no keypunching may be required; if partial payment is made, the amount of the payment is punched, but verification is not necessary for any fields other than the amount. The same approach is used for turn-around documents which are read optically when returned.

Another approach to reducing verification, used with statistical data, is to verify only if the card punching error rate is above an acceptable level. Each operator's work is checked on a sample basis. If her error rate is acceptable, no verification is made; if it is not, complete verification is made.

Verification can also be conducted by visual inspection of the printing on the card or a visual review of a listing of the cards. Other control procedures (explained below) may be substituted for verification—a check digit on an account number or a batch control total, for example.

Some techniques for data recording produce a punched card or a punched paper tape as a byproduct of the recording operation. For example, the typing of an invoice may, by the use of a device hooked up to the typewriter, automatically produce a punched card or punched paper tape for inventory control, sales analysis, etc. Proofreading of the invoice serves also to verify the punched card byproduct, though not to the same extent as mechanical verification.

When data conversion is performed by an optical character reader, the correctness of the original document is critical since there may be no separate encoding into machine-readable form. Optical readers are used to read data encoded in a special format, such as marks on a form, and to read special stylized characters or ordinary typed or written characters. Since there is no separate verification, applications having high accuracy requirements use checks such as check digits, batch controls and programmed tests to detect reading errors.

Check Digit   In most applications involving identification numbers, each number may be verified for accuracy by a check digit, which is essentially a redundant digit added to the normal number. The check digit is determined by performing some arithmetic operation on the number in such a way that the usual errors encountered in transcribing a number will be detected. There are many possible procedures, a simple example of which follows:

1. Start with a number without
   the check digit   57648

2. Multiply every other digit by
   two   10 12 16

3. Sum the digits in the resulting
   numbers and the digits not
   multiplied $1+0+7+1+2+4+1+6=22$

4. Subtract sum from next high-
   er number ending in zero $30 - 22 = 8$

5. Add check digit to number
   (at end or elsewhere)   576488

Note that a check digit procedure is not completely error proof. In the example given above, 57846 or 54678 give the same check digit. It is unlikely, however, that transpositions of this sort will occur. The check digit does not guard against the possible assignment of an incorrect but valid code, such as the assignment of a wrong valid identification code to a customer.

The checking of the code number for the check digit may be performed by the input device (a keypunch or a paper tape punch) or it may be programmed into the computer. Using the check digit as part of the input device has the advantage that an incorrect code is detected before it enters the computer process. Using a check digit on a keypunch, for example, removes the necessity for verifying that portion of the data being punched. Numbers with check digits are frequently termed "self-checking" numbers. Examples of their uses are charge account numbers, employee pay numbers and bank account numbers. A disadvantage of check digits is the necessity of providing new identification numbers when converting to their use. The check digit may be added to an existing code number but this also creates a new number. In most instances, a check digit should be built into any new identification number system that may be used in input data.

Control over input data read into the computer

When data is read into the computer, the program usually checks the file labels to see that the proper file is being used, makes certain checks to ensure that the data fields being read are valid and establishes and checks control totals.

To ensure that the proper transaction or master file is used and that the entire file is processed, file labels are usually used at the beginning and end of files (especially magnetic tape files). In fact, many operating systems specify standard file labels. A file label is a record at the beginning and/or the end of the file which records identification and control information. Reel labels may be used for each reel of a multi-reel file. The label at the beginning is the header label which identifies the file (see Figure 5-3, page 65). Typical information on a header label is:

File Label Controls

1. Name of file

2. Creation date

3. Identification number

4. Reel number

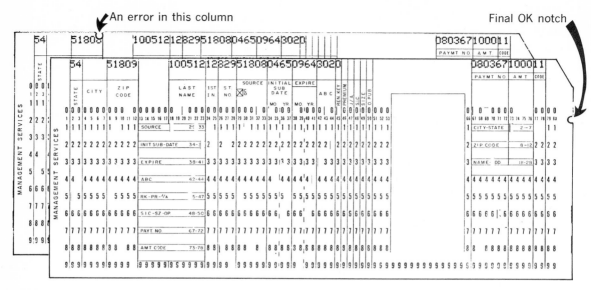

FIGURE 5-2. Punched card showing verification notch

The trailer label is the last record and summarizes the file. Typical information on a trailer label is:

1. Record count

2. Control totals for one or more fields

3. End-of-file or end-of-reel code

Note that these are internal labels. External labels are a separate feature and are explained in Chapter 7.

Tests for Valid Data

Once read by the computer, the data items can be subjected to tests to ensure that they are within the limits established for valid data. Some examples of the checking which can be done are:

1. Valid code. If there is only a limited number of valid codes (say, for coding expenses), the code being read may be checked to see that it is one of the valid codes.

2. Valid character. Certain characters only are allowed in a data field, so the computer can test the field to determine that no invalid characters are used.

3. Valid field size, sign and composition. If a code number should be a specified number of digits in length, the computer may be programmed to test that the field size is as specified. If the sign of the field should always be positive or always negative, a test may be made to ensure that the sign is correct. If the field should contain only numerics or only alphabetics, a test may be made to determine that the field does indeed contain the proper composition of characters.

4. Valid transaction. There is usually a relatively small number of valid transactions processed with a particular file. For example, there is a limited number of transaction codes that can apply to accounts receivable file updating. As part of input error control, the transaction code can be tested for validity.

5. Valid combination of fields. Combinations, besides individual fields, may be tested for validity. For example, a salesman code that can be associated with only a few territory codes can be checked for invalid combinations.

6. Missing data test. The program may check the data fields to make sure that all data fields necessary to code a transaction have data.

7. Sequence test. In batch processing, the data to be processed must be arranged in a sequence identical to that of the file. Both the master file and the transaction file may be tested to ensure that they are in correct sequence—ascending or descending, as the case may be. The sequence check can also be used to account for all documents numbered sequentially.

8. Limit or reasonableness test. This is a basic test for data

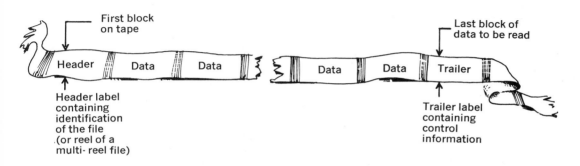

FIGURE 5-3.   Header and trailer labels for file on magnetic tape

processing accuracy. Input data usually falls within certain limits. For example, hours worked should not be less than zero and should not be more than say 50 hours. The upper limit may be established from the experience of the particular firm. Input data may be compared against this limit to ensure that no input error, or at least no input error exceeding certain pre-established limits, has occurred. The following are sample situations:

The total amount of a customer order may be compared with his average order amount. If this order exceeds say three times the amount of his average order then an exception notice may be printed.

A material receipt which exceeds two times the economic order quantity established for the particular item may be subject to question.

An amount on a receiving report may be compared with the amount requested on the purchase order. If there is more than a small percentage variance, an error in the input data can be assumed.

In a utility billing, consumption is checked against consumption in prior periods to detect possible errors or trouble in the customer's installation.

9. Check digit. The check digit is checked on identification fields having this control feature.

Control Totals   Control totals are used as a basic method for detecting data errors. The control total process requires that a control figure be developed by some previous processing and that the current data processing recompute this amount, comparing the resultant total with the previous total. Control totals are usually obtained for batches of data. The batches are kept to a reasonable size so that errors can be isolated easily. In batch processing, one or more control totals are prepared for each batch of source documents before they enter data processing. The control totals are written on a batch ticket along with other control information. (Figure 5-4 (page 67) and Figure 5-5 (page 68)) which accompanies the batch. The control totals are normally keypunched or otherwise converted to machine-readable form and accompany the batch as it enters computer processing. The control totals are

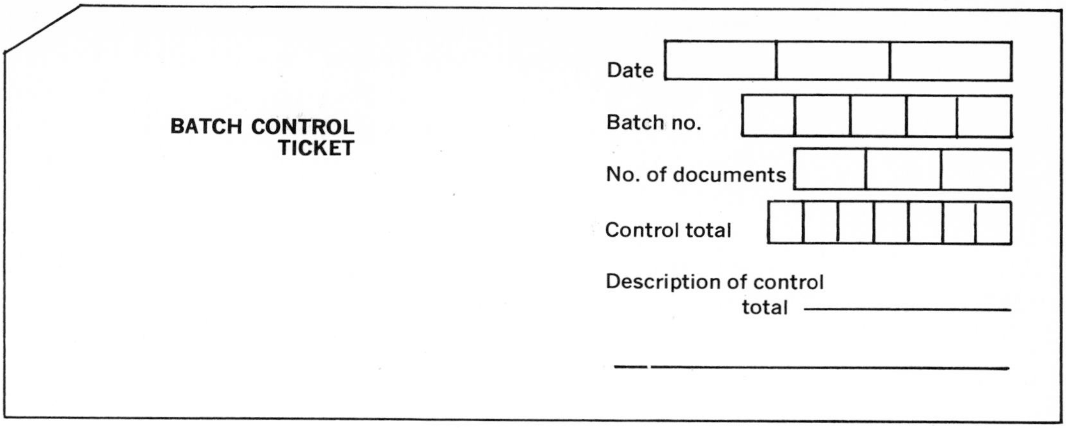

BATCH CONTROL
TICKET

Date

Batch no.

No. of documents

Control total

Description of control
total ————————————

——— ——————————

FIGURE 5-4.   Punched card used as batch control ticket

read by the computer for use in checking the batch of input data. Sales slips to be processed by computer, for example, are first added on an adding machine so that a control total for the sales in the batch may be reached. A control total for payroll might be the number of employees for which checks should be prepared. Control figures may be financial totals, hash totals, or document or record counts.

Financial totals. Financial totals are totals such as sales, payroll amounts, inventory dollar amounts, etc., which are normally added together in order to provide financial summaries.

Hash totals. Hash totals are totals of data fields which are usually not added. The total has meaning only as a control and is not used in any other way in data processing. To determine that all inventory items are processed, a control total may be developed of the inventory item numbers and this control total compared with the sum of the item numbers obtained during the processing run.

Document or record count. In many cases, instead of obtaining a financial total or hash total, it may be sufficient merely to obtain a count to ensure that all documents or records have been received and processed.

The comparison of the control totals obtained prior to process-

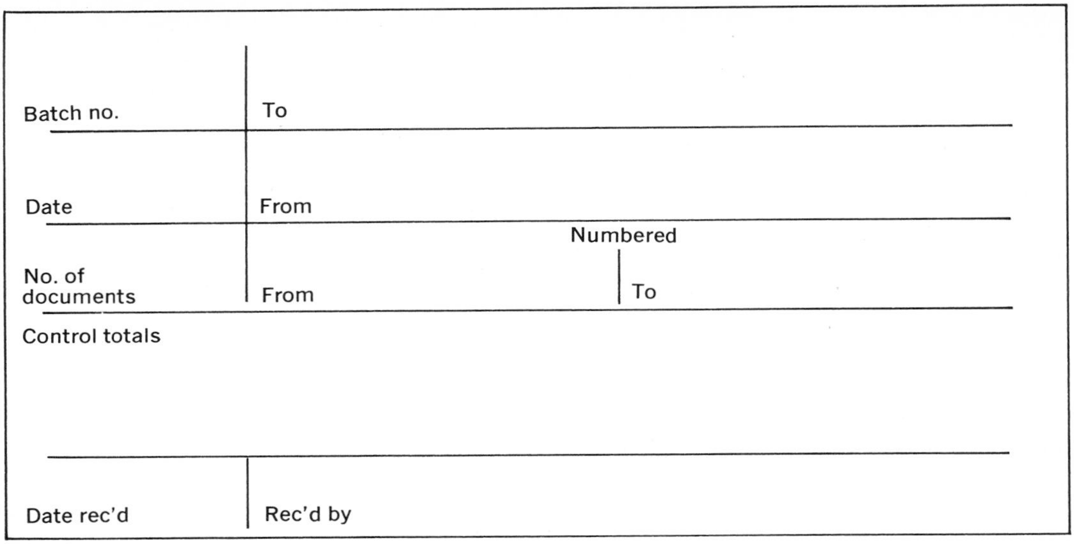

Batch no.	To		
Date	From		
		Numbered	
No. of documents	From		To
Control totals			
Date rec'd	Rec'd by		

FIGURE 5-5.   Batch control ticket to accompany source documents

ing with the control totals computed by the computer may be handled by the computer or performed by the control clerk. When trailer labels are to be used on magnetic tapes, a record count and other control totals are established by a prior processing run and are available for checking purposes when the tape is read. When the output of one run becomes the input of another run, run-to-run control totals are established. These control totals can be used to determine whether or not all items in the batch have been received and processed.

In general, it is desirable to have the computer perform the control comparison. Control totals are read as input data items and the computer is programmed to accumulate control totals internally and make comparisons. A message confirming the comparison and showing the totals should be printed out even if the comparison does not disclose an error. These messages are then subject to review by the control clerk.

Control over handling of input data

Transmittal controls, route slips, control totals and external file labels are examples of controls over the handling of input data.

Control totals have already been explained and external file labels are described in Chapter 7. The transmittal controls and route slips are discussed in this section (see Figure 5-6, below).

When data is moved about in an organization there is always a possibility that it may be lost or otherwise diverted from the proper processing channels. To ensure proper identification of data as it moves through the company, and more especially as it moves through the data processing steps, it is customary to use some form of status identification. As they enter the data processing center, batches of data may be logged on a listing showing the date received. As each batch passes a data processing station it is registered to record the fact that the batch has been processed. The batch itself usually carries a route slip which indicates both the path of processing it should follow and a record of processing performed.

The input controls should provide for some method of indicating the fact that a document has been processed through a

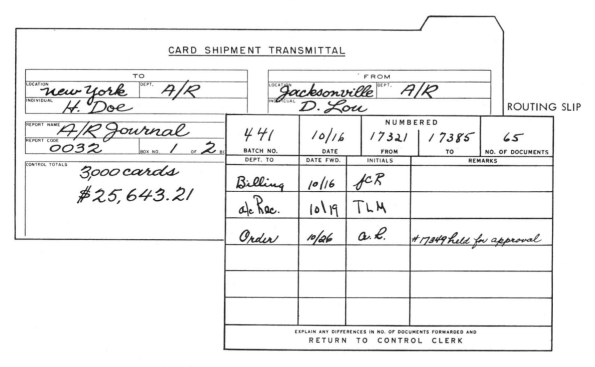

FIGURE 5-6.   Examples of transmittal and route slips
(from IBM C20 — 8060 Document and Accounting Controls)

given department or past a control point in order to prevent the accidental or fraudulent reuse of the document for initiating data processing. Examples of methods include document numbering, cancellation stamps, and processing marks.

Uses of input controls

Three examples illustrate some of the controls discussed above.

Department Store Accounts

In this example of accounts receivable input preparation procedure for a department store, the use of a control total plus a check digit eliminates the need for separate verification.

1. A clerk writes the sales slip which contains the description of the sale (amount, customer account number, date, etc.). The credit sale is also entered in a cash register.

2. The sales from the department are batched and visually checked and a control total for the batch, prepared on an adding machine, is attached to the batch.

3. The batch goes to data processing where a paper tape punch operator first enters the control total in her machine and then prepares a punched tape of transactions by punching (a) the customer account number (checked automatically by the tape punch device using a check digit procedure) and (b) the amount of sale. All other data such as the date, department number, etc., is constant for the batch and is entered only once.

4. At the completion of the punching of the batch, the dollar sales amounts just punched are checked in total by automatic comparison with the batch total. If the two totals are the same the batch of input data is considered to be correct.

5. The control total for the batch is included as part of the input data to be used for computer input and processing controls.

A Statistical Analysis

A questionnaire was sent for market research purposes to customers of a company. There were over 15,000 replies which were to be tallied and analyzed. Most of the questions could be answered in one of six ways. The impact of a small number of errors in coding was not great because of the type of analysis performed. The company used the following procedure:

1. The questionnaire results were punched onto cards but not verified.

2. A simple edit program was written in to examine each card for (a) answers out of the possible range (for example, a 3 or any higher number answering a question with a yes or no response coded 1 or 2), (b) absence of answer to a question and (c) inconsistent answers to three control questions. The cards were then counted.

3. Corrections were made based on this simple edit routine and the revised deck was used in the analysis. Each analysis included a count of the cards. This count provided a control against loss or non-processing of a card.

In data processing, a common processing run is the placing of punched card data onto magnetic tape. In the following example, the hourly payroll data, punched on cards, is mailed by each of the various locations of a multi-location firm to a central computer center for payroll preparation. Each location sends a deck of cards (no batch more than 300) with each employee's payroll data punched into a separate card. The first card of the deck is a control card giving the date of the payroll, the location code of the sender and two control totals (the number of cards transmitted in the batch and the sum of hours worked). The cards are verified at the sending location. A system flowchart for the run is shown in Figure 5-7 (this page).

In the card-to-tape computer run, the computer program performs the following input checks:

1. The number of cards and the number of hours worked in each batch are tallied and compared with the appropriate batch control total. If there is a difference, the batch is copied onto an error tape. An error message is also printed by the console typewriter. In order to avoid a delay in preparing the checks, the discrepant batch is allowed to continue but the checks are not released until the error is resolved.

2. The information on each card is examined for (a) missing

Card-to-Magnetic-Tape Computer Run

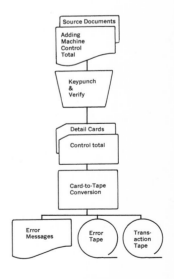

FIGURE 5-7. System flow-chart for card-to-magnetic-tape run

71

data for fields always required, (b) field size for payroll account number and (c) reasonableness of hours worked. Records not passing the tests are copied onto the error tape together with the originating location code.

3. Two control totals (number of records and number of hours worked) are prepared for the tape trailer label which is written as the last record.

4. A summary of errors is typed by the console typewriter. The computer-generated error report reconciles differences between input control totals and output control totals.

5. The data processing control clerk obtains information in order to resolve all batch or other errors. These corrections are added to the payroll run as miscellaneous inputs in place of regular inputs to the card-to-tape run.

The payroll run itself includes tests against invalid or duplicate payroll account numbers, unreasonable rates or hours, etc. It also prepares various controls for a location to use in the distribution of the payroll.

Control over output

Controls over input data, controls over processing (Chapter 6) and built-in hardware controls (Chapter 4) give a high degree of assurance that the computer output is correct. Output distribution should be controlled to ensure that those, and only those, authorized to receive the reports (or other output) do receive them. Persons receiving the output form an important error detection control point, so provision should usually be made in system design for error feedback from recipients of output.

Distribution Controls   The documentation for a run specifies the number of copies to be prepared by the computer operator. Multiple copies must be separated and the carbons removed (decollation). Continuous forms are sometimes separated (burst), but are also frequently bound unburst. Mechanical equipment is available for removing the carbons and separating the individual sheets.

Normally, the documentation for a data processing run also

describes the distribution of the output. A report distribution sheet (Figure 5-8, below) or similar control may be used to record the distribution of the output. A transmittal or release form may be attached to the document, especially if it contains confidential information.

The output should be subjected to review before it is sent from data processing. It may receive an additional review by a control function established in the user department. The receiving departments also tend to detect errors in the normal course of their use of the data.

The person charged with processing control inside the data processing installation checks for completeness of output, correct number of copies and agreement of control totals and also cross checks with output from related programs (for example, he checks reductions of inventory in an inventory control program against cost of sales quantities in a sales analysis program). This review prior to distribution includes scanning of the output for obvious errors, such as lines of meaningless characters or missing fields.

In certain cases it may be desirable (as explained in Chapter 2) to have additional tests performed on the output before ac-

Report Distribution Control

Job No. _____ Job Title _____

Report Title	Copies	Destination	Deleave	Burst	Bind	Remarks

FIGURE 5-8.   Control sheet for report distribution

73

cepting it. These tests are usually either reasonableness tests using approximations developed independently of data processing (for example, total statistical tests) or comparisons with independently maintained control figures.

Persons using output frequently detect errors. These employees should not redo the processing but should apply a visual reasonableness test. If, as in the case of inventory, cash, etc., the physical count is made available, a comparison of this count with the computer prepared records will disclose any errors.

Control over error investigations and corrections

Computer installations normally try to have programs written so that errors will not halt processing. An error procedure written into the program usually provides for a temporary halt—for error identification and listing to facilitate subsequent follow-up—and then a continuation of processing. The procedure followed in any particular case depends on the nature of the errors detected. It is not usually considered good practice to have the operator initiate data corrections.

If there are errors in input data, an input error listing or report which explains the reason for each rejected item should be prepared. The rejected data and the error report should be returned to the originator for correction and resubmission. Personnel receiving the error reports should be instructed in the handling of them. The data processing organization should log out or prepare error listings to establish a control over follow-up and to make sure corrections are made. The data processing organization may make a follow-up check for resubmission or they may leave the responsibility for correction and resubmission entirely to the originator. In either case the responsibility should be defined specifically.

When faulty records are detected, one method of ensuring correction is to write the faulty records on a suspense file for subsequent analysis. Another method is to flag the faulty items but leave them in the file. An error in control totals may be handled through a suspense entry which temporarily corrects imbalances between debits and credits or between control totals. If there are dummy or suspense records maintained in the file to hold balancing entries or unmatched items, such items should be identified clearly and the purpose of each should be investigated promptly.

Master file changes, such as changes in employee pay rates, customer credit limits, etc., should be closely controlled. All master file changes or changes in program data factors should be authorized in writing by the department initiating the changes. A notice or register of all changes should be furnished to the initiating department to verify that the changes were made and to subject the changes to their review.

If an error suggests a faulty program, correction is usually made through a formal request for a programming change. After approval of the request the program change is written, tested and approved as explained in Chapter 2.

Input/output controls and the audit

To determine the reliance he can place on the operation of the data processing system, the auditor should take particular care to evaluate input/output controls because of their importance and because input control is such a common problem in data processing. A point to be remembered is that some of the available input controls (such as card verification) are relatively expensive, so controls in an application should be chosen in relation to the consequences of an error.

The basic points of interest to the auditor are:

1. The consequences of an error (these should usually be considered for each field in the input data)

2. The points in the data processing at which an error may be introduced into the data

3. The adequacy of controls introduced for prevention, detection and correction of input errors

A basic source of background information on the operation of a system's input controls at the computer input stage is the error listing produced when data is rejected. This usually shows the items rejected and the reason for their rejection. It serves as an indication of operative controls but can tell the auditor nothing about controls not operative.

The use of control totals is a basic control method used at all points of input/output control. Since control totals generally require some manual checking, the auditor should review carefully the manner in which control totals are compared and the procedures followed when differences are found.

The follow-up on errors detected by the controls explained in this and the following chapter is of concern to the auditor. He should understand the error follow-up procedures used in the organization and should ascertain that they are operating satisfactorily. He should investigate such points as:

1. What happens to input data found to be in error

2. What happens to an unmatched transaction

3. What happens if control totals do not balance

4. Whether any dummy records or suspense entries are being used to hold erroneous data

5. What procedure is followed when an error is reported in an output.

Summary

Although input data accuracy is a continuing problem in data processing, there are various control techniques which may be built into the data processing procedures.

Input errors can occur when the data is recorded, when it is converted to machine-readable form, when it is read into the computer, or when it is handled, moved or transmitted.

Controls over input creation and conversion may include procedural controls over data recording, review or verification of transcription or conversion and the use of a check digit.

Controls at the point of entry into the computer may include a file label, tests for valid data and control totals. The validity checks are performed on the data fields of each record and may include tests for valid codes, characters, field sizes, transactions and combinations and tests for missing data, sequence and limit.

File labels, transmittal slips, route slips and control totals are used to keep track of batches of data and to prevent loss or nonprocessing of items as they move through the data processing installation.

Controls over output include distribution controls and reviews of the output. The reviews may be performed within the data processing organization and by the users of the output.

The auditor must evaluate input/output error controls as part of his evaluation of the data processing system. In general, he is concerned with the adequacy and operation of the controls. In order to make his judgment, the auditor must understand how errors might be introduced, what the consequences might be of possible errors, and what correction procedures are used when errors are detected. The handling of error corrections should be well controlled in order to avoid the introduction of new errors or the accumulation of uncorrected errors in suspense accounts.

CHAPTER 6

PROGRAMMED CONTROL OVER PROCESSING

IF THERE ARE ADEQUATE input controls for detecting input data errors and adequate equipment controls for detecting equipment errors, what is the need for programmed control over internal processing? A program performs exactly as written, and if it is properly debugged and tested there should be no program-based errors. However, large programs are so complex that there may be latent errors in the program which may not show up for weeks, months, or even years after the program has been accepted. For example, a large payroll program worked well for several years but failed when it was required to process name changes for two newly married female employees whose names were on adjacent records in the master file. The program was unable to handle this somewhat unusual situation. Another reason for having programmed controls over processing is that a program may be modified incorrectly—intentionally or accidentally—while the data is being processed. It is sensible, therefore, to put various processing error control features into the program.

Sources of errors in computer programs

Errors in the coding of instructions usually show up in the assembly or compilation process during which the program is translated from symbolic to machine language form. Errors

Errors in Coding

79

(other than syntax errors) in written instructions are usually detected in the debugging phase of program preparation.

Errors in Processing Logic

During programming, every path which the processing can possibly take should be accounted for—but there may be literally thousands of possible paths. Thus, a program may be written with incorrect logic for several processing paths and the defect detected during the debugging phase only if there is a test of that path. Test data used in debugging is designed to test all processing paths, but it is unlikely that all possible sets of conditions for a large program can be tested in advance.

Incomplete Program Logic

Although a program should handle all possible processing conditions, it may happen that the system designer and the programmer overlook some conditions which may occur. For example, a field which should not be negative may, through some combination of events, take on a negative value. If this possibility is not anticipated in the computer program and does occur, the results of the processing may be incorrect and the error never detected.

Failure to Test For Machine Conditions

The equipment controls described in Chapter 4 do a good job of detecting equipment-based errors. There are other equipment-based conditions which may or may not be considered errors, depending on circumstances or the conditions themselves. Most computer systems, therefore, have the computer program handle certain internal conditions and machine conditions associated with the input/output equipment. If the program does not provide for the testing and handling of machine conditions, an undetected error may result. In many computer systems, the operating system performs much of this function, relieving the individual programmer of most of this responsibility.

The following situation illustrates this type of program requirement. A computer program performing arithmetic may produce a result larger than the storage location assigned to the result can hold. This circumstance is called overflow. The excess digit produced in an overflow will be lost unless program action is taken to restore it. The overflow condition may set an internal switch. This switch can be tested by a program instruction to find out whether or not overflow has occurred. If the test of the switch is not made, the correction for overflow cannot be made and the results of the program may be in error. An alternate computer design automatically causes processing to be interrupted temporarily when a condition such as overflow occurs; the program then determines the reason for the interruption, makes the necessary adjustments, and returns control to the program step which was interrupted.

Improper Program Modification

One of the characteristics of a computer program is that instructions can be modified during the running of the program. In many cases, therefore, some steps required for computer processing are not put into the computer in the form in which they are actually executed. One programming technique using the concept of modification is the loop. Say, for example, that a program must compare an account code with a list of valid account codes in order to check the validity of the account code data item. A straight line coding would require a separate instruction for each comparison. For 100 codes, this would mean 100 to 300 (or more) instructions, depending on the type of computer involved. A loop may be written containing only a few—perhaps four to six—instructions, but these few instructions are executed repeatedly. Each time they are executed, the instructions governing the task (in this case, making the comparison) are modified so that on each turn through the loop the computer executes a revised set of instructions. A loop has the form shown in Figure 6-1 (this page). Instruction modification may become quite complex. If it is not handled properly or if the procedure is not terminated correctly, the modification may alter the program in a way not anticipated by the programmer.

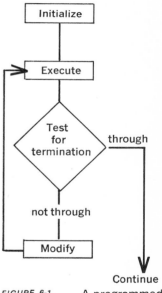

FIGURE 6-1.   A programmed loop

Incomplete or Unauthorized Program Changes.

Another source of errors in computer programs is the changing of programs without proper authorization and without proper checks to foresee the impact of each change. There may be interaction among various parts of a complicated program such that a change in one part of the program may affect steps in another part. Unless there is a proper evaluation of changes and a proper post-change debugging, minor changes may result in the introduction of major errors into the program.

Program tests for errors in computer processing

When an error is detected during processing, it should be indicated by an operator message. This message—or the operator instructions associated with it—should specify a recovery procedure. Processing may be halted or continued, depending on the type of error and the recovery steps to be taken.

Where feasible, programs which require a long running time should be written so that an error occurring late in the run will not necessitate an entire rerun. This is accomplished by including rerun points in the program. At each rerun point, all intermediate results obtained so far are preserved. They may be written on a magnetic tape or punched into cards, for example. If the run is aborted because of some error following a rerun point, the processing can be restarted at that point by a procedure that reads in the preserved data.

The types of program controls that test computer processing are the limit and reasonableness test, the crossfooting or cross-testing check, and the control figures check. Other programmed checks primarily designed to detect input errors have been described in Chapter 5.

Limit and Reasonableness Test

As in the case of input data, a control over processing may be exercised by program instructions which test the reasonableness of the results of processing by comparing them either with predetermined limits or with flexible limits. The net pay in a payroll application may be checked against an upper limit such that any paycheck exceeding it is probably in error. In a billing operation for a relatively homogeneous product, such as steel bars or plates, the weight of the shipment may be divided into the billing in order to develop a price per pound. If the price per pound differs from the average by more than a predetermined percentage, a message should be written for subsequent follow-up to determine if the billing is in error.

Crossfooting Test

It is frequently possible to check computer data processing by a method similar to the manual method of crossfooting. Individual items are totaled independently and then a crossfooting total is developed from the totals. In a payroll application, for example, the totals are developed for gross pay, for each of the deduction items and for net pay. The total for net pay is also obtained independently by taking the total for gross pay and deducting the totals for each of the deduction items. If this crossfooting result does not correspond to the original result for net pay, some error in the program of processing is indicated.

Control figures developed in the same manner as the input control totals can be used for testing the data processing within the machine. For example, the number of items to be invoiced in a billing run may be used as a control total and compared with the number of items billed on the invoices.

Control figures developed during processing should, where relevant, be in a form which can be compared with related input control totals. If input controls are on gross debits and credits, then the program should also develop gross debit and credit totals.

Program control over operator error

An operator may introduce errors into a program run by setting console switches incorrectly, by loading incorrect files, by loading incorrect batches of transactions, or by putting the files of transactions on the wrong piece of equipment (such as the wrong tape unit). The program controls attempt to reduce the possibility of such operator errors by supplying console messages for directing the operator, by testing for proper equipment and switch settings, and by testing each file for a file label (as discussed in Chapter 5).

For the initial setup of a job, the operator makes use of directions in the computer operator instructions book. This specifies the equipment to be used, the files to be loaded, etc. For computers with an operator console I/O device, a console message should describe any steps to be performed by the operator during the running of the program. The console input/output unit is usually a typewriter or a cathode ray tube display. (If a computer does not have a console input/output device, the regular printer must be used for messages.) The console operator should usually be required not only to perform the task but also to verify via the console input device that the task has been performed.

If files such as magnetic tapes are to be placed on specific units, it is correct procedure to program a test of the equipment to check that the files are loaded. If program sense switches (manual switches on the computer which can be tested for setting by a program instruction) are used, the program should test the switch settings to see if they correspond to switch settings which are appropriate for that particular program.

Program control by an operating system

An operating system is, in its simplest form, a program which supervises the running of other programs. In third generation equipment, the operating system is vital to the effective use of the computer. A typical operating system consists of a control program and a number of processing and service programs which are executed under the supervision of the control program.

The control program automatically supervises job flow through the system; controls the location, storage and retrieval of data; and schedules the use of the equipment to ensure efficient and continuous operation. There is a scheduling routine which assigns input/output units to jobs and processes job control instructions, for example, and an input/output control system which services all input/output operations.

The standard input/output control system is significant for error control. It moves data between the input/output units and the central processing unit, regulates input/output priorities, provides error detection and correction, and stops and restarts operations when a malfunction occurs. Procedures for testing for file labels, for recovering from card reader errors and for handling tape-write errors are examples of error procedures contained within this system which therefore do not need to be written by the programmer. This control reduces the chance for error and standardizes the error messages and procedures.

Most third generation equipment of medium or large size can perform in multiprogramming mode; that is, more than one program can be executed concurrently. Supervision of multiprogramming is part of the control program. When the central processor, while executing a program, must wait for input or output operations to be completed, this waiting period (a few milliseconds) may be used for work on a second program, and, if the latter must wait, on a third, and so on. The switching back and forth between programs is performed by the control program.

The operating system establishes a certain amount of discipline in programming and operating. For the programmer it provides standard routines for handling all error checking and recovery procedures when the data is moved between the input/output device and the central processor. The operating system moves the data, but the programmer must still perform tests to evaluate the validity and correctness of that data. For the operator, the operating system requires standard control cards, issues standard messages, and requires standard recovery procedure.

Summary

To obtain reasonably high assurance that a program will do what is intended, there should be proper organization and supervision of programming and proper debugging of programs before use. In addition, the program itself should provide for the detection of errors which may go undetected during preparation and debugging. The programmed tests are relatively simple but can be very effective in detecting logic errors, incomplete processing errors, and errors introduced by incompletely debugged program changes. The programmed error controls can also detect certain types of operator errors, such as the loading of incorrect data files or the incorrect setting of sense switches.

The operating system is an important development with respect to processing control because it takes over, using standard routines, many processing tasks which would otherwise have to be detailed by the programmer. The standard procedures, standard error messages and standard responses eliminate many of the errors which come from the use of inconsistent, non-standard methods.

CHAPTER 7

SAFEGUARDING RECORDS AND FILES

A DATA PROCESSING INSTALLATION should follow procedures for safeguarding the program and the data files from loss or accidental destruction. Advance provisions should be made for reconstruction of records in the event of loss or destruction. Computer data processing introduces additional safeguarding problems which are not present in manual data processing systems. This chapter surveys the problem of safeguarding records and files and describes various possible control measures. These include physical safeguards, procedural controls, a retention plan, a reconstruction plan, and insurance.

Need for file protection

The machine-readable records and files of a computer data processing system might typically consist of punched cards, magnetic tapes, magnetic disks, magnetic drums, or plastic strips. Except in the case of punched cards, information is recorded on these file media in patterns of magnetized spots on iron oxide coatings. The computer-based media are more easily destroyed than manually prepared records and are more subject to misuse because the contents are not recognizable without the use of the computer. The situations in which file losses can occur are:

Ways in Which
File Loss Can Occur

1. Presence in destructive environment

87

2. Operator mishandling

3. Machine malfunction

A destructive environment can result from fire, excessive variation in temperature, power failure, etc.

Operator mishandling may range from careless physical destruction of file media to loss of information through incorrect or premature use of files. Since most file media are reusable, careless use of an incorrect file could result in the obliteration and destruction of its prior contents. A data processing magnetic tape may be read from and written on hundreds of times; it is similar in concept to the magnetic tape of a voice recorder. The recorded tape may be played (read) many times, but the recording (writing) of new information automatically erases the previously recorded data.

Machine malfunctions in file handling devices can lead to the destruction of recording media. Most file handling devices operate at high speed. Speed is a benefit to data processing, but it also presents a danger to the recording media. The device which can read cards at a rate of 1000 per minute can also shred cards beyond any possibility of reconstruction. A high-speed magnetic tape drive can, through a slight timing error, begin to rewind before all the slack has been taken up. As a result, the backlash may peel off some of the oxide coating, stretch the tape, or break it. In such cases, the data on the magnetic tape will be lost.

Auditing Considerations

The client's practices for safeguarding of files are important to the independent auditor. Unsound practices may lead to operating problems for the client and may interfere with the audit by not providing an adequate audit trail. The client's retention practices for safeguarding files may also provide data for audit tests.

The auditor should alert management to any deficiencies in procedures for safeguarding records and files and providing file reconstruction in the event of loss. Even though no loss or destruction may have occurred, a weak system endangers the records and, consequently, jeopardizes future operations and audits of the company.

Proper management of file safeguards aids in the preservation of an audit trail. An audit trail is a trail of files and references which allows for the tracing of transactions from inception to final recording in the accounts, or from final recording backwards to inception. This concept is discussed further in Chapter 9.

A client's control procedures must be understood if the auditor is to make use of the computer to test client files. Without this knowledge, the auditor can very easily plan to run a test on files which no longer exist. Of course, the auditor should not depend on the retention practices of the client but should specify in writing the files that must be retained for recurring audits. Otherwise a change of file retention practices during the year may destroy data desired for the audit.

Physical safeguards

The physical safeguards for computer files may be classified as environmental control, fire protection, security protection and off-premises storage. A discussion of fire insurance protection is included later in the chapter.

Cards, tapes and disks can be affected by extremes of temperature and humidity. Punched cards, for example, tend to hold static electricity and stick together if the humidity is too low, but, if the humidity is too high, they swell in size and can jam the input mechanism on the card reader. Therefore, it is desirable to control the temperature and the humidity in the areas used for storing machine-readable records. Standard building temperature and humidity control equipment is adequate.

Environmental Control

A magnetic field arising from a power generator or a nearby high voltage electrical source can destroy the magnetically encoded contents of media such as disks and tapes. This possibility, though it seldom occurs, should be considered when environmental safeguards are established.

Tape files, card files and disk packs can be easily destroyed by fire. These records are even more subject to fire damage than the printed or written records of manual or tabulating systems. A small fire which chars only the edges of paper or books can melt a tape or warp a disk. Both fire and water can damage a card file so that it can no longer pass through the input reader. In the

Fire Protection

case of computer equipment, "over-heating to as little as 140° can cause malfunction of some transistors and temperatures above 300° Fahrenheit can permanently damage these devices."[1]

A most spectacular example of fire damage occurred in 1959 in the Air Force Statistical Division Offices at the Pentagon. Seven thousand reels of magnetic tape were destroyed. The tape itself was valued at $.25 million; the information on the tape was probably worth many millions.

The National Fire Protection Association has made extensive recommendations concerning computer installations.[2] In general these call for:

1. Housing of the computer in a non-combustible environment

2. Use of smoke or fire detectors

3. Availability of carbon dioxide extinguishers

4. Storage of vital records in storage cabinets having a class C rating (one hour at 1700° Fahrenheit)

5. A separate air conditioning system for the computer or a shut-off switch for cutting off the air conditioning fans

6. A separate emergency shut-off switch to control electrical power for the computer system

7. Personnel trained in fire control procedures

Care should be taken to include program files and documentation in provisions for fire protection. In one case, a company purchased an excellent vault for storing magnetic tape and felt they had done a good job of ensuring fire protection. However, a magnetic tape can be read only by using a computer and a computer will not function without a program. The company's programs were stored in a steel cabinet next to the computer. In the event of a fire, the data would have been safe, but there would have been no way to process it.

Security Protection

Many organizations always lock their general ledgers in their vaults each night, yet leave the same information on a tape reel

---

[1] Robert E. Meyer, "Fire Protection for Computer Systems," *Proceedings of Univac Users Association*, April 1965.

[2] *Standard for the Protection of Electronic Computer Systems*, Bulletin No. 75, National Fire Protection Association, 60 Batterymarch Street, Boston, 1964.

sitting on a rack in the machine room. Interestingly enough, a tape reel is considerably more portable than an old general ledger. If important corporate information is kept in machine-readable format, it should be subject to the same security precautions applied to written, hard copy records. Security precautions should be especially strict for machine records, since these can be duplicated easily or even altered in such a way that no trace of the change is left.

At best, fireproof storage will only guarantee protection of files or documents for a limited period of time. An intense fire, or some other disaster such as flood can still destroy data processing records in "fireproof" storage. For this reason, off-premises storage is used to provide a further safeguard for essential data processing records.

Off-premises storage can be implemented by renting space in a secure, fireproof, remote location. Some organizations use bank vaults. This is usually quite expensive and therefore suitable only for selected information. Another method is to use a different storage location within the same company. One organization which follows this policy mails copies of magnetic tape files and documentation each day to another location of the company, where they are stored in a fire-resistant room. Tape files no longer needed for back-up are returned to the computer center for reuse.

The method of providing files for remote storage is chosen according somewhat to the type and portability of the media being used, whether punched cards, magnetic tape, disk packs or strip file packs. This topic receives further treatment later in the chapter.

Procedural controls

Procedural controls can be used in the management of a computer center in order to minimize the possibility of data or program file destruction through operator errors. Some common methods surveyed here involve external labels, magnetic tape file protection rings, tape library procedures, internal labels and boundary protection.

External Labels   Files should be clearly labeled so that the operator can be sure of their contents. External labeling can be used on punched card and magnetic tape files, for instance.

Punched card files should be clearly labeled as to date created and file name. Such information is usually written on the top of the deck with a felt marking pen. The first and last cards of the deck are marked "FIRST CARD" and "LAST CARD," respectively, and both carry the file identification number.

All magnetic tape reels should be clearly labeled for easy identification. An unlabeled tape is assumed to be a "scratch" tape (one available for erasure and reuse). External tape labels (see Figure 7-1, below) indicate the date written, the file number, the file name and the release date. Large installations may have so many tapes that it is convenient to identify tapes by reel number, rather than by file name.

It is possible to use the color of the plastic tape reel itself as a further identification—but not as a substitute for external labels. Reels can be obtained in six to eight different colors. An installation may work out an identification code, such as red for master files, yellow for system files, etc.

File Protection Rings   Another physical safeguard is used to prevent erasure of information prior to the release date for a magnetic tape. This device is a removable plastic or metal ring, the presence or absence (depending on the computer manufacturer) of which will prevent

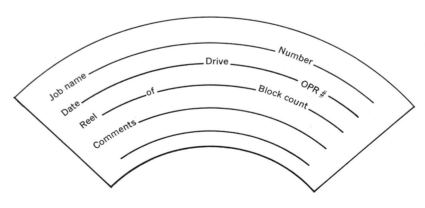

FIGURE 7-1.   External magnetic tape label

an employee from writing on the tape. The most common method consists of the insertion of the ring to allow writing and the removal of the ring to inhibit writing (Figure 7-2, this page). The ring is used with the external label as an added protection. The procedure for writing a file includes instructions about the external label and a reminder to remove (or insert) the file protection ring.

In large tape installations, it is common to have a tape librarian, or a library staff, charged with the responsibility of keeping track of tapes and their uses. Good library practices should also be employed in medium or small tape systems, even if no single person is specifically charged with the library function. Tape racks and cabinets should be available for storing all tapes in the installation. Tapes released for use and tapes to be saved should be strictly segregated. Within these two basic classifications, the racks may be further separated according to tape function. It is also desirable to have each reel case labeled on its outside edge so that reels may be identified without removal from the racks. Some installations use an out-of-file card which is placed in the rack whenever a reel is removed; of course, this is not required for scratch tapes.

A reel of tape is moderately expensive (about $30) and in a tape installation it is normal to have several hundred reels. So procedures should be established to control this asset. Ideally, each tape reel should be assigned a permanent reel number when it is placed in service and a control card (see Figure 7-3, page 94) should be set up for it. This card should show the date placed in service, the manufacturer, the manufacturer's reel number, and the installation reel number. A record should be made of each use of the reel of tape. If a tape is broken or damaged, or if it causes any operating problems, entries should be made on its control card. The information on these cards is used:

1. To provide a record of reel use, including
   (a) a record of current and prior use
   (b) a record of reels which have completed the retention period and can be made available for reuse
2. To provide a record of errors and difficulties in order to

Tape Library

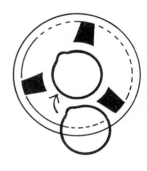

FIGURE 7-2.   File protection ring for magnetic tape

93

(a) evaluate performance of various brands of tape
(b) determine if tapes need reconditioning
(c) determine if tapes should be permanently removed from service

TAPE HISTORY CARD				
Date purchased	Mfg.	Length		Reel number
Density	Date	Length stripped		Remaining length
Date Certified				
Density				
Date out	Program no.	File no.	Program and file name	Errors

FIGURE 7-3.   History card for tape reel

A careful tape procedure is thus a protection against the loss or destruction of a file. It is also a useful housekeeping procedure; it minimizes tape investment by avoiding excessive back-up retention and promotes operating efficiency by removing error-causing tapes and having them cleaned or replaced, depending on their condition.

Internal file labels, which have been explained in Chapter 5, serve as programmed checks for safeguarding files from misuse. The header label is a special record at the beginning of a magnetic tape (or other file). It identifies the tape and provides information which the program can check to ensure that the tape is the one required or that it has reached the release date. Program tests of internal labels supplement external labels and file protection rings as safeguarding measures.

Internal Labels

Boundary protection is the protection of one file or program from another when they are stored on a common medium. In internal storage, a memory protection feature, if available, can prevent one program from entering the storage area assigned to another. In disk storage, a similar situation must be handled by programming. For example, when several files or tables are stored on the same disk module or pack, all programs which read or write on the disks should provide boundary protection. If a disk file contains an inventory file on disks 1-9 and a payroll master file on disks 11-17, the inventory programs should provide for a halt if an attempt is made to read any disk other than disks 1-9 and the payroll programs should likewise confine reading to disks 11-17. Such protection should be provided where more than one file is stored on a single disk file.

Boundary Protection

Retention plan

The retention plan, aside from legal considerations, should provide the basis for file reconstruction and for reference or audit trail tracing. Since the retention plan is affected by the characteristics of the media involved, this discussion considers source documents, punched cards, tape files, disk files and dumps (copying of contents) to other media.

Source Documents

The source documents on which an input file is based must be retained intact until such time as the file is proved and balanced with its controls. At this point, the data may be filed or otherwise disposed of. However, the traditional audit and regulatory retention requirements still prevail and must be observed.

Punched Card Files

Any important master file, such as an accounts receivable master file, should be reproduced and the copy should be stored outside the installation as a back-up or reserve deck. Two copies of any revision to the file should be prepared, one for processing against the current master file and one for filing with the reserve deck. Should it be necessary to use the reserve deck, all changes made since it was prepared could be processed to create an updated deck. A complete new copy of the master file should be reproduced periodically (say, every six months) for storage in the outside location. Each time, the previous master deck and intervening revisions may be destroyed. Some installations punch master files into plastic-coated cards which last longer. Plastic cards cost 3 to 4 times as much as regular cards but they can be used for about 6 times as many computer passes.

It is not possible to make any blanket statements about card file retention. In each case the overall system and the importance of the file together dictate how long the file should be retained. Original card files from source documents are usually retained longer than other files since they are more difficult to recreate. Machine output card files can be recreated by reprocessing, but source files from written documents can only be duplicated by the laborious process of repunching. If a card file is correctly transcribed to another medium, such as magnetic tape, the card file may be released and the replacing medium preserved.

Magnetic Tape Files

Back-up support for tape files is usually accomplished by use of the son-father-grandfather concept (Figure 7-4, page 98). An organization usually produces an updated master file at each processing by reading the previous period's master file, making changes according to the transactions being processed, and writing the new file. The following is an example of the normal back-up available for daily processing after processing of Wednesday's transactions (keep in mind that the processing creates a new file tape but does not destroy the old one):

1. Wednesday's file   (son)
2. Tuesday's file   (father)
3. Monday's file   (grandfather)

If the Wednesday tape is destroyed during Thursday processing, Tuesday's tape is processed again with Wednesday's transactions in order to recreate Wednesday's tape. This type of back-up is basic to all magnetic tape processing.

If files are to be recreated under the son-father-grandfather approach, the transaction records used to update the original files must also be retained. In the example cited above, Tuesday's and Wednesday's transaction records must be available, since file recreation is accomplished as follows:

Monday's master + Tuesday's transactions = Tuesday's master

Tuesday's master + Wednesday's transactions = Wednesday's master

In the son-father-grandfather back-up procedure, the old grandfather tape may be released when a new one is produced. Thus, two back-up tapes are in holding at any particular time. Sometimes, a great grandfather may also be saved, but this is not usually necessary.

There are other considerations important in the establishment of a retention schedule for magnetic tapes. First-of-the-month files and other critical records may be saved in order to preserve data which is likely to be needed for the preparation of special analyses, etc. Once a master file is released, its associated transactions can usually be released also.

Disk Files

Disk files are of the fixed module or the removable module (disk pack) type. A characteristic of disk file processing is that the old record is destroyed. When there is an updating, a record is read into storage, altered, then copied back onto the same part of the file, thereby wiping out the old record. To obtain a back-up copy

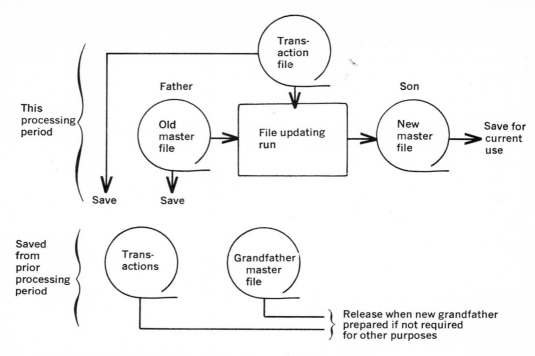

This
processing
period

Father

Trans-
action
file

Son

Old
master
file

File updating
run

New
master
file

Save for
current
use

Save   Save

Saved
from
prior
processing
period

Trans-
actions

Grandfather
master
file

} Release when new grandfather
prepared if not required
for other purposes

FIGURE 7-4.   Grandfather, father and son in magnetic tape files

a special recording must be performed. Unlike magnetic tape processing, disk file processing does not automatically produce a duplicate copy.

Compared to tape, disk packs are expensive and do not readily lend themselves to duplication. Under certain circumstances, however, a back-up copy is necessary for adequate safeguarding of files. Take, for example, a client with a small disk installation which has no magnetic tape capabilities. He maintains his complete inventory file on a disk pack. Inventory is updated every day but there is no need to prepare daily printouts detailing inventory balances. In this case, it may be advisable to duplicate the disk pack each night in order to provide a back-up for reconstruction purposes. Such a procedure would be the best method of providing the inventory file with full support, without which the loss of the disk file would mean the loss of all inventory detail. Like tape files, duplicate files plus transactions allow for reconstruction. The back-up file copy should be protected adequately, preferably in storage off-premises.

In many cases, daily duplication of the disk pack may involve more time and expense than is justified by file retention requirements. As an alternative, a weekly or bi-weekly disk duplication schedule, coupled with a plan for retaining intervening transactions, may provide adequate support. Since this alternative makes considerable reprocessing necessary before a duplicate file can be available, it may not be satisfactory if rapid file replacement is essential.

Where a fixed disk file is used, the method of duplicating and of utilizing off-premises storage is not suitable. A dump procedure (described below) is used instead.

Requirements for transaction retention in disk systems are similar to requirements in tape systems. Basically, transactions must be retained until the related files have been proved and until they are no longer required for purposes of support or other processing needs.

A file may be retained by reproducing (dumping) it on another file medium. This procedure requires extra processing and is therefore used primarily with fixed disk files (or with a single disk pack drive). The common dumps are from disks to tape, cards, or printer paper.

Dumps to Other Media

A very effective form of fixed-module disk file back-up is provided by a magnetic tape drive attached to the computer system. The file can be dumped onto magnetic tape in a matter of minutes and the tape file can then be given fireproof, off-premises storage. This combination of disk file with tape support makes a very powerful system from the standpoint of file control, but the addition of the tape unit and tape control increases the system cost.

If tape is not available, a disk-to-cards dump can be used to provide support. However, such a dump is very time-consuming and should be undertaken only infrequently, say, monthly. In this case, it is necessary to retain transactions for a month in order to permit a rebuilding of the file.

The least satisfactory disk dump support is a dump to the printer. While this procedure is faster than a dump to cards, the information is not in machine-readable form and must be repunched before it can be used to recreate a file. Such a process is very inefficient and time-consuming, but should be used if no other form of back-up is available. However, printer dumps may be useful for other purposes, such as manual reference. If the number of transactions is not too great, the printed copy of the file may be used for a selective manual reconstruction while the computer system is being restored.

To serve as back-up for a fixed disk file, the printer dump, magnetic tape dump, or punched card dump of the file should receive protected or off-premises storage along the same lines as that specified for tapes and disk packs.

Reconstruction plan

If an installation prepares file back-up and safeguards it properly, it has the raw materials for reconstruction. The implementation of reconstruction may require two additional elements:

1. Physical back-up facilities

2. Programs to facilitate reconstruction

Physical Back-up Facilities

The installation should have arrangements for the use of back-up facilities. These may involve the use of:

1. Manufacturer's installation

2. Data processing service center equipment

3. Another organization that has the same equipment (perhaps a reciprocal arrangement)

Plans should be included for the transportation of personnel, data and records to these facilities.

Procedures to Facilitate Reconstruction

Reconstruction is frequently necessary on a day-to-day basis to handle errors which have affected the file. In the case of magnetic tape, the most common reason for rerun is that one or more records on a tape cannot be read. The file may be reconstructed by using the back-up and the normal processing program to reprocess the transactions and produce a new updated file, or a few correcting transactions can be inserted in the next updating run.

In the case of disk files, an incorrect entry alters a file. To correct it, an installation may have a separate program which reverses the transaction and returns the record to its previous state. This may not be possible in other systems where the erroneous record must be restored from the data in the back-up copy of the file.

Insurance

Insurance should be included in the plan to safeguard files. Of course, the details of an adequate insurance program should be explored with a competent insurance representative but, in order to review the plan for safeguarding files, the auditor should be aware of the types of coverage available.

The risks against which the organization should be protected arise primarily from fire and, if work is performed for others, from liability for errors or omissions. The risks from fire are covered in varying degrees by three different types of policies:

1. Fire insurance

2. Valuable papers and records insurance

3. Data processing insurance (all risk) with media and records section

A summary of coverage by specific risk is summarized in Table 7.1 (page 102). This table shows that data processing risks from fire are not well covered by regular fire or valuable papers insurance, whereas the all-risk data processing insurance is designed specifically for the losses that are associated with computer data processing.

Organizations (service centers, banks, CPA firms) which rent time or provide data processing services for outsiders are exposed to two liability risks:

1. Losses caused by errors in the work performed

2. Losses caused by programs written by a consultant

Both of these risks can be covered by data processing liability insurance.

There are currently four insurance companies writing data processing insurance. Two determine premiums on the basis of an engineering survey of the installation and two quote a flat rate with a $5,000 deductible clause. In all four cases, actual

TYPE OF RISK	FIRE COVERAGE	VALUABLE PAPERS COVERAGE	DATA PROCESSING COVERAGE
Damage and/or loss of equipment whether leased or owned	Cost of equipment	None	Cost of equipment
Loss or destruction of programs (software)	Cost of materials (cards and tapes) and labor (keypunching). No coverage for costs of programming or systems design	Extent of coverage in doubt. May exclude recovery for loss of data stored on disks, tapes, or drums. However, may cover loss of software in punched card form	Cost of reconstruction under critical conditions, provided that remote storage is employed for key files and documentation
Loss or destruction of data when reconstruction will be costly, time consuming and difficult	Cost of materials on which data was recorded	Extent of coverage in doubt	Cost of reconstruction under critical conditions, provided that remote storage is used
Extraordinary expenses incurred to return to normal operation	None	Extent of coverage in doubt	Covered
Loss sustained by interruption of business	None	None	Covered

premiums are percentages of the current fire insurance rates paid by the installation.

Apparently, the number of losses arising from the dishonesty of data processing employees is quite small. However, the risks associated with the concentration of the data processing function in a relatively small number of people suggest that bonding of these employees is a desirable practice.

CHAPTER 8

EVALUATING INTERNAL CONTROL

The general framework of internal control

MANY READERS of this report will be already familiar with principles of internal control. It will be advantageous, however, to survey these principles generally before describing their application to internal control in a computer-based data processing environment.

The auditor's primary purpose in evaluating internal control is expressed in the second standard of field work of generally accepted auditing standards:

> "There is to be a proper study and evaluation of the existing internal control as a basis for reliance thereon and for the determination of the resultant extent of the tests to which auditing procedures are to be restricted."[1]

A secondary, but nevertheless important, purpose is to provide constructive suggestions to clients. Of course, these two purposes are related, but it must be understood that the former is required by professional standards, while the latter is a matter of discretion.

The Purpose of Evaluating Internal Control

---

[1] *Auditing Standards and Procedures*, American Institute of Certified Public Accountants, 1963, p. 27.

Because of this distinction, attention given to evaluation must be adequate for each client each year, but attention given to suggestions may vary from client to client, or from year to year for a particular client.

Types of Controls

It has been common in auditing to make a distinction between accounting controls and administrative controls. The accounting controls "comprise the plan of organization and all methods and procedures that are concerned mainly with and relate directly to safeguarding of assets and the reliability of the financial records."[2] Since these controls bear directly on "the reliability of the financial records" they require evaluation by the auditor. In the context of a computer system, the "accounting" controls are those data processing system controls whose aim is to ensure that processing is performed without undetected error (i.e., to ensure that input data is correct, that there is no loss or non-processing of data items, that the program uses the proper files, that the processing is correct, and that the output is distributed to the persons authorized to receive it).

Administrative controls "comprise the plan of organization and all methods and procedures that are concerned mainly with operational efficiency and adherence to managerial policies . . ."[3] Since these controls relate only indirectly to the financial records, evaluation is not required. However, if certain administrative controls have a bearing on the reliability of the financial records, the auditor may include them in his evaluation.

Elements of an Internal Control System

The principal elements of an internal control system are:[4]

A plan of organization which provides appropriate segregation of functional responsibilities

A system of authorization and accounting procedures adequate to provide reasonable accounting control over assets, liabilities, revenues and expenses

Sound practices to be followed in performance of duties and functions of each of the organizational departments

Personnel of a quality commensurate with responsibilities.

---

[2] *Ibid.*, p. 28.
[3] *Ibid.*
[4] *Ibid.*, pp. 28-29.

104

The data processing system controls with which the auditor is most concerned relate directly to the safeguarding of assets and to the reliability of financial records. This idea is expressed somewhat differently as follows:

> "A function of internal control, from the viewpoint of the independent auditor, is to provide assurance that errors and irregularities may be discovered with reasonable promptness, thus assuring the reliability and integrity of the financial records."[5]

A suggested general approach, which focuses on internal control's function of preventing and detecting errors and irregularities, involves the following steps:

1. Analysis of possibilities for errors and irregularities in (a) the general system of data processing and (b) each area of accounting transactions and data processing operations

2. Evaluation of existing controls over such possibilities

3. Evaluation of weaknesses (error possibilities not covered by existing controls) to determine their effect on (a) auditing procedures to be applied and (b) suggestions to be made to client

Regardless of the means by which the data processing operations are performed, the steps above comprise a logical approach for the auditor's evaluation of internal control. They can be particularly useful for distinguishing the essential and non-essential control aspects where computers are used.

In considering specific types of accounting transactions, the experienced auditor should be able to identify the various kinds of errors and irregularities that could result in unreliable financial records or improper disposition of assets. The effects of errors provide a basis for distinguishing critical (for the auditor's purposes) weaknesses of internal control from non-critical weaknesses. Critical weaknesses are those that cause the auditor to include additional auditing procedures, or to change the timing or increase the extent of application of other auditing procedures.

Application of an error impact criterion to the administrative and control techniques discussed in Chapters 2-7 may, in some cases, place a number of them in the non-critical category.

---

[5] *Ibid.*, p. 32.

Those that are so classified in particular cases may be regarded as aspects of administrative control in that they relate primarily to operational efficiency. For instance, the effect on the audit of inadequate documentation depends on the application involved and the audit approach used. Lack of documentation may or may not influence the auditor's evaluation of internal control, but it will certainly cause internal inefficiency in making revisions of programs. In another case, there may be no audit impact from the absence of certain processing controls; but this lack may force the client's data processing personnel to take excessive time for correcting errors which could have been prevented or detected earlier. Controls in the administrative category are not usually the auditor's primary concern, but they are an appropriate area for constructive suggestions to the client.

Possibilities of errors and irregularities that could affect the financial statements require special study by the auditor. For each error possibility, he should determine the control procedures that might be applied effectively and ascertain whether or not such procedures are in use. Each error or irregularity possibility for which appropriate accounting controls are not in use constitutes a weakness requiring the auditor's attention.

The framework of internal control in a computer system

The controls in a computer data processing system should provide reasonable assurance that the processing is carried out correctly. They should detect errors and irregularities promptly and ensure proper corrective action.

The controls in an EDP system include both "administrative" controls for promoting operational efficiency and "reliability" controls for preventing and detecting errors (similar to "accounting" controls). It is frequently difficult to categorize a given control as one or the other of these types unless its use in the system is known. Though a computer time log is usually an administrative control, it is sometimes utilized primarily in connection with procedures to spot unauthorized or unexplained computer usage. Other controls such as limit check, check digit, control figures, etc., are designed primarily for prevention and detection of erroneous processing.

The general elements of internal control—plan of organization, system of authorization and accounting, sound practices in performance of duties, quality of personnel—are applicable to the computer-based data processing system. However, such a system concentrates in a small staff many functions which, in other systems, are widely dispersed. A useful distinction in considering internal control in computer data processing is the difference between the controls required for computer equipment and the controls which substitute for traditional controls based on division of duties, human judgment and alertness.

Controls for Automated Equipment

The purpose of these controls is to detect and control errors arising from the use of EDP equipment. Examples (described in previous chapters) are:

1. Controls to verify conversion of data to machine-readable form for input

2. Controls to detect the loss or nonprocessing of data items

3. File controls to guard against the misuse of files stored on machine-readable media

4. Controls to detect hardware malfunctions

5. Programmed and procedural controls to guard against operator error

If any of these controls are absent, the system may be exposed to undue risk of error. If an omission is considered serious, the scope of audit procedures is affected.

Program Controls That Substitute for Human Controls

In a manual system, internal control relies upon such factors as human alertness, care, acceptance of responsibility and division of duties. Computer processing, however, reduces the number of persons involved in data processing, so that many controls based on human judgment or division of duties are no longer available. The computer program provides alternatives for these human controls. Take for example the following situation: the lowest level clerk usually reacts when she receives a shipment document on which to insert prices and cannot relate the description of the item to the price list; in a computer operation, a non-match must be programmed lest the shipment be invoiced at $0 and accounts receivable updated with a "no charge" invoice. In most instances, the computer checks can be more extensive than those performed manually. Examples (described in previous chapters) are:

1. Data validity tests and check digits

2. Limit and reasonableness tests

3. Sequence checks

4. Error routines for unmatched items, erroneous data, violations of limits, etc.

Controls in a computerized system

The controls in a computerized data processing system may be divided into those which relate to organization and management and those which relate to processing activities. This concept is diagrammed in Figure 8-1 (page 110).

Organization and
Management

This aspect of internal control relates to the assignment of responsibility and authority for the various functions to be performed within the organization. Generally, internal control requires a segregation of duties so that the functions of authorizing and processing transactions and of maintaining custody of assets are effectively separated.

Where computers are used, the auditor's review of internal control should determine whether the organizational structure includes any incompatible combinations of functions. Sources of information and techniques available for reviewing those aspects of internal control to do with organization are generally similar whether or not computers are used. Certain matters that require special consideration in this respect have been discussed in Chapter 2. In general, separation of the systems design and programming duties from computer operating duties is desirable. This separates the preparation of programs from their use in processing.

Further control based on division of duties is achieved by keeping the performance of control functions from the programmers or operators. The control function should include such duties as maintenance of manual controls which account for all input data, reconciliation of manual and machine control figures, reconciliation of run-to-run control totals, investigation of violations, and control over transmission of output. In larger installations, control over data files and programs may be increased by employing both a tape librarian and a program librarian.

Control practices associated with data processing organization and management are:

1. Documentation

2. Program changes controls

3. Scheduling of personnel

4. Procedures for reviewing error log, time log, etc.

5. Maintenance of adequate audit trail

6. Provision for file protection

Proper authorization of transactions is the starting point for establishing internal control over them. The authority of any level of management to commit or disburse assets is associated with its responsibility for achieving the objectives assigned to it. In a computer system, proper authorization is required for input data, programs and possibly output data. The authorization of transactions is based on their desirability, validity and proper classification. The authorization of programs is based on the desirability of the programs or applications and is shown by management's approval to proceed with the writing of the programs.

Input data may relate either to individual transactions (sales or disbursements) or to changes in master files (credit limits set for new customers, increased salary rates, or revised selling prices of products). In these and similar examples, input is usually authorized by signatures or initials on the documents from which the input data is prepared. If the input data may be introduced directly into the computer system without the preparation of any related documents, an alternative means of authorization is necessary. It must include some form of physical control over access to the recording devices or access to the means by which the recording devices can be activated.

Authorization of programs and program changes is as important as authorization of input data, since both are integral parts of the processing operations in computer applications. Evidence of proper authorization of programs and program changes is usually included in the program documentation.

Controls Over Processing

The control points at which specific data processing controls are applied to prevent or detect errors are presented in Figure 8-1 (below). These are the controls imposed on original source document preparation, on conversion to machine-readable form, on processing, on distribution of output, and on uses of output. Typical controls associated with each control point are outlined here; they have been discussed specifically in Chapters 2-7.

1. Source data preparation: (a) traditional controls such as document numbering, review, etc., and (b) records of documents sent to data processing

2. Conversion of source data to machine-readable form: (a) control over receipt and conversion of documents, (b) verification of conversion to machine-readable form and (c) control over handling of errors detected during or after verification

3. Control over processing: (a) tests for validity of input data,

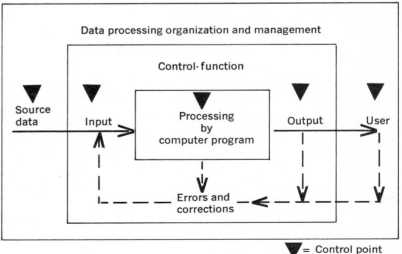

FIGURE 8-1.   Control in a computer data processing system

(b) controls to ensure use of correct files, (c) controls for completeness of processing, (d) controls to detect incorrect processing and (e) control over handling of rejected items and other errors

4. Control over output: (a) controls over distribution of copies and (b) controls over errors and handling of corrections and resubmissions

5. Control exercised by users: (a) user special control comparison and (b) detection of errors during routine use of data

There are programmed controls at only one of these control points (No. 3). These programmed controls may be very significant (depending on the application), but they make up only a part of the complete set of controls. It is important for the auditor to avoid viewing each control separately; he must view the entire set of controls which apply to an application as well as the organizational and management environment in which they are applied.

Review of computer system controls

"Adequate evaluation of a system of internal control requires (1) knowledge and understanding of the procedures and methods prescribed and (2) a reasonable degree of assurance that they are in use and are operating as planned" (Numerals added).[6] These two phases in evaluation are referred to hereafter as "investigation of the system" and "testing for compliance," respectively.

In order to obtain a knowledge and understanding of the procedures and methods prescribed for a data processing system, the auditor should investigate (1) general aspects of control that apply to the computer system as a whole and (2) controls associated with specific applications. Since there is some overlap between these two types of control, the following division is not strict:

Investigating the System

---

[6] *Ibid.*, p. 32.

Each of these topics is discussed in a separate chapter which provides background information to assist the auditor in his evaluation.

Obtaining Information

The auditor's principal sources of data for making his review of the computer system controls are organization charts and related material, documentation, inquiries of responsible data-processing personnel, and inquiries of accounting and other personnel. The manner in which the auditor obtains the necessary information and records it in his working papers is largely a matter of individual or firm preference (as is also the case where computer systems are not involved). Techniques ordinarily include questionnaires, check lists, flowcharts and narrative memoranda. An example of a questionnaire designed for this purpose is included as Appendix E.

The sample questionnaire is divided into two sections—one for general system controls and the other for specific application controls. The questions in the general section relate to the general control framework present in data processing organization, documentation, hardware, file protection, and general policies and procedures for input and output. The other section is used in connection with each computer application within the scope of the auditor's examination (i.e., each application that affects the financial statements). The extent of the review of different applications may vary, depending on circumstances.

The error listings made in connection with computer application runs are a basic source of information about the system and its performance. They have no direct counterpart in a manual system. However, similar information can be found in a manual system by examination of adjusting journal entries for error correction, error memoranda, corrections in the records and suspense account entries.

Organization is investigated in order to obtain information on the segregation of duties or practices such as rotation of personnel, on the organization of the control function and on the operators' control procedures. This information forms a basis for evaluating the control provided by the organization and management of the EDP installation.

A review of documentation provides information relevant primarily to operating efficiency. Inadequate documentation exposes the installation to operating hazards but may not affect the audit steps unless a review of error listings and reports raises questions about the adequacy of program controls which can only be resolved if there is adequate documentation, or unless the independent auditor wishes to test the program directly. If documentation is inadequate to support the audit procedures (such as test data), additional audit procedures may be required. Moreover, inadequate documentation may indicate poor management, which may be indicated elsewhere in inadequate controls.

Hardware controls are usually reliable. However, the auditor should be aware of possible problems, particularly where program tests are necessary for the detection of errors. He does not usually gather information on hardware controls unless his examination discloses hardware-based difficulties.

File protection and file reconstruction are important for preventing hazards to the processing of data. However, these controls do not usually affect the audit procedures unless some information needed for the audit has been destroyed. The auditor should report any uncovered weaknesses to management as items to be corrected in order to safeguard the organization against failure caused by a data processing breakdown.

Other general topics may be investigated to aid in assessing the operating procedures. When examining input and output controls for review of application, for instance, the auditor may also examine certain overall policies. His investigations reflect his concern with the organization of input control procedures and with the administrative procedures for controlling distribution of output and for handling error feedback based on review of the output. The adequacy of control over error investigations is of great concern to the auditor, since a procedure for independent review and approval of error corrections reduces the risk of introducing undetected error conditions through corrections.

The auditor must make an evaluation of the adequacy of the

controls associated with a particular application in order to establish the extent to which audit test procedures should be applied. The general area of data processing may be viewed as the subject of a separate control review. Review of a computer application, however, should consider together the information from the regular internal review questionnaire (or other source) and the data processing information. The EDP application questions thus form a supplement to the regular application questions. For example, the EDP questions relating to processing of payroll should be evaluated in terms of the entire payroll application (including all manual procedures).

Whatever technique is used for obtaining and recording the necessary information about any computer control system, the most important and difficult task is the evaluation of this information. Evaluation so far is preliminary, based on the system purported to be in effect. The next stage, therefore, consists of tests of compliance to see if the supposed system does exist.

Tests of Compliance

Ordinarily, the information obtained by the auditor in his preliminary investigation can be tested by supplemental inquiries and discussion with data processing personnel and by personal observation of their activities during the course of his examination.

In non-computer systems, tests to establish the performance of specific control procedures are made by examination of documentary evidence, such as signatures or initials indicating authorization, approval, verification and reconciliation of details with control totals. Such forms of visible evidence are also available for many control procedures in computer data processing. Examples of compliance tests using such evidence are:

1. Examination of cards for end notch if they are to be key verified

2. Examination of machine room log book for proper recording of control information

3. Examination of documentation for completeness and evidence of proper authorization of program changes

4. Examination of control and error listings and tracing of control totals to sheets used in reconciliation to check compliance with reconciliation procedure

5. Examination of control and error listings for evidence of control totals said to be used.

For the testing of controls contained in computer programs, evidence that the controls exist and are operative during the period of the examination is necessary. There are two methods for obtaining this evidence—one which does not use the computer and one which does.

The method which does not involve the use of the computer program makes use instead of computer printouts and error listings to obtain evidence of the processing actually performed. Transactions are traced from input to regular output or to an error listing. This procedure tests a sample of processed items rather than the program itself. The program's processing and control steps are inferred from evidence of its handling of selected transactions (both correct and erroneous). This approach is described in more detail in Chapter 10.

The second method makes use of the computer to test the program or to test the results of processing with the program. This approach is described in Chapter 11. The different methods may be used separately or in combination, as appropriate.

Summary

In carrying out the internal control review, the auditor evaluates both the possibilities for errors and the existing controls against these errors. His review should result in a determination of the nature and extent of audit procedures to be followed; it should also enable him to offer appropriate suggestions to the client for eliminating the weaknesses in existing controls.

The review consists of two major phases: investigation of the system and testing for compliance. The investigation of the system makes use of inquiries of responsible data processing personnel and of documents such as procedures manuals, organization charts, etc. Its purpose is to discover what the system is supposed to be. The tests of compliance check the system to determine whether or not it complies with the description obtained during the investigation phase.

The internal review should provide the auditor with an understanding of the system sufficient to allow him to evaluate the extent to which he may rely upon the system of internal control and the extent to which he must perform audit tests of the records.

CHAPTER 9

THE AUDIT TRAIL IN AN EDP SYSTEM

ONE ASPECT OF electronic systems which has been of primary concern to the auditor is the audit trail. The auditor is concerned with the changing nature of the trail since source documents and visible historical records can now be altered or eliminated. Changes in the trail have been slow in coming and have frequently been exaggerated by writers on auditing and systems design. This chapter examines the effects of EDP on the audit trail and the problems and opportunities the changes present to the auditor.

The audit trail in non-EDP data processing

The audit trail in non-EDP data processing systems consists of documents, journals, ledgers and worksheets (Figure 9-1, page 118) which enable the auditor to trace an original transaction forward to a summarized total or to explode a summarized total backward to the original transaction. Using the trail, he can perform tests to determine whether or not the summary accurately reflects the transactions carried on by the business enterprise. Unfortunately, the term "audit trail" is somewhat misleading. Perhaps a better term would be "management trail or inquiry trail" because management almost always makes more use of trails in the normal operation of the business than the auditor does in his examination. Business concerns are constantly subjected to inquiries and demands from external sources (customers, employees, vendors, government agencies, etc.). Trails, therefore, are essential. The following are typical day-to-day inquiries which make it necessary for companies to be able to trace either from summary to transaction documents or from transaction to summary:

1. Request from customer for copy of invoice supporting a billing

2. Request from management for method used in classification of a transaction (expensed or capitalized)

3. Request from division manager for detail supporting the amount charged to entertainment account

4. Order for reclassification of tooling expenses based on change in company policy regarding capitalization.

To evaluate the system of data processing and its internal controls and to substantiate the propriety of the balance of a particular account, the auditor has been able traditionally to start at the general ledger and, by reference to specific journal entries, trace back to selected source documents which support the general ledger postings. In this tracing process, he has become accustomed to certain facilities, viz.:

1. *Source documents.* These records of the originating transactions are used to classify and summarize information for posting to journals and ledgers. They are useful to the auditor for providing underlying details of account balances

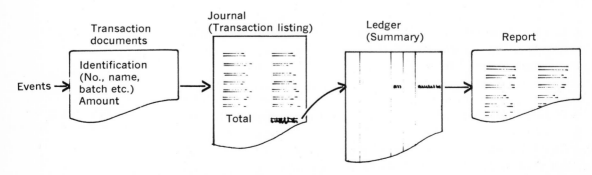

FIGURE 9-1.   The traditional audit trail

and for aiding analysis of the existence and effectiveness of internal controls.

2. *Detailed chronological journal.* A record of all events is provided as a regular step in the accounting cycle or as a byproduct of posting operations.

3. *Ledger summaries.* These give not only the current balance but also a record of the accumulation of amounts leading to the balance. The historical references in the ledger are unnecessary for showing the current status of an account, but the individual postings form a documentation of the stream of events that affect the account over a period of time.

4. *Accessible records.* Files containing records are accessible to the auditor. They can be read without special arrangements involving the use of machines. Furthermore, the search for records and the examining of them does not normally interrupt regular processing.

5. *Observable activities.* Many of the data processing activities are performed manually. The auditor can observe transactions being recorded, listings being prepared, ledgers being posted, files being maintained and inquiries being serviced. The controls are based on division of duties, human judgment and alertness.

In non-EDP systems the audit trail does not impose special requirements because its elements must be present anyway for internal purposes.

The effect of the computer on the audit trail

Changes in internal inquiry requirements and/or changes in methods of data processing may cause changes in the available audit trail under EDP.

The capabilities of the computer can change certain key elements in data processing that relate to the audit trail. These possible changes have mainly to do with the use of machine-readable records.

General Impact of Computers on Audit Trail

1. Source documents, once transcribed onto a machine-read-

able input medium, are no longer used in the processing cycle. They may be filed in a manner which makes subsequent access difficult.

2. In some systems, traditional source documents may be eliminated by the use of direct input devices.

3. Ledger summaries may be replaced by master files which do not show the amounts leading up to the summarized values.

4. The data processing cycle does not necessarily provide a transaction listing or journal. To provide such a listing may require a specific action at a recognizable cost.

5. It is sometimes unnecessary to prepare frequent printed output of historical records. Files can be maintained on computer media and reports prepared only for exceptions.

6. Files maintained on a magnetic medium cannot be read except by use of the computer and a computer program.

7. The sequence of records and processing activities is difficult to observe because much of the data and many of the activities are contained within the computer system.

The Audit Trail in a Sequential Batch System

The batch processing approach requires that transactions be accumulated into batches for processing. A batch usually consists of all transactions of a given type for a period of time (say, a day). The processing may be performed sequentially or randomly (see Appendix A, page 239, for a discussion of methods). The following explanation is based on sequential batch processing using punched cards or magnetic tape. In sequential processing, the transactions in the batch are sorted into the same order as the items in the file to be updated. An updated file, a file of transactions and the prior non-updated file are available after a file updating run, as illustrated in Figure 9-2 (page 121).

The original input documents may be filed as a batch or, bearing batch references, in some other order. A journal or transaction listing is not automatically produced, but it is fairly simple and inexpensive to prepare one. Such a listing is a reference for the input to a run. As explained in Chapter 7, the transactions and the old file should be retained for a time for file reconstruction purposes.

An historical record of changes in the balances is often a

missing element in computer data processing. It is possible to keep an historical ledger-type account of all the transactions processed against each record in the file, but this is frequently left undone or done only for summary accounts. Instead, such information is obtained from transaction listings or similar records. Since it is time-consuming to search daily transaction listings, the installation may combine the transactions over a period of time and prepare a summary reference listing. In instances where there is a management need for a ledger chronology, a record of all changes can be prepared and can also be made available to the auditor.

In contrast to sequential batch processing, the direct (random) processing method (requiring a direct access file such as disk, drum or strip) can process items in any order (see Figure 9-3, page 122). In practice, the direct access equipment may be used in several ways—with batches of sorted transactions, with batches of unsorted transactions and with unbatched transactions. In each of these methods, a record on the file is physically altered by the replacement of its former contents with the updated record.

The Audit Trail in a Simple Direct Processing System

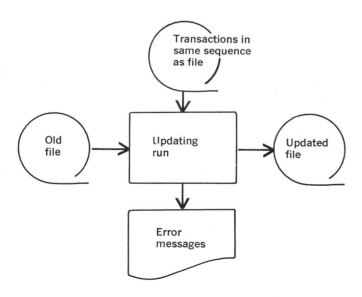

FIGURE 9-2.   A batch updating run for a serial access file medium

If the transactions to be processed are batched, batch identification may be provided and a batch listing may be produced in much the same way as in sequential batch processing. However, sequenced transactions may be in an order which minimizes seeking time for the file device but which is not useful for reference purposes. In other words, the direct access method of processing does not eliminate the need for a transaction listing for management reference and file reconstruction purposes. The fact that the transactions may not be in an order which facilitates reference will, in many cases, present no serious difficulty; in other cases the transactions must be sorted into a reference order before listing.

Where transactions are processed without batching, transactions of different types and from different locations are usually mixed together. If the transaction documents are filed in random order, they are not suitable for reference. In order to provide a management inquiry trail, therefore, the transactions are usually sorted and sequenced in a useful order. The documents can be given numbers (or other references) for the transaction list.

The Audit Trail in an Advanced System

The advanced system discussed here is an on-line, integrated, communications-oriented system. The connecting of individual input/output units by communications lines to the computer allows data to be put directly into the computer system, thus eliminating the need for source documents. In actual practice, source documents are not usually omitted; if they are, their

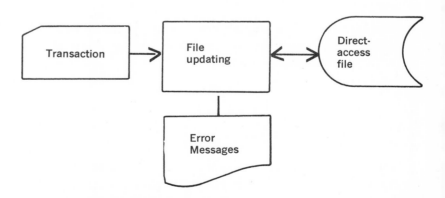

FIGURE 9-3.   A direct access file updating run

absence does not mean a lack of input record. On the contrary, management usually considers it essential that the system maintain a transaction file that records all input into the system and identifies the device and the individual involved. This file is a source document file. It may be sorted, and a record of all input for each unit may be printed out and preserved as a transaction listing substituting for source documents.

The integrated processing concept involves the updating in one run of all files affected by a particular transaction. In this case, the audit trail must provide information on all files affected by the transaction. This topic receives further discussion in Chapter 13.

Summary of guidelines for the design of audit trails

The general principles governing the design of proper audit trails are as follows:

General Principles

1. For all transactions affecting the financial statements there must be a means for establishing the account to which the transaction is posted.

2. For all accounts reflected in the financial statements there must be a means for tracing the summary amount back to the individual transaction elements.

3. For all transactions and accounts drawing a large number of inquiries, regular provision should be made to supply the records necessary for answering the inquiries.

4. For all transactions and accounts not typically subject to inquiries there must be a means for tracing, even though regular provisions are not made.

The methods by which these general guidelines may be followed are limited only by the ingenuity of the system designer. There are, however, three basic methods:

Implementation Methods

1. File record gives current balance and references all changes by transaction listing or batch number (see Figure 9-4, page 124). This is similar to the ledger system as each

change in the file balance is recorded by a reference to the transaction listing or batch. The transaction listing provides the details for tracing back to the documents.

FIGURE 9-4.   One type of audit trail

2. File record gives balance only. Changes in the balance are obtained from transaction lists. Use of transaction listing is the only method by which the changes in an account may be traced. Therefore, the changes may be combined and summarized for time periods such as a week or a month (see Figure 9-4 below).

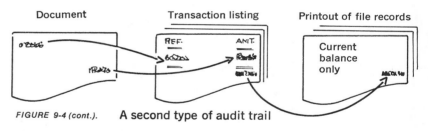

FIGURE 9-4 (cont.).   A second type of audit trail

3. File record gives balance and contains document references for each transaction. No transaction listing is used for reference. This method is appropriate where the number of transactions for each record is small (see Figure 9-4 below).

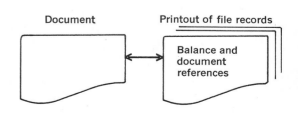

FIGURE 9-4 (cont.).   A third type of audit trail

Records, documentation and audit trails must be provided in order to satisfy the requirements of regulatory authorities. The requirements of the Internal Revenue Service are of particular interest. Revenue Procedure 64-12, issued by the IRS in February of 1964, is shown in Figure 9-5 (page 126). Note that the requirements emphasize the capacity for tracing transactions forward to summary totals and back from summaries to individual source documents. There is a specific requirement for a printout of the general ledger and subsidiary ledgers coincident with the date of the financial report. In cases such as inventories, a printout reasonably close to the statement date would presumably be acceptable.

Documents can be filed in any way as long as they can be made available to the examiner within a reasonable period of time. Data concerning the handling of transactions can be printed out, or retained on machine-readable media, or not retained at all if the processing steps can be reconstructed on request. This requirement suggests that an organization should make specific provision for obtaining and retaining records of the processing performed on items which are usually examined by the IRS. Issues from stores of production materials and supplies are of little interest, for instance, but issues for maintenance, repairs and construction are likely to be scrutinized carefully.

The IRS guidelines require adequate documentation. The preferred practices described in Chapter 3 are probably acceptable to the taxing authorities.

The IRS guidelines emphasize the necessity for reconstructable trails to the documents. In integrated systems—even though the progress of processing between end-products and original source inputs may not be well marked by intermediate printouts—there should be no difficulty in satisfying the guidelines as long as the processing of source documents to summaries and back to detail can be demonstrated clearly (see Chapter 13).

An important audit trail consideration in an EDP system—as in any system—is the problem of determining how long files and transactions should be kept. Both operating and legal requirements for record retention must be considered in the solution of this problem.

From an operating standpoint, the answer to this problem is generally along the following lines: Discard the file when the

REVENUE PROCEDURE 64-12

Reprinted from Internal Revenue Bulletin 1964-8
February 24, 1964

26 CFR 601.105: Examination of returns   Rev. Proc. 64–12
    and claims for refund, credit or abate-
    ment; determination of correct tax
    liability.
(Also Part I, Section 6001; 1.6001–1.)

> **Guidelines for record requirements to be followed in cases where part or all of the accounting records are maintained within automatic data processing systems.**

SECTION 1. PURPOSE.

.01   The purpose of this Revenue Procedure is to set forth guidelines specifying the basic record requirements which the Internal Revenue Service considers to be essential in cases where a taxpayer's records are maintained within an automatic data processing (ADP) system. References here to ADP systems include all accounting systems which process all or part of a taxpayer's transactions, records, or data by other than manual methods.

.02   The technology of automatic data processing is evolving rapidly; new methods and techniques are constantly being devised and adopted. Accordingly, the five points set forth in section 4 of this Revenue Procedure are not intended to restrict or prevent taxpayers from obtaining the maximum benefits of ADP provided the appropriate information is present or can be produced by the system. These guidelines will be modified and amended as the need indicates to keep pace with developments in automatic data processing systems.

SEC. 2. BACKGROUND.

The inherent nature of ADP is such that it may not be possible to trace transactions from source documents to end results or to reconstruct a given account unless the system is designed to provide audit trails. Taxpayers already using ADP or contemplating its use have requested information concerning the types of records that should be developed and maintained in order to meet the requirements of section 6001 of the Internal Revenue Code of 1954 and the corresponding regulations. This section of the Code reads in part as follows:

> **Every person liable for any tax imposed by this title, or for the collection thereof, shall keep such records, render such statements, make such returns, and comply with such rules and regulations as the Secretary or his delegate may from time to time prescribe * * ***

SEC. 3. OBJECTIVES.

Modern machine accounting systems are capable of recording business transactions much more rapidly and with greater accuracy than manual systems and they are capable of retaining and producing vast amounts of data. The ability to produce in legible form the data necessary to determine at a later date whether or not the correct tax liability has been reported must be carefully considered in designing and programming a machine system. This factor may add to the com-

     FIGURE 9-5.   **Internal Revenue Service guidelines**

plexity of the system and require additional cost, but this cost may be negligible in comparison to the expense that may be incurred at a later date if the system cannot practically and readily provide the information needed to support and substantiate the accuracy of the previously reported tax liability.

SEC. 4. ADP RECORD GUIDELINES.

.01 ADP accounting systems will vary, just as manual systems vary, from taxpayer to taxpayer. However, the procedures built into a computer's accounting program must include a method of producing from the punched cards or tapes visible and legible records which will provide the necessary information for the verification of the taxpayer's tax liability.

.02 In determining the adequacy of records maintained within an automatic data processing system, the Service will consider as acceptable those systems that comply with the guidelines for record requirements as follows:

(1) *General and Subsidiary Books of Account.*—A general ledger, with source references, should be written out to coincide with financial reports for tax reporting periods. In cases where subsidiary ledgers are used to support the general ledger accounts, the subsidiary ledgers should also be written out periodically.

(2) *Supporting Documents and Audit Trail.*—The audit trail should be designed so that the details underlying the summary accounting data, such as invoices and vouchers, may be identified and made available to the Internal Revenue Service upon request.

(3) *Recorded or Reconstructible Data.*—The records must provide the opportunity to trace any transaction back to the original source or forward to a final total. If printouts are not made of transactions at the time they are processed, then the system must have the ability to reconstruct these transactions.

(4) *Data Storage Media.*—Adequate record retention facilities must be available for storing tapes and printouts as well as all applicable supporting documents. These records must be retained in accordance with the provisions of the Internal Revenue Code of 1954 and the regulations prescribed thereunder.

(5) *Program Documentation.*—A description of the ADP portion of the accounting system should be available. The statements and illustrations as to the scope of operations should be sufficiently detailed to indicate (a) the application being performed, (b) the procedures employed in each application (which, for example, might be supported by flow charts, block diagrams or other satisfactory descriptions of input or output procedures), and (c) the controls used to insure accurate and reliable processing. Important changes, together with their effective dates, should be noted in order to preserve an accurate chronological record.

SEC. 5. COMMENTS OR INQUIRIES.

Comments or inquiries relating to this Revenue Procedure should be addressed to the Assistant Commissioner (Compliance), Attention: CP: A, Washington, D.C., 20224.

U. S. TREASURY DEPARTMENT · INTERNAL REVENUE SERVICE

FIGURE 9-5 (cont.).   **Internal Revenue Service guidelines**

cost of keeping it exceeds the probable value of having the data on hand. Application of this general rule is difficult, however, because it is not simple to forecast when and what demands will be made on the files and documents that are saved. As explained in Chapter 7, the necessity for file reconstruction capabilities establishes a minimum retention period. The internal inquiry requirements define a second need for retention. A third need is that of the legal requirements.

If records are retained in machine-readable form, their admissibility as evidence to meet legal requirements is pertinent. Writers on the subject generally agree that sufficient legal basis is available within the various "business records" statutes or the equivalent common-law exception to the hearsay rule to establish the admissibility in evidence of information prepared or maintained on an EDP system. Since the nature of the data—rather than its form—is the significant factor from an evidential point of view, it is anticipated that there will be no major problem about the admissibility of machine-readable evidence merely because of its form.

Management must carefully evaluate the significance and materiality of each type of record considered for elimination. Legal counsel should be consulted when any significant question arises. For instance, internal expense distribution listings, small materials requisitions and updating details of magazine subscriptions may usually be destroyed. Organizations such as insurance, banking or brokerage houses, however, probably require retention of original signed documents for customer accounts. Companies which perform government work (particularly those under "cost-plus" or "price redetermination" contracts) must exercise particular discretion. Management should consider its own past experience when estimating the possible need for specific records to provide proof in contract, tax or court matters.

The audit trail and audit procedures

To date, auditors have found that audit trail conditions in most electronic systems have not changed enough to require significantly different audit procedures from those used in non-EDP systems. In most cases, sufficient printed records, detailed journals and source documents have been available to allow the auditor to audit in a fairly conventional manner. Current developments in data processing equipment, systems design and programming are providing greater opportunities for change in the form of the audit trail, which will not disappear but which may be incorporated more in the computer and less as a separable trail of printed records. Special audit procedures are needed to access the information contained in machine-readable files.

One method of extracting information from machine-readable files is by means of the company's regular interrogation process. In direct access processing, a request may be honored immediately. In sequential access processing (with magnetic tape, for example), a request for file data must usually wait for a regular processing run. The interrogation request is merged with the other transactions affecting a given file. It is interpreted as a call for a printout of a particular file record rather than as a change in the file. Thus, with a little planning, the auditor may have his file-searching needs met by the routine procedure of the organization. He disturbs such a system only if he lengthens processing time by presenting a large number of requests.

The auditor is usually able to obtain a complete printout of the contents of particular files. Clients usually have "utility" programs to perform this printout. Before using this method, the auditor should weigh the value of the information he will receive against the cost of printing the detailed listings. A less desirable variation of this method involves the use of the client's file "dump" routine. This routine prepares a listing of the records in a file in an unedited form, which is generally very difficult to read and analyze.

Perhaps the best method of obtaining audit information from large machine-readable files is by means of special audit computer programs. These programs are developed by the auditor and include audit criteria and procedures for analysis and selection of records for audit purposes. The auditor thus uses the computer as an audit tool. Such programs can be used to analyze both transaction files and master files. The development and use of such computer programs is discussed in detail in Chapter 12.

It is desirable for the auditor to have an opportunity to review proposed new data processing systems before implementation. The audit trail will usually be found in a well designed system simply because management inquiry requirements usually satisfy audit requirements also. A poorly designed system, on the other hand, may satisfy neither management's nor auditor's needs. Suggestions from the auditor's review may therefore benefit management immediately besides facilitating future audit work.

Summary

The advent of EDP systems has brought changes in audit trail form. The extent of the changes varies according to different system design concepts. The substance of the audit trail has been retained, however, because of management's need of inquiry trails for reference purposes.

General guidelines for the audit trail emphasize that there must be a capacity for tracing any transaction to a summary account and for tracing a summary account backward to its individual elements. These guidelines are consistent with those of the Internal Revenue Service.

The changing form of the audit trail involves an increased retention of data in machine-readable form. Given machine-readable records for examination, the auditor may read them by using the client's inquiry programs, by obtaining file printouts, or by using a special audit computer program. This last possibility is the subject of Chapter 12.

CHAPTER 10

AUDITING A COMPUTER SYSTEM WITHOUT USING THE COMPUTER

THIS CHAPTER EXAMINES an approach in which the audit procedures for computer-connected phases of an audit are performed without using the computer. The term "auditing around the computer" has been avoided. This term has often been used to signify audit procedures that are conducted in the traditional manner by making use of computer printouts in the same way as manually prepared records. Use of the term has sometimes implied that the auditor need not consider computer controls as long as he performs the tracing and proofing of printouts. The term itself suggests that the independent auditor may ignore the computer altogether. The view presented in this chapter, however, stresses that although the auditor may choose not to make use of the computer in conducting audit tests, he must nevertheless consider the control framework in which electronic data processing is performed.

An auditor may choose to use the computer for testing some records but not for testing other records or the system itself. This chapter discusses the case in which the computer is not used at all. The next two chapters deal with the use of the computer in testing the system and in evaluating the records.

Summary of auditing approach without using the computer

This audit approach to a computer-based system may be summarized as follows:

1. Evaluation of internal control, involving (a) review of the system to ascertain how it is purported to work and what controls should be operable and (b) tests of the systems to accumulate evidence of how the system actually does work

2. Evaluation of computer-prepared records.

A system which performs relatively uncomplicated processing and produces detailed output can be audited without examination or direct testing of the computer program. The computer processing system is tested indirectly by tracing transactions and examining error and control lists. The auditor views the computer program as a black box, that is, an unknown which can be understood by inferring what must take place in order for a known input to result in a known output (see Figure 10-1, below). The records produced by the computer are evaluated by comparison with source documents, by outside confirmations, or by similar tests which do not depend on the program. All computer records to be used must be available in printout form (or at least capable of being printed out at the auditor's request). The tests also furnish additional evidence on the processing which has taken place.

Auditing by testing the input and output instead of the program itself does not detect program errors which do not show up in the output sampled. An erroneous input transaction rejected by the program (as shown by the error listing) is evidence that a control to detect such an error is present in the program, but missing controls are not revealed. However, the auditor can rely upon procedural and output controls to detect many errors

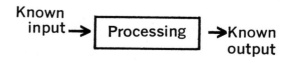

FIGURE 10-1. The computer program as a black box

even if some program controls are missing. Batch totals or ledger controls are examples.

An audit which does not use the computer is implemented by the following general steps:

AUDIT APPROACH	IMPLEMENTATION
Review of system	Interviews with personnel in data processing
	Use of questionnaire (see Appendix E)
	Examination of general system description
	General review of major controls
	Review of controls for each application vital to the audit
Tests of systems	Examination of evidence for controls (error listings, batch control records, authorizations, etc.)
	Use of printouts to trace items in output to source documents, source documents to reports, report totals to controls, etc.
	Checking of transaction sample for correct processing
	Other typical tests
Evaluation of records	Tests to check correctness of summary accounts (foot, crossfoot, etc.)
	Tests of samples of detail items by confirmation, reasonableness tests, etc.

The system review is not limited to the electronic data processing portion. The work steps and procedures for an application are traced through the entire processing system—manual, electromechanical and computer—and through all departments involved. Thus, the specific controls for an application are considered within the framework of general controls imposed by the organization and management of the business.

In the area of computer data processing, an application is reviewed for:

1. Adequacy of control over input and output

2. Adequacy of control over processing

3. Adequacy of control over programs and files

4. Adequacy of audit trail

These data processing controls are evaluated within the framework of controls established by the organization and management of the data processing department.

When to audit without using the computer

The data processing systems which may be audited without the use of the computer are usually batch-processed or batch-controlled systems having detailed audit trails. This type of system is characterized by:

1. The collection of transactions in batches, to be sorted and processed sequentially against a master file (this process normally involves the development of batch totals to control the movement of data within the system)

2. The recording of transactions manually, followed by conversion to machine-readable form

3. The production of numerous printouts (often at each processing run).

The feasibility of auditing the processing without testing the program directly depends on the auditor's being able to obtain evidence about the quality of processing by means of tests on the input and output, sample computations, tests of the controls, etc. Complicating conditions which obscure or impair the auditor's ability to obtain such evidence may include the following:

1. Processing may result in a summarized end-product output, so that individual items are not identifiable by manual means. A knowledge of the computer program is then necessary for tracing items from source to output or from output to source.

2. There may be so many transactions and transaction types that the tracing of processing becomes difficult without the use of the computer.

3. The system may be integrated so that a transaction is posted to several files at the same time without intermediate printout. It may also trigger a variety of systems responses. Tracing transactions and testing the system without an understanding of the computer program may be difficult. The number of printouts is reduced and the feasibility of using printouts for understanding system performance is usually lessened in comparison to simpler non-integrated systems.

This auditing approach can usually be applied even when systems are quite complicated, but alternative approaches may be more satisfactory. Methods described in Chapter 11 explain how to test the computer program directly as part of the evaluation of the system; alternatives described in Chapter 12 utilize computer routines to test the computer-based records.

Requirements for audit tests without using the computer

There is no detailed discussion of the performing of audit tests without the use of the computer, since these tests can be conducted in essentially the same manner as those for a non-computer system. The few changes include new or extended requirements for planning in advance and use of the error listing.

The audit of an EDP system usually requires more extensive planning than a conventional audit. The additional planning is due primarily to the mechanization of processing and to the attendant changes in the system of internal control. Before developing an audit approach, the auditor should make inquiries to ensure his awareness of conditions (an altered audit trail, for example) which might affect the audit.

Planning in Advance

The audit trail in a batch processing system is usually similar to the audit trail in a punched card or manual system. Sometimes, however, certain necessary information is retained in the system for a limited period of time only, and/or is not printed out at all in the normal course of system processing. In this uncommon case, the auditor must make prior arrangements for data to be saved and specific printouts to be made.

The audit requires a complete trail of visible records of items to be tested. If these records are not regularly printed out, the auditor should request well in advance that a printout be made. When the account balances run at the closing or at other occasions are to be included in the examination, the client should be requested to run an extra set which can be used as an audit working copy.

While conducting the review and evaluation of computer controls, procedures and administration, the auditor also reviews the procedures and controls associated with each application affect-

Use of Error Listing

ing the financial statements. He performs the audit verifications by using accepted techniques, such as the examination of source documents.

In performing both the review and the audit tests, the auditor usually makes use of the error listings produced during data processing runs. Those listings of all transactions rejected or found to be in error during processing are retained as controls to ensure that corrective action is taken. They also form valuable documentation on the effectiveness of system controls by indicating the types of errors detected by the computer. If any step (such as the tracing of transactions) uncovers an error, reference to the error list may disclose that no error of this type has been detected and, therefore, that some control feature is absent.

Evaluation of approach to auditing without using the computer

The advantage of auditing without using the computer lies in the fact that the auditor is using simple and familiar techniques. He must review the control framework of data processing, but he does not need to work with the intricacies of the computer program. This approach, under proper conditions, has been the most economical and has proven to be satisfactory.

Auditing without using the computer depends upon records which adequately detail the input and output of computer processing. The counterparts of manually produced journals, registers and ledgers must be available as computer listings and reports. There is usually little need for the auditor to request special printouts or analyses, since his needs are usually satisfied by documents produced to meet the internal requirements of the organization.

The existence of computer-based systems which can be audited without the use of new techniques is a result of factors such as the following:

1. Many computer applications are not much more complicated than their punched card or manual predecessors.

2. There has been, and to some extent still is, a tendency to move into computer processing by ways which are known

and easily understood. Batch processing, printed journals and registers, conventional ledgers and so forth are often relied upon even with equipment which is capable of operating more efficiently by other methods.

3. Company personnel have a tendency to need or want visual records.

4. Journal and register printouts are often essential for answering inquiries, tracing and correcting errors, etc. The need for a management trail has been discussed in Chapter 9.

The disadvantages of auditing a computer-based system without using the computer are (1) the fact that the auditor may neglect to use the capabilities of the computer to assist in the audit and (2) the fact that the audit may be difficult to implement if the system is quite complicated or has no well-defined visible audit trail.

Two case studies are included here as illustrations of the types of procedures an auditor might follow for performing an audit without using the computer. The object of these studies is to discuss pertinent aspects of the use of this approach, not to present a model set of audit procedures. The steps described are merely illustrative and may be performed differently from year to year.

CASE STUDY A

AUDITING WITHOUT USING THE COMPUTER: PAYROLL

This study is not intended as a detailed documentation of payroll processing. Detail has been kept at a minimum for illustrative purposes in order to avoid obscuring the principal issues.

Description of payroll processing

The payroll processing system is described here in terms of computer runs (separate tasks). Run numbers refer to the runs shown in the schematic diagrams in Figure 10-2 (page 139).

These runs are interconnected because the output from one run may be the input for another run. The computer system is a simple tape-oriented configuration. Run Nos. 1-4 cover the pay calculation and check writing. Run Nos. 5-11 cover labor distributions and other processing.

Run No. 1: Card-to-Tape

Payroll detail cards showing employee numbers, number of hours worked, job number, work code, etc., are keypunched and verified and then converted to magnetic tape along with the associated batch control totals punched from transmittal tapes. The control totals are a record count and a hash total of hours worked. During the conversion run, control totals for the same items are accumulated by batch and compared with the pre-established amounts. Controls and out-of-balance batches are printed for clerical review, correction and re-entry. All transactions are listed.

Run No. 2: Sorting

The payroll detail records are sorted into employee number sequence within departments.

Run No. 3: Data Validation

The sorted transactions are checked for correctness and completeness of the data. Control totals are also checked. Invalid data and control discrepancies are printed for clerical review. (Note that data validation is often performed as part of the card-to-tape run, not after sorting as in this application.)

Run No. 4: Calculation of Payroll and Updating of Master File

Gross and net pay are calculated; year-to-date and period-to-date data are accumulated and written on the new payroll master file. A payroll register is printed showing such items as name and number, hours worked, deductions, gross and net pay both for the current period and on a cumulative basis. A payroll tape is produced containing the data required for printing employees' checks and earnings statements. Errors (a missing master record for an employee, for example) are printed at the end of the register.

Run No. 5: Printing of Checks

The payroll tape data is formatted for the printing of checks and earnings statements. A copy of the entire earnings state-

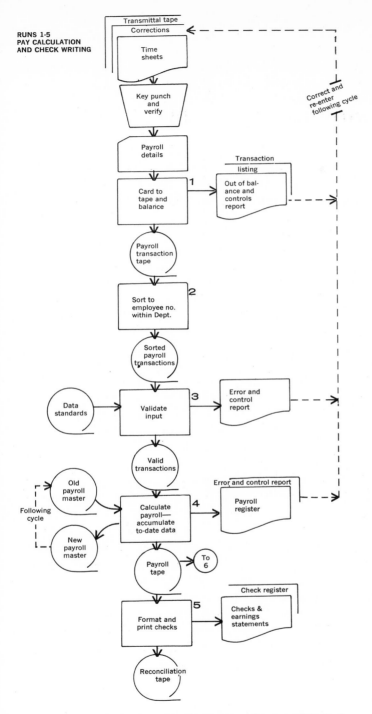

FIGURE 10-2. Payroll processing system for Case Study A

139

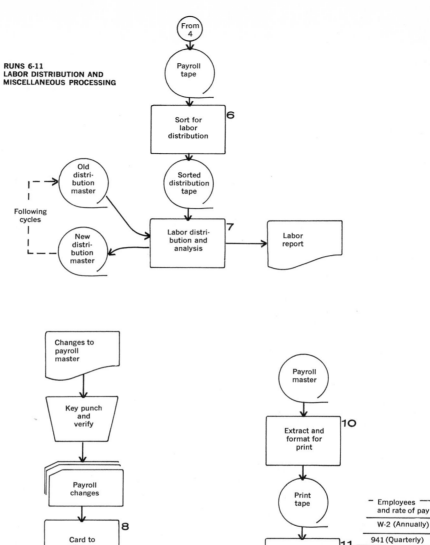

RUNS 6-11
LABOR DISTRIBUTION AND
MISCELLANEOUS PROCESSING

140   *FIGURE 10-2 (cont.).*   Payroll processing system for Case Study A

ments serves as a check register. A magnetic tape copy of the check register is produced and held for subsequent processing against cashed checks during the reconciliation procedure (not shown).

The payroll detail records produced by Run No. 4 are sorted into the account order for labor distribution analysis.

Run No. 6: Sorting for Labor Distribution

Labor hours and dollars are summarized by appropriate accounts. Cumulative and current period data are written onto a new distribution tape and a labor analysis report is printed from this tape.

Run No. 7: Preparation of Labor Report and Updating of Labor Distribution Master File

Changes in the payroll master file are keypunched and verified and converted to magnetic tape. Changes in rate, department, deductions, etc., are included.

Run No. 8: Placing of Payroll Change Cards On Tape

The payroll master file is updated periodically to reflect changes in the semi-constant portions of the record (pay rate, department, deductions, etc.). These changes are listed to provide documentation of the prior and current contents of changed records.

Run No. 9: Updating of Payroll Master File With Changes

At appropriate intervals, information is extracted from the payroll master file to prepare management and government reports.

Run No. 10: Extraction of Data for Reports

Form 941 (Employers' Quarterly Federal Tax Return) is printed quarterly; a W-2 Withholding Tax Statement is produced annually; management reports are produced as needed from the payroll master file.

Run No. 11: Report Printing

The audit of the computer processed payroll

In any audit, whether mechanized or not, the first step is to review the payroll procedure from the hiring of an employee

Review of General Internal Control

to the payment of wages. This review should be directed toward an evaluation of the system of internal control. The major purpose of control over payroll is to ensure payment of the correct amounts to the correct employees. Much of the internal control review can be conducted in the same manner for either mechanized or manual systems. A typical internal control questionnaire for payroll should cover those control points not directly involved with computer processing.

Review of Computer Internal Control

A review of internal control in a computer environment should cover the points listed below as well as those covered by the general review. The list includes comments relating each point to the case example. (See Appendix E for a sample questionnaire.) A control review sheet for Run Nos. 1-5 is shown as Figure 10-3 (page 143).

1. Adequate control over transmittal of payroll transactions from remote locations and within the data processing center

   Example: A record count of the number of employees to be processed and a hash total of the number of hours they have worked is prepared on an adding machine tape prior to the keypunching of the data. These control totals accompany the batch and are used to detect the loss or non-processing of payroll transactions (Run No. 1).

2. Adequate verification (key or sight) of payroll transactions, including changes made in the semi-constant portion of master records

   Example: For Run No. 1, the payroll detail cards are keypunched and verified. Errors detected in verification are repunched and reverified before the batch is released for processing. The same verification process is required for Run No. 8.

3. Verification that all payroll transactions received are processed once and once only; provision for error correction and for control over the re-entry of corrected transactions

   Example: The batch control totals (record counts and hash total) are computed by the computer in Run No. 1 and compared to the input control totals. The same control totals continue with the

APPLICATION __PAYROLL ~ RUNS 1 to 5__   Prepared by __MBO__ Date 8/23/67   Reviewed by __ Date __

RUN NO. AND RUN NAME	DESCRIPTION OF CONTROL FIELD OR CONTROL ITEM	TYPE OF CONTROL	CONTROLS ESTABLISHED BY				CONTROLS VERIFIED BY			
			DEPARTMENT SENDING DATA	DATA PROCESSING DEPARTMENT CONTROL SECTION	COMPUTER PROGRAM	PRECEDING RUN (RUN-TO-RUN)	COMPUTER PROGRAM		DATA PROCESSING DEPARTMENT CONTROL SECTION	USER OR OTHER OUTSIDE DEPARTMENT
							CONTROL INFORMATION OUTPUT	EXCEPTION OUTPUT ONLY		
#1 card to tape	Processing batch	Record count	✓				✓		✓	
	Hours worked	Flash total	✓				✓		✓	
#2 Sorting	Processing batch	Record count				#1 ✓	✓		✓	
#3 Data Validation	Processing batch	Record count				#2 ✓	✓		✓	
	Hours worked	Hash total				#1 ✓	✓		✓	
	Payroll number	Duplicates			✓			✓		
	Hours regular	Validity			✓			✓		
	Hours overtime	Validity			✓			✓		
	Labor code	Validity			✓			✓		
	Employee code	Validity			✓			✓		
#4 Payroll Calculation + Updating	Processing batch	Record count				#3 ✓	✓		✓	
	Hours worked	Hash total				#3 ✓	✓		✓	
	Gross pay	Control total			✓		✓		✓	
	Gross pay	Limit check			✓			✓		
	Records on tape	Record count			✓		✓		✓	
#5 Printing of checks	Processing batch	Record count				#4 ✓	✓		✓	✓
	Gross pay	Control total				#4 ✓	✓		✓	✓
	No. of checks	Record count				#4 ✓	✓		✓	✓

FIGURE 10-3.   Data processing control review sheet for Run Nos. 1-5 of Case Study A

batch for Run Nos. 2, 3, and 4. Run No. 4 prepares a count of the number of records on the new payroll master tape and compares this count to a control total on the old master tape trailer label. The same type of control is applied to the master tape prepared in Run No. 9. The transactions are sorted, then validated. Duplicate transactions should be detected in this step. Transactions to be corrected are listed on the error and control report. Re-entry is handled the next time the job is run. A check for an employee whose record has been rejected is prepared manually and corrections are entered in the computer the next time the payroll is run.

4. Validity (and other) tests of regular hours, overtime hours, labor codes, employee codes, calculated pay, etc.

Example: These tests are part of the processing in Run Nos. 3 and 4. The error and control reports from these runs indicate the reasons for record rejection and provide some evidence that controls such as these are operable in the programs.

5. Specific provision for control over changes to the payroll master file (additions, deletions, rate changes, etc.)

Example: Run No. 8 input is prepared from an authorized list of changes. The updating in Run No. 9 produces a change register which is subjected to a control review.

6. Provision for a transaction register (printed or available on demand) for the audit trail

Example: Transaction listings are prepared by Run No. 1 (input transactions), Run No. 4 (payroll register), Run No. 5 (check register) and Run No. 9 (change listing).

7. Adequate run-to-run control over record count and amount fields

Example: Once the record counts and hash totals of Run No. 1 are established, they are automatically carried forward to the succeeding runs, with adjustments for rejected records. The amount of the payroll is computed in Run No. 4 and this control total is carried forward to Run No. 5. A record count and control total on earnings to date is maintained on the master file and updated and checked in Run Nos. 4, 9 and 10.

8. Standardized, uncomplicated computer operating instructions and up-to-date documentation of the payroll application (see Chapter 3)

9. Adequate back-up procedures in case of destruction of key files (see Chapter 7).

For his examination of employment records, the auditor usually needs a list of all employees and their rates of pay to be used as a basis for selecting an audit sample. In the case study, this list could be a listing of the payroll master file prepared periodically in Run Nos. 10 and 11 for review by the personnel department, who use it to ensure that employment records and payroll records are in agreement. In his investigation of termination methods, the auditor can, for example, compare the change listings from Run No. 9 with the personnel department's records of termination to ensure that ex-employees are not maintained on the payroll.

Inspection of Employment Records

The payroll register from Run No. 4 allows the auditor to compare the total of the period payroll with the total of checks drawn for this purpose. He can also use it for tests of individual deduction amounts (social security taxes, state unemployment taxes, hospitalization fees, union dues, etc.). To ensure that the deducted amounts have actually been remitted to the appropriate agencies, remittance amounts should be checked against the totals shown on the payroll register for the deduction items.

Comparison of Payroll With Cash Disbursed

A representative number of employees should be selected from the payroll register from each class of employee for which a different calculation routine is required (hourly, salary, commission, etc.). Using the computer prepared register, the auditor should make such tests as the following:

Tests to Validate Computer Processing

1. Comparison of name, job classification, time card number, etc., with employment authorization

2. Comparison of pay rate with wage authorization, union contract, or other appropriate records

3. Checking of number of hours worked with time sheets (appropriate approval of hours worked by a foreman or other supervisor should be noted)

4. Testing of payroll deductions by examination of W-4 forms and withholding tax tables for income tax withheld, by recomputation of social security taxes and by examination of authorization forms for other payroll deductions such as bond purchases; review of the change listings from Run No. 9 and corresponding payroll registers to test that authorized changes are properly reflected in the payroll

5. Manual computation of gross and net pay and comparison with computer printed payroll checks from Run No 5

6. Comparison of payroll checks with labor allocation listings (Run. No. 7) for each of the representative employees and departments.

Completion of the Audit Utilizing Validated Computer Output

After appropriate testing of the processing has been completed, the computer listings and registers can be used in performing audit steps such as the following:

1. Examination of a summary of payroll totals by pay periods and preferably by departments (Run Nos. 4 and 7); investigation of any unusual variations among periods

2. Checking of the footings and crossfootings for the applicable portion of the payroll registers (Run No. 4)

3. Review of the payroll register for unusual entries, adjustments, checks to non-employees, etc.; examination of appropriate explanations and support

4. Tracing of hours or labor dollars to appropriate labor distribution (cost)records (Run No. 7)

5. Examination of paid and endorsed payroll checks for agreement of number, date, payee and amount with data in the the payroll register

6. Checking of the footings of the labor distribution record and tracing of the totals to general ledger or cost ledger accounts; reconciliation of total labor charges distributed with total pay shown on the payroll register.

CASE STUDY B

AUDITING WITHOUT USING THE COMPUTER:
ACCOUNTS RECEIVABLE

This study is not intended as a detailed documentation of accounts receivable processing. Detail has been kept at a minimum for illustrative purposes in order to avoid obscuring the principal issues.

Description of accounts receivable processing

The accounts receivable system is described here in terms of computer runs. A total of 10 computer runs are required to process accounts receivable. Run numbers identify the runs shown in the schematic diagrams in Figure 10-4 (page 148). The computer system is a tape-oriented configuration and all processing is in sequential batch mode. Processing is performed frequently (say, daily) except for Run No. 10, aging, which is performed periodically (say, monthly).

Prior to the input of data into the system, the dollar effect on accounts receivable for all input transactions is determined manually. These figures are used as controls throughout the processing. Another control figure is a record count established by the first run.

Sales and other entries to the accounts receivable file are keypunched and verified before being converted to magnetic tape. Control totals for dollar amounts are accumulated by batch during the conversion run and then compared with input totals. Out-of-balance batches are noted on the transaction balance report and subjected to clerical review, correction and re-entry. Detail transactions in the out-of-balance batches are not posted to the master file until the batches are corrected and re-entered.

Run No. 1: Card-to-Tape

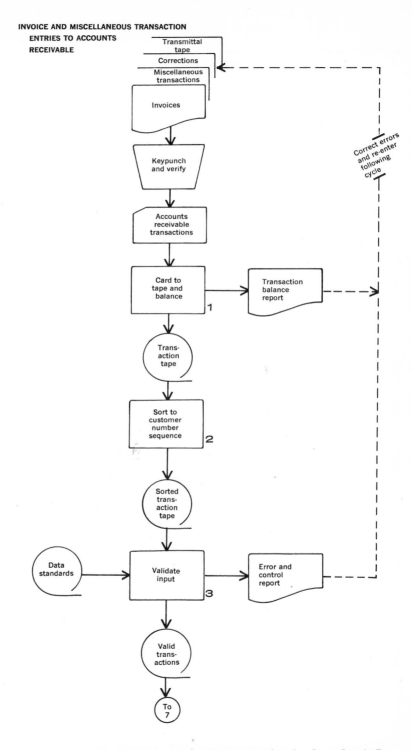

INVOICE AND MISCELLANEOUS TRANSACTION
ENTRIES TO ACCOUNTS
RECEIVABLE

Transmittal tape

Corrections

Miscellaneous transactions

Invoices

Keypunch and verify

Accounts receivable transactions

Card to tape and balance 1

Transaction balance report

Correct errors and re-enter following cycle

Transaction tape

Sort to customer number sequence 2

Sorted transaction tape

Data standards

Validate input 3

Error and control report

Valid transactions

To 7

FIGURE 10-4. Accounts receivable processing for Case Study B

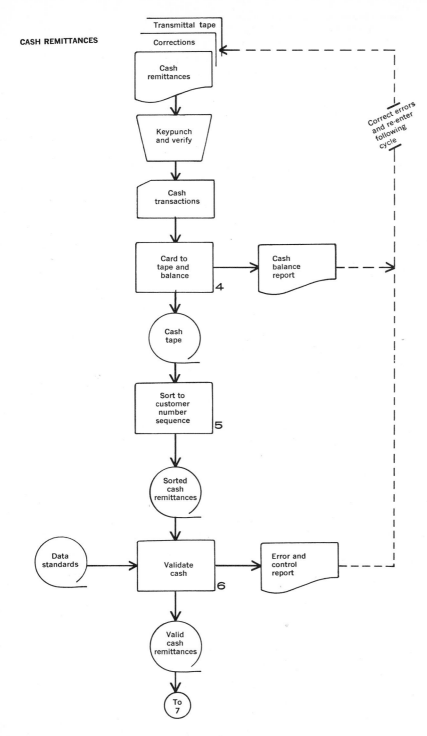

CASH REMITTANCES

FIGURE 10-4 (cont.).   Accounts receivable processing for Case Study B

149

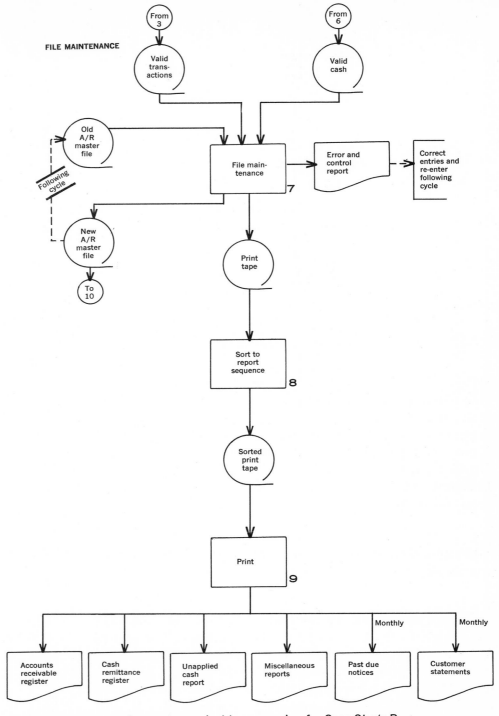

FILE MAINTENANCE

FIGURE 10-4 (cont.).   Accounts receivable processing for Case Study B

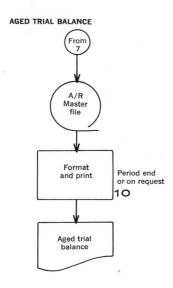

AGED TRIAL BALANCE

From 7

A/R Master file

Format and print

Period end or on request

10

Aged trial balance

FIGURE 10-4 (cont.). Accounts receivable processing for Case Study B

Run-to-run record count controls are created by Run No. 1 and used throughout the runs in the application. The checking of control totals is performed automatically by the computer which is programmed to print out the totals after each run and manually by a control clerk who keeps a reconciliation sheet in order to record and reconcile control totals as the processing moves from run to run.

Transactions on the transaction tape are sorted in customer number sequence.

Run No. 2: Sorting

The sorted transactions are analyzed to check for the correctness and completeness of the data. Invalid transactions are printed on an error and controls report. The control totals (dollar effect on accounts receivable) and record count are also printed— divided into error transactions and valid transactions—and are compared with manually maintained control totals.

Run No. 3: Data Validation

Run Nos. 4, 5 and 6: Card-To-Tape, Sorting And Validation for Cash Remittances

The card-to-tape, sorting and data validation runs for cash remittances include processing similar to that which is used for sales entries to the accounts receivable file in Run Nos. 1, 2 and 3.

Run No. 7: Updating of Accounts Receivable Master File

Invoices, changes to customer accounts and cash remittances are posted to the accounts receivable master file. Data for eventual printing of the different registers and reports is assembled on the print tape. Invoice transactions for which no master record can be found are printed on the error and control report. Mismatches on cash transactions are assembled on the print tape for later printing on the unapplied cash report.

The following control totals are printed on the error and control report for comparison with manually maintained control totals:

1. Accounts receivable control totals on input master file (to be compared with output master file of previous cycle)

2. Changes to master file accounts receivable control totals as result of (a) cash transactions and (b) noncash transactions

3. Accounts receivable control totals on output master file (to be compared with manual control totals)

4. Control totals on cash and noncash errors located in this run (to be used to adjust manual controls).

Once a month, data is assembled on the print tape to produce past due notices and customer statements showing monthly activity.

Run No. 8: Sorting for Report

All data assembled for reports is sorted into proper report sequence.

Run No. 9: Printing of Registers and Reports

The accounts receivable register shows all the postings to the master file. The register is used to provide a management trail, to facilitate the answering of inquiries and to resolve error situations. The cash remittance register contains an itemization of all posted cash.

Miscellaneous reports—on overextension of credit, new accounts, deleted accounts, transactions requiring special authorization, or accounts referred to attorneys for collection—are also printed.

At the end of the accounting period—or on request—the master file is analyzed to produce an aged trial balance. This trial balance is compared with the manual control totals and also with the accounts receivable control totals on the last accounts receivable output master file.

The audit of the computer processed accounts receivable

The first step in the audit of accounts receivable is to review procedures, paying particular attention to the adequacy of the internal controls. The major controls over receivables are intended to ensure that (1) shipments are properly reflected in receivables, (2) collections are applied to the correct accounts, (3) credit and collection policies are correctly applied and (4) separation of duties is maintained among those responsible for transaction authorization, sales activities, collection activities, and maintenance of accounts receivable files. Much of the internal control review can be conducted in the same manner for either mechanized or manual systems. A typical internal control questionnaire for accounts receivable records, credits and collections should adequately cover those control points not directly involved with computer processing.

The internal control review in a computer processed accounts receivable operation includes many points not present in the audit of manual systems. These additional points are listed below. The list includes comments relating each point to the case example. (See Appendix E for a sample questionnaire.)

1. Sufficient control over transmittal of invoices and cash remittances from preparation and/or collection points to the first computer run

   Example: In Run Nos. 1 and 4 the input transactions are balanced with batch control totals which have accompanied the transmittal of the transactions from the operating departments.

2. Adequate provision to ensure that all transactions requiring

special authorization are checked for proper approvals on entry into the system (documentation must also be produced for review to ensure that unauthorized transactions have not been processed)

> *Example:* Run No. 9 produces listings of all transactions requiring special authorization. These listings are sent to those individuals responsible for authorizing the transactions.

3. Adequate provision for validating input transactions for correctness and completeness at the earliest possible point in the system

> *Example:* Run Nos. 3 and 6 validate the input after it is converted to magnetic tape and sorted into sequence. If nothing is to be gained by having the transactions in a prescribed sequence for validation then the validation can take place in the card-to-tape run. In the case example, however, the sorting operation comes first so that a check may be made for duplicate invoices and duplicate remittances.

4. Adequate control over system rejections to ensure that they are researched, corrected and re-entered into the system within a reasonable time

> *Example:* Run Nos. 1 and 4 produce balance reports; Run Nos. 3, 6 and 7 produce error reports; Run No. 9 produces an unapplied cash report. All these reports contain system rejections which should be researched and cleared by a control clerk. He should note on the reports the correction which was made, when it was made and when the transaction was re-entered into the system. The source document should also contain the date the data was re-entered into the system and the new batch number.

5. Adequate controls to ensure that input transactions (invoices, adjustments and cash remittances) are properly posted to the accounts receivable master file

> *Example:* Before input transactions are entered into the system, their eventual dollar effect is de-

termined for control batches small enough to enable efficient error research. The figures obtained are adjusted for system rejects and then compared with the controls from the actual results of Run No. 7.

6. Verification that the accounts receivable master file is properly reflected in the control account per the general ledger

   Example: Run No. 7 accumulates the details in the accounts receivable master file and prints the control figures for manual comparison.

7. Adequate audit trail to enable source documents to be traced to the results of the posting and vice versa

   Example: Run No. 9 produces an accounts receivable register showing the results of all transactions posted to the master file and providing references to the source documents. References are made by date processed and batch number, which is also the sequence in which the source documents are stored. The documents can be traced forward using the same references. Run No. 9 also produces a cash remittance register showing additional details for cash transactions. This is done because of the frequent inquiries received on cash transactions.

8. Adequate documentation of the receivables application to ensure proper maintenance and accurate operation (see Chapter 3)

9. Adequate back-up procedures in case of destruction of key files or extended machine failure (see Chapter 7)

10. Controls to ensure that the monthly customer statements and the aged trial balance are balanced to the accounts receivable controls

    Example: The control figures from Run Nos. 9 and 10 are compared with the receivable control totals produced by Run No. 7.

11. Appropriate follow-up on collection of receivables

    Example: The accounts receivable register and the

aged trial balance provide documents which aid the tests for past due accounts, for sending of notices, etc.

The auditor follows regular audit procedures for reviewing propriety of miscellaneous entries, checking trial balance to statements, and so on.

Confirmations—based upon the controls in effect and the overall reliability of the client's records—are sent to a representative sample of the accounts. The selection can frequently be made from the aged trial balance.

In the case example, the aged trial balance can be used, but it does not contain any information on type of customer or any indication of accounts in litigation or dispute. These items, however, are coded in the records on the customer master file. The auditor should request (1) a copy of the aged trial balance as of confirmation date, with the above two items indicated on the report or (2) separate reports indicating type of customer and accounts in litigation or dispute. This request should be made well before the confirmation date.

In the case of negative confirmations, the auditor should also request that the customer statements (Run No. 9) for the customers selected should be pulled out of the normal mailing to be mailed with the confirmations. Copies of the statements are available for normal positive confirmation procedures.

Nonreplies to confirmation requests and replies reporting exceptions can be analyzed by use of the various reports from the system, especially the accounts receivable register, the cash remittance register and the subsequent months' customer statements (all produced by Run No. 9). For instance, the cash remittance registers printed after confirmation date will contain subsequent payments which are useful in clearing exceptions. The register also provides a trail back to the source document. The same is true of the accounts receivable register for all transactions to an account.

Error and control reports (Run Nos. 6 and 7) and cash balance reports (Run No. 4) may explain unusual delays between receipt of payment and posting to the customer's accounts. It is also possible that lost payments are on these error lists and have never been corrected. The same points apply to the processing of invoices in Run Nos. 1, 3 and 7.

Unusual differences between the aged trial balance at confirmation date and at balance sheet date can be reviewed by references to the accounts receivable register produced between these dates. It will show what transactions caused the difference and will provide references to the source documents.

The aged trial balance (Run No. 10) should be reconciled with controls on the customer statements (Run No. 9) and controls produced by the file maintenance run (Run No. 7) as well as with the general ledger. This will ensure that the computer system's output is in balance with the company's books.

Other normal audit procedures should be followed. The aged trial balance should be test footed and cross-footed, for instance, and the aging of a number of representative accounts should be verified by reference to accounts receivable registers and source documents.

The audit procedures to test the adequacy of the allowance for bad debts can use the aged trial balance (Run No. 10). Examination of activity on marginal accounts can be performed by the use of subsequent accounts receivable registers (Run No. 9) and cash remittance registers (Run No. 9).

Detailed Tests of the Aged Trial Balance

Review for Adequacy of Allowance for Bad Debts

CHAPTER 11

USING THE COMPUTER TO TEST THE DATA PROCESSING SYSTEM

THE COMPUTER PROVIDES an opportunity for the auditor to automate certain audit procedures. For the major audit tasks outlined in Chapter 8, the auditor can make use of the computer (1) to test the data processing system as part of his evaluation of internal control and (2) to test the computer-maintained records as part of his evaluation of the records of the organization. The first of these topics is discussed in this chapter; the second is covered in Chapter 12.

In the testing of the data processing system, the computer is used primarily to obtain information about the operation of the computer program (or set of programs in an application) and about its built-in controls. The auditor must still use other techniques to examine the organizational and procedural controls and obtain evidence that they are functioning properly.

Two methods for testing the program by using the computer are discussed in this chapter: (1) by test data and (2) by controlled processing or reprocessing. For implementation, both techniques require of the auditor a reasonable degree of expertise in computer methods. In addition, there are practical limitations which suggest that the auditor should carefully consider (1) the applicability of the technique for a particular application and (2) the technical competence required by the audit staff for performing the tests.

The test data method

The test data approach involves the preparation of test data which is then processed under auditor control by the clients' computer programs. The test data consists of transactions illustrating all the valid and invalid conditions which the auditor wishes to test. Only one transaction of each type need be tested since a given program consistently processes all transactions of a particular type in exactly the same way.

The use of test data (sometimes referred to as "test decks") is somewhat analogous to the audit procedure of tracing actual transactions. In both cases, the object is to obtain "competent evidential matter," as required by auditing standards, that a system and its controls are operating as represented. However, the underlying rationale and the scope of the two tests are different.

The tracing of transactions involves scrutiny of source documents, processing and output for a sample of transactions processed during the audit period. The items traced provide sample evidence of the activity of the period.

The use of test data involves the testing of programs for an application at a single point in time (during or after the audit period). Performance during the audit period is inferred from this test. To make a valid inference, the auditor must have evidence about the condition of the program during the audit period. The possibility in advanced on-line systems of continuous tests during the period is sufficiently unique that it is dealt with separately in Chapter 13.

The test data method tests the procedures contained within the program, not the input data processed by the program. *In order to satisfy auditing standards, use of the test data method must be coupled with an examination of source documents and other source evidence supporting the records that are being produced.*

The Applicability of the Test Data Method

The use of test data represents one of the methods available for assisting the audit of a computer-based system. The auditor can use it, in conjunction with other methods, to determine whether or not the programs and their related controls have operated as represented; or he can use it merely to gain information about the operation of particular programs. Because of theoretical limitations and practical difficulties in implementation, its applicability is severely restricted.

The test data method is most probably applicable under the following circumstances:

1. A significant part of the system of internal control is embodied in the computer program.

2. There are gaps in the audit trail, making it difficult or impractical to trace input to output or to verify calculations. This situation is possible in simple applications as well as in complex integrated systems (see Chapter 13).

3. The volume of records is so large that it may be more economical and more effective to use test data methods (and related procedures) instead of manual testing methods.

Say, for example, that an insurance company maintains a master file of insurance policies in force. At the end of each month, the file is processed to calculate unearned premiums for each policy and the total for all policies. Only the total is printed out and the general ledger is adjusted to this amount. The auditor can use test data to satisfy himself that the program provides an accurate calculation and summarization of the unearned premiums. He can also perform other tests to satisfy himself (1) that source data is properly prepared and enters the system without loss or non-processing and (2) that the tested program is the one used for the processing.

The difficulties of applying the test data method should be kept in mind. In addition to the points discussed in the next section of this chapter, relevant factors include availability of computer time, availability of auditor's time to prepare and run test data and his ability to use the method effectively.

Given the same program and the same data repeatedly, the computer consistently produces identical results. An auditor can use test data as a valid basis for inference about processing performed by a particular program if and only if he is sure that that program tested was the one actually used. If changes have been made in the program during the audit period, the auditor must be able to ascertain their impact on the processing.

Three methods are available for checking whether or not a given program was in use during the period under audit. The

The Problem of The Program

applicability of each depends upon the type of application and the type of processing performed.

1. *Controlled processing or reprocessing.* The auditor checks the program using test data and then has the tested program run under his control. (This approach is explained later in the chapter.)

2. *Repeated use of test data during the audit period.* This method is seldom practical for the outside auditor. He may use it for an on-line system with remote terminals. (See Chapter 13 for discussion.)

3. *Reliance upon client's internal control.* The auditor examines the client's controls over the program, program changes, etc. If these are satisfactory the auditor may infer that the program tested is representative of the program used during the audit period.

To be able to rely fully upon the client's internal control, the auditor must have independent corroboration that the controls have been operable during the audit period. An arrangement to use test data on a surprise basis during the period covered by the examination would usually provide the required evidence. Implementation of surprise testing is difficult for the independent auditor but it may be feasible for the internal auditors. If the independent auditor can satisfy himself as to the procedures of internal auditors who have performed such tests, he may reduce the amount of independent testing performed. In addition, tests of adherence to documentation and change procedures, library procedures and other control features all provide evidence about the use of the program during the audit period.

Implementing the test data method

Test data is a set of sample transactions to be processed by the computer program being tested. The application being tested usually involves the use of master records. For instance, the processing of a test transaction which represents a payment received from a customer will update a customer record contained in a master file of accounts receivable records.

Test data can take whatever form is appropriate for a particular processing system. The term "test deck" is frequently used for referring to test data and implies the use of punched cards.

However, there are other media that may be used:

1. Media with machine-readable encoding (punched cards, punched tape, or magnetic tape)

2. Machine-readable hard copy (magnetic ink characters or optical characters)

3. Hard copy which must be converted (appropriate if the test data is being used to check the data conversion operation as well as the computer program).

The general steps in developing and using test data are as follows:

1. Determine types of master records to be used (if required)

2. Determine types of transactions to be included in the test data

3. Develop appropriate working papers

4. Obtain the master records which are to be processed with the test transactions; pre-compute the results for comparison with the actual output from the test processing

5. If test transactions are run with regular master files or with the regular processing run, investigate the effects that the test processing will have on the output of the system

6. Obtain the programs to be tested; verify that these programs are used for the processing of the test transactions

7. Make arrangements for the preparation of test transactions and for the production of output in a useful form.

For testing programs which update master records, the auditor may choose from four basic types of master records.

The possible choices are:

Types of Master Records

1. Use of current master records

2. Use of special audit records maintained in the current master file

3. Use of obsolete master records or copies of current master records

4. Use of simulated master records on separate test file.

When using method (1) or (2), the auditor includes his test transactions in the client's normal processing run. When using method (3) or (4), he obtains a separate master file for later use. The characteristics and problems of each approach are discussed.

Use of Current Master Records

The auditor includes the test data in the file of current "live" transactions. This data is processed against current master records during the regular processing cycle. The main advantages of this approach are:

1. That the test can be performed on a surprise basis (subject to management's approval)

2. That it is not necessary to load programs and perform other set-up work solely for the purpose of processing a small volume of test data

3. That a rigorous test of the entire system under normal operating procedures is possible.

The main disadvantages are:

1. That insofar as test data is used to update master files, it must subsequently be reversed out of the system—a time-consuming process, requiring the highest order of competence, coordination and precision

2. That the reports produced by the normal processing cycle for various levels of management must be adjusted clerically to correct for the presence of test data

3. That the dangers of running tests during normal processing are so great that it should not be attempted except by an auditor expert in computer methods

4. That the auditor's tests may be blamed for any complications in the computer run when the tests are made.

Use of Audit Records in Current Master File

For this approach, a small number of simulated records are maintained (for audit purposes only) in the current master file. They are easily identifiable because they are assigned references which are obviously simulated (references to non-existent cost centers or departments, for example). During normal processing they remain inactive because "live" activity does not affect fictitious cost centers or departments.

The auditor builds his test data around the contents of these simulated master records and conducts his testing in the same manner as with current master records.

The advantages of using dummy records rather than current "live" records are that in this case the test data does not affect regular records and does not have to be reversed. It may affect the reports, however. A disadvantage is that since live master records (or copies thereof) are not involved in the tests, live masters in poor condition (having missing data fields, invalid data, and so on) are not revealed. Other disadvantages are (1) that the EDP operating personnel may object to having these audit records "clutter up" their master files, (2) that the approach requires much pre-planning and client participation and (3) that the audit records may be used for fraudulent purposes by EDP personnel.

These master records come from (1) an obsolete ("great-grandfather" or earlier) master file set aside for the auditor or (2) a copy of the current master file made for the auditor. In a sequential access processing system involving, for example, punched card or magnetic tape input, actual master records can easily be reproduced for the auditor. Since an "old" master file is not destroyed during an updating run, as many actual master records as are required may be duplicated without the use of the current master file. In a direct access system, an old master record is immediately updated, destroyed and replaced by the new master record. In order to protect the master records, there is usually a periodic transfer of data from the direct access storage device to another device (frequently magnetic tape). This transfer process can be used to provide the auditor with a copy of master file records.

Use of Obsolete Master Records or Copies of Current Master Records

If the system does not provide printouts of the contents of the master file, a special printout of the portion of the file to be used in the test must be arranged. A number of records are selected from the printout and the test data is constructed around them. The prepared data is processed with the copies of the files containing the selected records.

This method is relatively simple and avoids many of the dangers of running test data in the regular processing run. One disadvantage is that programs must be loaded and equipment set up and operated for audit test purposes only. Provisions must be made to copy a current file or to obtain a copy of an obsolete file before it is released.

Simulated master records in a separate test file, created for audit purposes only, contain a small number of fictitious records against which the test data is processed. The client may have simulated masters available for processing his own test transactions. The auditor may review and use these records or create his own. The exact record layout should be found in the client's documentation. One company uses 24 simulated master records as a test model of a 20,000 employee master record file. The assumption underlying the use of simulated records is that the computer cannot distinguish between these records and actual client records. The advantages of this approach are:

1. That it is a relatively simple method which avoids the difficulties of processing test data in the normal processing run

2. That theoretically these master records can be used over and over again, thus eliminating the recurring expenditures of time needed for copying files.

The disadvantages are:

1. That the use of a simulated master does not provide any evidence about the "live" master file

2. That it can be time-consuming to prepare test records if the records are large

3. That the programs must be loaded and the equipment set up and operated for audit test purposes only.

Each of the four methods discussed has its advantages and disadvantages. Methods (3) or (4), however, which involve use of copies (current or obsolete) of the master file or simulated master records in a separate test file, and which do not attempt testing as part of a regular processing run, are recommended for the auditor who has no substantial experience or who is testing a particular program for the first time.

Types of Transactions

The auditor must determine carefully the types of transactions to be included in his test data. He must consider all of the

166

possible significant data variations in order to fully test the programs in an application. A review of the basic documentation should provide information on the nature of the processing and on the exact record layout of the data processed by the programs.

There are several methods by which the auditor can determine the types of transactions to be included in his test data. He may analyze the data used internally for testing the client's computer programs. The client's test data usually tests processing steps and controls which the auditor is also interested in testing. This method is the most expedient, since many transactions can be devised merely by duplication or slight modification of the client's test data. It has the added advantage of serving as a review of the client's procedures for testing programs. Such a review may uncover outdated tests or areas in the program which are not being tested at all; it may therefore be highly informative and beneficial to EDP operating personnel.

As data processing systems become more integrated and complex, greater emphasis will probably be placed on formalizing a client's procedures for testing his computer programs. If these tests are well documented and kept up to date, the auditor may be able to use the client's test data to perform a more effective and efficient audit. Of course, he will have to review the data and satisfy himself that it contains all the conditions which he wishes to test. It is reasonable to assume that any test the auditor wishes to make is also a desirable, if not a necessary, test for the client to include in his test data.

Another method of determining the types of transactions to include in the test data involves an analysis of the client's source documents, records and system requirements. This method is more time-consuming than the method which makes use of the client's test data. Usually, a combination of the two approaches is necessary in order to ensure the inclusion of all the transactions which the auditor would be interested in processing.

The test data should include transactions which determine the processing and handling of the following general conditions:

1. Valid conditions

2. Out-of-sequence conditions

3. Out-of-limits conditions

4. Alternative processing which takes place as a result of the comparison of transaction records with master records (for

example, comparison of the transaction identification number with the identification number on the master record)

5. Units-of-measure differences (for example, tons instead of pounds)

6. Incomplete, invalid, or missing input information

7. Incorrect master and/or transaction files

8. Fields containing numeric characters instead of alphabetic characters (and vice versa)

9. Fields containing too many characters

10. Illogical conditions in data fields which should be logically related

11. Conditions where transaction codes or amounts do not match the codes or amounts established in internally stored tables.

There should be programmed controls to handle each of these conditions (see Chapter 6).

It is not necessary for all possible combinations within all data fields to be set out as separate transactions. Distinction should be made between data fields which merely represent identification data (account numbers, social security numbers, and so on) and those which represent variable data. In the former case, only a limited number of possibilities need be included to test the identification routines in the program. To test sequence checking and identification comparison routines, for example, a transaction which has a valid transaction code and employee number and which contains valid information may be placed out of sequence in the test deck. Additional tests for sequence checking and identification comparison are not necessary. In the case of variable data fields, also, not all combinations need be tested. To illustrate, Figure 11-1 (page 169) shows and describes the fields for a rate change input card used in a payroll system. The purpose of the transaction is to change an employee's hourly rate and pay code. The transaction is checked by the program to disclose any invalidity of change date, alpha name, old pay code or old pay rate and to determine whether the new rate is equal to the old rate and whether the new rate is greater than $10. Although these five conditions theoretically represent 32 combinations, fewer tests need to be made because not all combinations are relevant. For instance, if the new rate is over $10, no

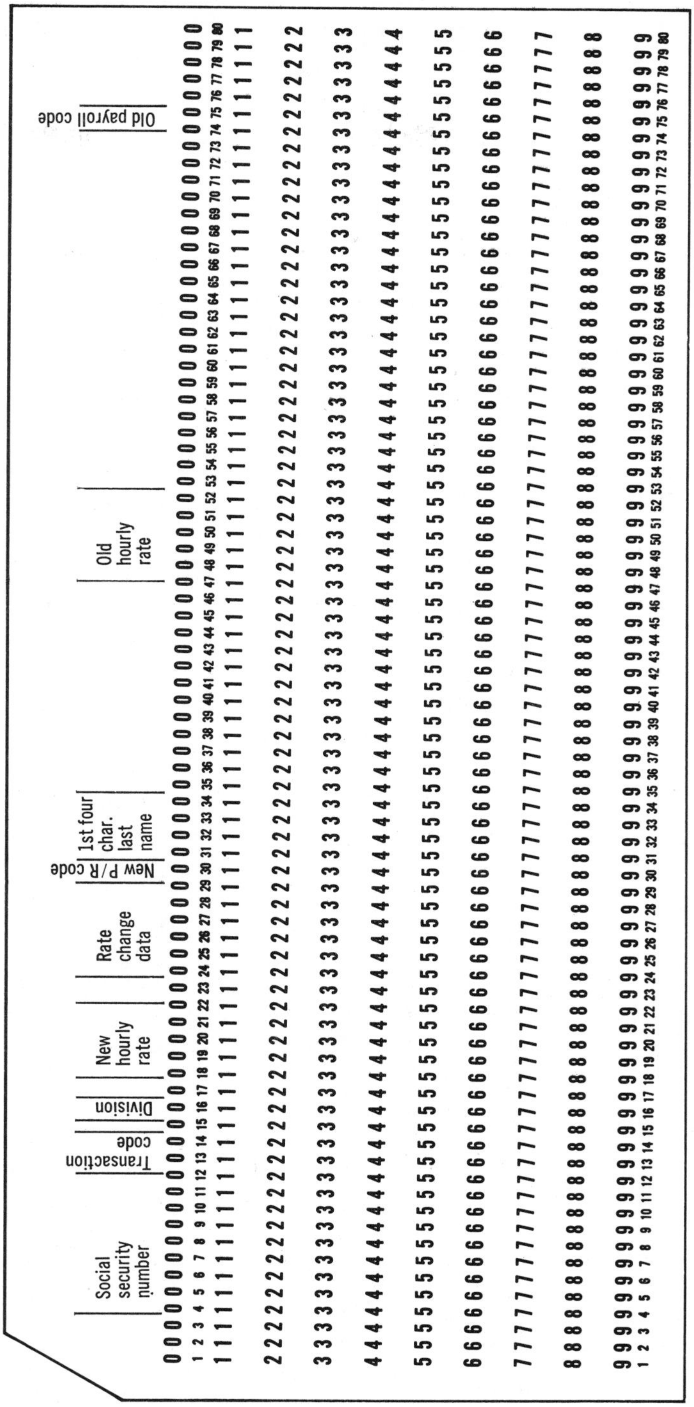

FIGURE 11-1. Rate change card format

169

further tests are made and an error exception message is printed out; if the rate change is valid ($10 or less), the other conditions are tested. The test data therefore consists of transactions for the following six conditions:

1. All data valid, including new rate

2. Invalid rate (over $10)

3. Valid rate change and invalid old rate

4. Valid rate change and old rate equalling new rate

5. Valid rate change and invalid alpha name

6. Valid rate change and invalid date

Working Papers   For developmental and review purposes, tests should be documented in working papers. These papers should include schedules such as the following:

1. *Test data control.* This type of schedule describes the conditions which are tested, indicates the results expected and reports upon the actual results. It is illustrated in Figure 11-2 (page 171). It may also be combined with the transaction data and solutions schedule.

2. *Transaction data and solutions.* This type of worksheet lists and codes all the transactions which are to be processed, both valid and invalid. The solutions for valid transactions appear on this schedule. It is shown in Figure 11-2 for tests involving a payroll application.

3. *Master file data.* This type of worksheet includes a record format and the contents of the master file data used in the test. It is illustrated in Figure 11-2 for a payroll master file.

4. *Test data matrix.* This paper is useful for reviewing the test data to ensure that all substantive tests have been made.

   The top of the matrix indicates the transaction codes of the various transactions processed by the program being tested. The left side of the matrix indicates the types of conditions which may be tested. The matrix is completed by entering the conditions tested for transactions included in the test data. Figure 11-3 (page 172), for example, shows the types of conditions tested in the payroll rate change transaction described on page 168. Tests 3 (valid rate change and invalid old rate) and 5 (valid rate change and invalid alpha name) both test the invalid input condition (condition 6). The matrix should be completed for all payroll transaction codes.

Such a matrix indicates those conditions which are not being tested and those conditions which are being tested too

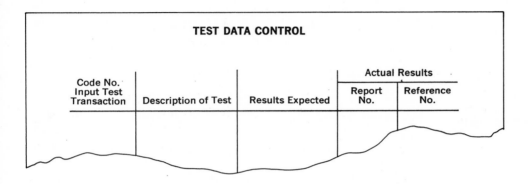

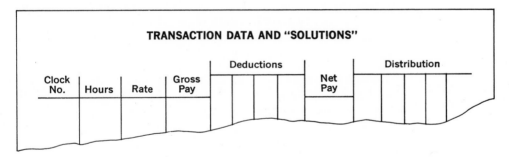

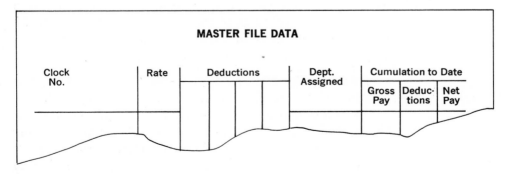

FIGURE 11-2.   Illustrations of test data working papers

much. It is also useful as a summary for review by the audit partner or manager.

An alternative to the test matrix is the decision table, in which the conditions to be tested and the actions to be taken by the computer are put in a tabular decision format (Figure 11-4, page 173).

5. *Computer printout.* The working papers should contain the computer printouts resulting from the tests (a transaction listing and the results of the transactions being processed, for example). These printouts should be cross-referenced to the test data control worksheet and the transaction data worksheet.

Obtaining the Master Records

Where the data processing application involves a master file as input, the auditor must obtain machine-readable master records against which to process his test transactions. The problem of choosing a type of master record to use has already been discussed. Advance planning is required to obtain copies of files or to prepare simulated records. (For instance, simulated records must be checked to ensure that they do not contain unintentional errors.)

Effect of Tests On the System

When using test data, the auditor must determine the effect of his tests on the operations of the system. This is a problem

Type of condition tested	Transaction code											
	0	1	2	3	4	.	.	.	.	.	.	. n
1 Validity				a								
2 Sequence												
3 Limit				b								
4 Decision												
5 Units												
6 Completeness				c, e, f								
7 Record Match												
8 Composition												
9 Field size												
10 Logic				d								
11 Code & amt.												

FIGURE 11-3.   Test transaction matrix

Decision table						
			Rules			
CONDITIONS	1	2	3	4	5	6
Rate $>$ \$10	y	n	n	n	n	n
Old rate on input not same as old rate on file		n	y	y	y	y
Old rate is not equal to new rate			n	y	y	y
Alpha name on input = alpha name on file				n	y	y
Date valid					n	y
ACTIONS						
Reject transactions	x	x	x	x	x	
Accept transactions						x

FIGURE 11-4.   Decision table documenting conditions to be tested

primarily when current master records are used or when test records are included in the master file. These methods should be used with great care, in consideration of their possible effects on the client's system.

The auditor must satisfy himself that the program he uses in processing his test data is the program presently in use. However, an assurance that the program tested is the one in use at the time of the test is not also an assurance that it was used during the audit period. The latter problem is discussed earlier in the chapter. There are several possible ways to gain reasonable assurance that the program tested is the one in use. Assuming that adequate organizational and administrative controls are present, the auditor can request the program from the librarian (preferably on a surprise basis) and process his tests with the program received.

Alternatively, the auditor may request that the operating program be left in the computer after the regular processing run has been completed, so that his test data can then be processed. This method is particularly appropriate in situations where program changes are frequent (especially shortly after a program is first put into operation), since it assures the auditor that the program version he is using is current.

The auditor should design the test data in a manner which will facilitate review of the processing results. He should consider

Obtaining and Controlling the Client's Program

Preparation and Processing of Test Data

the use of special codings or distinctive names which permit invalid test transactions to be easily identified, sorted from valid tests and listed as separate output.

Preparation of the test data frequently requires use of the client's equipment and/or personnel. In addition, computer time is necessary for the actual data processing involved in testing. Therefore, advance planning and consultation with systems and computer operations personnel is usually necessary.

The auditor should always observe the actual processing of his test data. This may involve some inconvenience, since such processing is frequently scheduled during the "grave-yard shift."

The controlled processing or reprocessing method

In a second method of testing the operation of a data processing system, the auditor controls the processing run using a program which has been tested. This method provides assurance that a particular program is or was used by the client. The procedures can take one of two forms: (1) control over the processing run which prepares data for the financial statements and (2) reprocessing of a sample of data from the period being audited.

In the first case, the auditor controls either the original processing run or a subsequent reprocessing run. The run uses a program which has been tested and is maintained under auditor control. This procedure provides assurance that the processing results to be used in the financial statements are based on the authorized, tested program. As an example of this procedure, the case of the insurance company mentioned previously is relevant. The auditing firm proved the client's computer program for computing unearned premiums at month end by the use of test data. The client was then requested to prepare a duplicate copy of the tested program for the auditor. At year end, the client was requested to use, under audit control, the auditor's duplicate copy of the program to calculate the unearned premium figure for the balance sheet.

In the second case, the auditor controls the reprocessing of transactions selected from the period under audit. The auditor's run uses a copy of the client's program which the auditor has reviewed, tested and controlled. The results obtained by the client are compared by the auditor with the results of the audit reprocessing run. This reprocessing of sample transactions proves whether or not the client company has followed—during the audit period—the processing procedures it has said were in use; that is, whether or not the company has used a program equivalent to the one furnished for the auditor's examination and use.

The use of controlled processing or reprocessing does not require the writing of a new program. The regular client program is used after the auditor has examined or tested it to assure himself that it is satisfactory.

This method does, however, require of the auditor a knowledge of computer data processing sufficient for obtaining assurance about the quality of the program and for controlling the processing or reprocessing. Advance planning is necessary to obtain, test and control a copy of the program and to obtain computer facilities, files and sample transactions for reprocessing.

When controlled processing or reprocessing is used to test the processing performed at the end of the audit period, the client usually has the data on hand in the appropriate form. Advance arrangements must be made for computer time, operators, etc. When reprocessing is used (in connection with interim work or at the end of the period) to test processing of transactions performed during the audit period, copies of transaction files should be obtained before they are released. Tests may be performed on as many sets of transactions as the auditor thinks necessary for obtaining sufficient audit evidence.

Controlled processing or reprocessing involves a substantial use of the computer in performing audit procedures (both for testing the program and for controlling the running of the program). The method is best suited for situations which justify use of the computer rather than the use of manual procedures based on visible audit trail printouts. Such situations are essentially the same as those described for use of test data. Therefore, the method should be considered (1) if the volume of data to be processed (and tested) is large or (2) if the processing to be verified is complex or otherwise difficult to follow by means of visible printouts.

The reprocessing during the audit period of samples of transactions is, from a logical standpoint, a very effective procedure for obtaining evidence that the processing is performed as claimed. However, since it is difficult to implement and since it requires considerable computer expertise, alternative procedures are often preferred by the outside auditor. Such a reprocessing procedure can also be carried out by an internal auditing group. If this is done, the outside auditor can follow usual audit practice with regard to the extent of his reliance on the work of internal auditors.

Summary

In certain circumstances, the auditor will find it either desir ble or necessary to make use of the computer for testing the pro- cessing performed by the computer. These circumstance: in- clude those applications for which:

1. A significant part of the internal control is embodied in the computer program

2. There are significant gaps in the visible audit trail

3. There are large volumes of records to be tested.

The purpose of using the computer to test the data proces system is to obtain assurance that the processing and the con are operating as represented and to obtain adequate evidei matter as required by auditing standards.

In some cases the use of the computer is optional, depend only on cost and effectiveness as compared to alternative cedures not directly using the computer. In other cases, the of the computer is advisable since alternative procedures difficult.

Two methods for using the computer in testing the c processing system have been presented: (1) test data and (2) c trolled processing or reprocessing. The test data method limited applicability since it is a test only of the program at t time tested. The auditor must conduct other tests to assure hi self that the tested program is the one actually used. O method of providing this assurance is to use the computer process data under auditor control. The results of the controll run are used in the financial statements or are compared wit processing performed by client personnel.

The use of the computer for testing the system concentrate on testing the program. Other parts of the system (input, con- trol framework, etc.) must also be tested. The use of the com- puter does demand of the auditor a reasonable level of understanding of computers. Such a method should be implemented only after careful planning and after an examination of the effect of the tests on the client's system.

CASE STUDY: USING THE COMPUTER TO TEST A
LABOR RECORDING AND PAYROLL APPLICATION

The EDP system reviewed and tested in this case study consisted of an automated labor recording and payroll system which recorded labor transactions and processed payroll for a major plant of a large manufacturer. In this case, simulated transactions were used and processed against special audit records placed in the current master file. Testing was performed during the regular processing run.

Automatic time recording devices were located throughout the shop areas. For the 11,600 employees covered by the system, these devices completely replaced the human timekeepers and manually-prepared time cards. Data from the system flowed through to the company's payroll and job-order cost accounting and control records. Basic timekeeping tools were (1) the plastic employee badge, prepunched with identifying information, and (2) the job card, prepunched with the charge number and other information about a particular job. See Figure 11-5 (page 178) for a flowchart of the system.

A badge was assigned permanently to each employee; job cards followed the parts or assemblies to be worked on. Exceptions were indirect labor cards and other special cards which were located in racks adjacent to the recording devices. When reporting for work, the employee inserted his badge into the recording device and depressed certain keys. When beginning work on a job, the employee inserted his badge and one or more job cards and depressed appropriate keys on the recorder keyboard.

All transaction recorders were linked electrically to a central control, a master clock and a key punch which automatically created a punched card for each entry. The cards were accumulated and then converted to magnetic tape to be processed by the computer. The first of these runs, a match against an employee

177

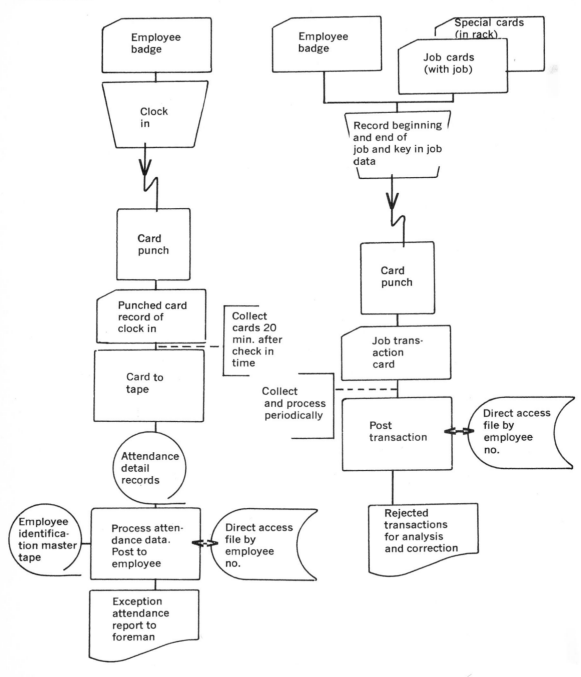

BEGINNING OF SHIFT
ATTENDANCE

JOB TIME RECORDING

Employee badge

Clock in

Card punch

Punched card record of clock in

Collect cards 20 min. after check in time

Card to tape

Attendance detail records

Employee identification master tape

Process attendance data. Post to employee

Direct access file by employee no.

Exception attendance report to foreman

Employee badge

Special cards (in rack)

Job cards (with job)

Record beginning and end of job and key in job data

Card punch

Job transaction card

Collect and process periodically

Post transaction

Direct access file by employee no.

Rejected transactions for analysis and correction

178   FIGURE 11-5.   System flowchart for labor recording application

FINAL ATTENDANCE REPORT

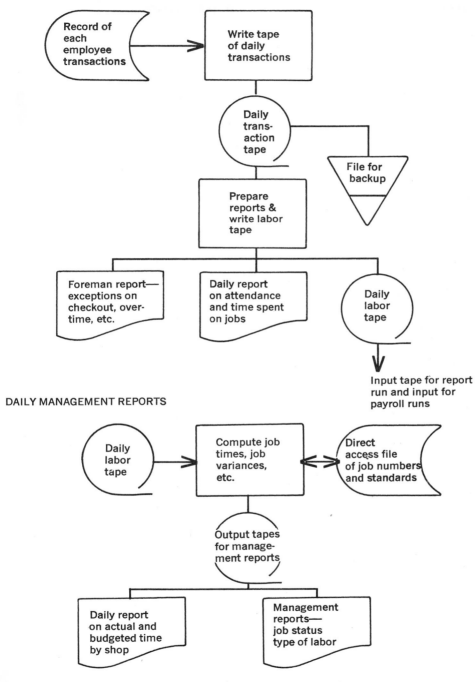

DAILY MANAGEMENT REPORTS

FIGURE 11-5 (cont.).   System flowchart for labor recording application

179

identification master tape, began half an hour after the beginning of each shift.

Within an hour after shift start, an exception report was prepared for distribution to shop foremen. This report indicated absences, tardy clock-in, pre-shift overtime and failure to check in on a job. Each exception had to be approved by the shop foreman. Transactions accepted in this first processing routine plus transactions accepted for the remainder of the shift were "posted" to a direct access file arranged by employee number. Transactions rejected were analyzed and corrected for re-entry into the processing cycle.

All labor transactions for the day were written onto a magnetic tape which preserved a record of all transactions and was used in further computer processing as follows:

1. Preparation of final daily report to shop foremen (again prepared for exceptions only, showing overtime, early clock-outs, and other items for approval by foremen)

2. Daily report which balanced job times by employees with the time between clock-in and clock-out

3. Daily labor tape prepared after (2) (later the input tape for the payroll runs)

4. Matching of job transactions against a direct access file of job numbers (this processing involved application of labor standards on certain jobs, accumulation of time by classification and preparation of output tapes for numerous reports; the reports included daily reports of actual and budgeted time to certain shops, summary management reports by type of labor and job status reports).

Audit Approach

To evaluate this labor recording and payroll system, the auditors decided upon a two-phased review:

1. Actual transactions were tested from their initiation through to final reports. The number and type of transactions for testing were selected by using the normal audit criteria for testing of labor charges and employees' payroll records and paychecks.

2. The labor recording and payroll system was tested in normal operations by using simulated but realistic transactions de-

signed to test not only routine processing but also the various exception procedures. Simulated audit master records were placed in the current file for the tests.

Emphasis was placed on the second phase because it enabled many facets of the operation to be tested with only a small number of test transactions. Before designing the simulated transactions, the auditors made a thorough review of the client's system flowcharts and documentation describing the programmed controls. Also, inquiries were made of responsible persons as to the various control points designed in the system.

For testing the labor recording system, 42 simulated transactions were developed, such as:

Tests of Labor Recording

1. Employee clocking in on time, working normally for full shift

2. Employee checking in on job without clocking in

3. Employee clocking in but failing to then check in on job

4. Employee absent

5. Employee tardy

6. Employee tardy but within 3-minute "grace period" allowed

7. Employee leaving before shift ends

8. Employee leaving early but returning

9. Night shift employee clocking in on day shift

10. Employee working overtime into next shift

11. Employee loaned to a different shop

12. Employee charging jobs improperly (for example, charging direct time as indirect time)

13. Employee using transaction recorder keys incorrectly when checking in on job

To process the simulated transactions, the auditors prepared a group of employee badges and employee master records on which information was entered to agree with the information on the badges. The transactions were entered into the system by using the prepared badges and job cards at actual shop locations.

Using the transactions outlined above, the test was carried out in two shops during normal working hours. Both day and night shifts were used. Data processing supervisors were made aware of the general nature of the test but not of the specific types of transactions being tested. Shop foremen were not informed until after they had questioned the simulated transactions which appeared as exceptions on attendance reports.

All transactions were traced through to reports which emerged from the data processing system on the same and on the following day. These included preliminary and final attendance exception reports, exception reports of erroneous job transactions and the daily balance report of correct job and attendance transactions.

The auditors identified—with two exceptions—every simulated transaction as correctly processed and concluded that the system was functioning as it had been described to them. The two exceptions point up the types of problems which may be encountered.

The auditors made extended tests on a subsequent day to determine the reasons for the two exceptions. The first discrepancy resulted in the rejection of certain apparently acceptable transactions as exceptions. This happened because the client had previously made a change in "leave early" cards but had failed to collect all the superseded cards from the rack placed in the shop. This change in the format of the "leave early" transaction cards caused the system to reject valid transactions recorded in the format used before the change. The second discrepancy was the result of a programming error. The erroneous program instructions resulted in the non-processing of the last employee in the file if the next to last employee had an exception transaction in the processing cycle. Such a programming error may exist in many systems, since the processing of the last employee is an atypical and complex processing routine involving end-of-file and end-of-job instructions in addition to the normal processing of the transaction. The testing of the system does not necessarily turn up such an error, since the tests cannot include every possible condition affecting the next to last and last employee records. In this case example, the error was revealed by the test prepared by the auditors. The simulated employee master records used by the auditor were the last on the master file and, since the simulated transaction for the next to last employee was an exception, the transactions for the last employee were not processed.

To test payroll processing, the auditors again designed simulated transactions to be processed with simulated employee payroll master records inserted in the file for audit purposes only. Payroll was processed by applying pay rates (included in the permanent portion of the employees' master payroll records) to the labor hour transactions accumulated in the variable portion of the employees' master records. The labor was accumulated by employee for payroll processing every two weeks and by job for weekly accounting distribution reports. The fixed portion of the master record included (in addition to the pay rate) name, social security number, number of tax exemptions, budget section, year-to-date amounts, and vacation and sick leave hours. The variable portion contained earnings and deduction data resulting from payroll transactions processed for the current payroll period.

When developing the transactions, the auditors first reviewed the client's flowcharts and other documentation which described the input formats, the programmed controls, the output and the exception reporting for all transactions processed by the computer payroll programs. They then reviewed the tests designed by the company's programmers to test the payroll programs. Many of the company's tests were selected by the auditors for inclusion in their tests. Additional tests were also formulated. All test transactions to be processed were then key-punched and listed in transaction number sequence. The nature and objective of each test was described on this transaction listing as an aid in review and in subsequent debugging of the test processing. The listing was included in the work papers. Several examples of the 196 transactions included in the test data are the following:

1. Employee hired on same day as terminated

2. Employee having rate change greater than programmed limit

3. Employee charging labor hours while on vacation

4. Employee not entitled to bonus charging bonus hours

5. Employee requesting vacation hours exceeding vacation hours balance in master record

6. Employee charging labor hours exceeding programmed limit

7. Terminated employee charging labor hours

8. Terminated employee requesting wage advances

9. Employee having accumulated year-to-date earnings and FICA tax at taxable limit prior to processing of valid labor hours

10. Employee requesting tax exemptions exceeding programmed limit

11. Valid employee charging normal labor hours

The auditors obtained the client's computer programs to be tested by requesting, on a surprise basis, the required programs from the EDP librarian. The tape reel serial numbers of the program tapes received were then traced to documentation in the EDP library, which included a program tape release record and a program tape journal. Such documentation provided information on the physical location of the program tapes and on their usage history. The auditors had previously reviewed the client's organization controls and EDP library procedures. Physically and organizationally, the EDP library and programming activity were segregated. Their review assured the auditors that the client's regular computer programs were being obtained. The auditors then controlled the programs and the test data, observed the processing of the test data and obtained the processing results.

Again, the results of processing proved highly satisfactory and enabled the auditors to evaluate the adequacy of the system of data processing and internal controls. A few areas were disclosed where programming changes would result in strengthened internal control. The suggested changes were largely concerned with input validity checks and reasonableness tests on incoming data. The tests also revealed that some of the documentation and some of the client's test data were no longer current.

As mentioned previously, the audit steps also included some conventional tests of labor charges and employees' payroll records. The procedures included (1) reconciling payrolls paid with distributed labor, (2) tracing labor distribution from accounting entries to weekly and daily reports and (3) tracing information from actual employee master records (selected randomly) to evidence supporting pay rates, exemptions and all deductions.

CHAPTER 12

USING THE COMPUTER TO TEST THE RECORDS PRODUCED BY A COMPUTER SYSTEM

THIS CHAPTER CONTAINS a discussion of the use of the computer by auditors for testing and evaluating the records produced by the data processing system. In the past, the records to be evaluated in an audit have been printed reports, listings, documents and written papers, all of which are visible output. Output and files in computer systems, however, are frequently in machine-readable forms, such as cards, tapes, or disks. Thus they present the auditor with an opportunity to use the computer in his analysis.

Any record maintained on a machine-readable medium can be transferred to a visible printed record. It is not necessary, therefore, for the auditor to use the computer for his tests. The decision whether or not to use the computer depends (1) on the cost of using the computer as compared to the cost of performing the tests by hand and (2) on non-cost factors such as improved audit procedures.

Uses for computer programs in auditing

A computer program can be used for any computational or comparison task for which quantitative criteria can be established. Examples of such tasks are:

1. Testing extensions and footings

2. Selecting and printing confirmation requests

3. Examining records for quality (completeness, consistency, invalid conditions, etc.)

4. Summarizing data and performing analyses useful to the auditor

5. Selecting and printing audit samples

6. Comparing duplicate data (maintained in separate files) for correctness and consistency

7. Comparing audit data with company records

A common characteristic of these applications is the fact that the auditor can define clearly and precisely what is to be computed, compared, summed, printed, etc. Each of the tasks is explained briefly.

Testing Extensions And Footings

The computer can be used to perform simple summations and other computations to test the correctness of extensions and footings. The auditor may choose to perform tests on all records instead of just on samples, since the speed and low cost per computation of the computer enable him to do this at only a small extra amount of time and expense.

Selecting and Printing Confirmation Requests

The computer can select and print out confirmation requests on the basis of quantifiable selection criteria. The program can be written to select the accounts according to any set of criteria desired and using any sampling plan. The format of the request can be designed to facilitate mailing and audit follow-up. For example, one auditing firm has designed a multi-part form which is prepared on the computer. A single printing by the computer prepares a confirmation request set which includes the first request, a mailing envelope, a return envelope, a control copy and a second request (should it be needed). The form is designed with carbons to eliminate further handling. The first request is printed on a form already inside the mailing envelope, which also contains the return envelope.

Examining Records for Quality (Completeness, Consistency, Valid Conditions, etc.)

The quality of visible records is readily apparent to the auditor when he makes use of them in his examination. Sloppy record-keeping, lack of completeness, and so on, are thus observed by the auditor in the normal course of the audit. If machine-readable records, however, are evaluated manually, a complete print-out is needed to examine their quality. The auditor may choose to use the computer for examining these records for quality.

If the computer is to be used for the examination, a program is written which examines the record for completeness, consistency between different items, valid conditions, reasonable amounts, etc. For instance, customer file records might be examined to determine those for which no credit limit is specified, those for which account balances exceed credit limit and those for which credit limits exceed a stipulated amount.

The auditor frequently needs to have the client's data analyzed and/or summarized. Such procedures age accounts receivable, prepare annual usage requirements, analyze for obsolescence of parts in an inventory, list all credit balances in accounts receivable and all debit balances in accounts payable, and so on. These procedures can be accomplished with a computer program.

Summarizing Data and Performing Analyses Useful to the Auditor

The computer may be programmed to select audit samples by the use of random numbers or by systematic selection techniques. The sample selection procedure may be programmed to use multiple criteria, such as the selection of a random sample of items under a certain dollar amount plus the selection of all items over a certain dollar amount. Other considerations can be included, such as unusual transactions, dormant accounts, etc. The samples selected in this way can be used for such audit tests as confirmations, price tests of inventory items, and so on.

Selecting and Printing Audit Samples

Where there are two or more separate records having identical data fields, the computer can be used in testing for consistency. For instance, the cost prices in the master inventory file may be compared with the cost figures used by the billing program.

Comparing Duplicate Data (Maintained in Separate Files) for Correctness And Consistency

Audit data such as inventory test counts can be compared with the company inventory records by using a computer program. For this procedure, the audit data must be converted to machine-readable form. Similar procedures can be used for tracing cash receipts to accounts receivable records or for comparing selected inventory costs with the cost data master file.

Comparing Audit Data With Company Records

Obtaining a computer program for audit use

One of three major approaches can be used for obtaining suitable computer programs for use in the evaluation of records. These are:

1. Programs written by the client

2. Generalized audit programs

3. Programs written by or under supervision of the auditor.

Alternatives (1) and (2) are discussed briefly below. Alternative (3) is discussed in the next section of this chapter (page 191).

Programs Written By the Client

Much of the analysis desired by the auditor is equally useful to the client. The client, therefore, frequently writes programs for his own use, or he prepares a program for his installation if there is an internal use for an analysis requested by the auditor. Programs to age accounts receivable or programs to analyze inventory turnover and obsolescence, for example, are often needed by both the client and the auditor.

If an auditor is to use the output of a client's analysis program, he must be able to assure himself that the program is performing what he wishes and is doing so correctly. He may obtain this assurance by manually testing samples of the analysis, tracing totals to controls and so on. Alternatively, he may review the coding or he may test the program by such a method as the test data method. As explained in Chapter 11, the auditor must also assure himself that the program used in the analysis is the same as the one tested. He may do this by relying upon internal controls (such as documentation, separation of duties, change procedures and tape library procedures) which are tested to determine that they have been operable, or he may use a copy of the program which he has tested and controlled. This latter method is implemented by steps such as the following:

1. *Preparation of an auditor's copy.* An auditor's copy may be a direct copy of the object program (on magnetic tape, for example), but, to avoid obtaining a program containing undocumented changes, it is desirable to obtain a copy of the symbolic program deck and to have it assembled separately to produce the auditor's copy of the object program. The auditor also obtains a copy of the client's run manual (which

includes operating instructions). Well in advance of running, an examination is made of the client's run manual to check any changes which have been made. If necessary, the auditor's program and operating instructions are updated before the run.

2. *Testing of program.* Testing involves either an expert review of the coding or the use of test data, as explained in Chapter 11. An added advantage of performing independent tests is in the operating experience obtained by the auditor before the programs are used.

3. *Obtaining records.* The records to be processed are the client records as of the end of the audit period (or perhaps, for interim work, as of the date of the tests). The auditor asks for a copy of the file or takes advantage of the client's file retention practices to obtain the needed records.

4. *Running the program.* The auditor should be present when the program is run.

There are many audit functions which change very little from client to client. This situation suggests the advantage of using general audit routines which the auditor adapts to each client. Attempts to apply the concept of a generalized program, however, reveal several difficulties:

Generalized Computer Audit Routines

DIFFICULTY	DISCUSSION
Different manufacturers make computers and each manufacturer makes different models.	Machine-readable programs written for one manufacturer's equipment generally cannot run on the equipment of another. In the past, there has not been compatibility even within a manufacturer's line. However, the following factors are favorable: (a) the trend is toward compatible families of computers; (b) the trend is for manufacturers to make provisions for compatibility through simulators and emulators; (c) a few computer systems dominate the business market; and (d) there is a trend toward the use of higher-order languages (such as COBOL).
Many different equipment configurations are possible for the same model of computer	Records maintained on a direct access file such as a disk are referenced and accessed differently from records on magnetic tape. The same audit program probably cannot handle both file media.

DIFFICULTY	DISCUSSION
There are problems in using common machine-independent languages such as COBOL	Even though COBOL is machine-independent, it is accompanied by the following difficulties: (a) the ENVIRONMENT and DATA divisions need to be rewritten for each use; (b) there is not yet complete compatibility in the implementation of COBOL (though progress is being made); (c) COBOL is not available for all machines; it is often not available for the smaller business data processing configurations.
Many different record and file layouts are used	Even if the other problems are solved, each customer still has his own formats for records and files. There must therefore be a means for "individualizing" a generalized program.

Generalized audit programs have been restricted in use. Two general methods are available. One method is to use an industry program which is applicable to all clients in an industry. In the brokerage field, for example, generalized audit programs have been used to perform standard audit procedures for confirmations, margin computations, etc. Each client's files are transferred to a standard format on magnetic tape by a simple conversion program which is unique for each different computer. In this standard form, the data file is processed by an audit computer program used for all clients. The client computer is used only if it fits the model and configuration specifications for which the audit processing program was written. Though two computer systems may not be program compatible, they are probably data compatible if the data is put on magnetic tape. In some cases, however, a processing run is necessary to adjust the data codes and make them compatible.

A second method is to use a generalized set of computerized audit routines[1] that can be run on a specified computer (and others compatible with it) which meets designated configuration requirements. The routines include programs to perform or verify footings or other mathematical calculations; to include, exclude, or summarize items having specified characteristics and/or to provide related subtotals; to compute and select statistical samples for confirmation or other audit tests; and to print out results in a form specified by the auditor. The auditor needs

---

[1] An example is the AUDASSIST System available for general use from the AICPA.

little understanding of computers to use these routines, since their purpose is to test and analyze the client's computer records, not his programs. The auditor obtains a description of the client's records (field sizes, scaling of numeric fields, codes and their meanings, etc.). He then fills out simple forms which describe the record format, the processing to be performed (fields to be totalled; fields to be tested for limit, completeness, etc.) and the type of sample to be taken, if any. The information is key-punched and read by the computer routines. The routines perform the specified processing and print out totals, record counts, records with violations, etc.

The use of generalized programs is developing rapidly. By mid-1970 more than a dozen audit software systems were available. This approach shows great promise. However, it will still be necessary for specific programs to be written for smaller equipment, non-compatible systems and unusual audit tasks.

Writing a computer program for audit use

Since a computerized audit program is written in the same way as any other program, the description of programming in Appendix A is applicable. The topics discussed here relate to the role of the auditor in the programming task (assuming he does not perform the actual detailed coding) and to the language used in the coding.

The writing of a special computer program for audit use is an extension of the method of using a tested and controlled copy of a client program. In both cases, the auditor must assure himself that the program performs what he wishes it to perform; he has additional responsibilities, however, in the preparation of a program written specifically for the audit.

The role of the auditor in the preparation of a computer program to perform processing on client records for audit purposes is summarized in Table 12.1 (page 192).

The Role of the Auditor in Preparing the Program

The audit objectives must be clearly defined by the auditor before the processing to be performed is decided upon. Once the audit objectives have been set, a review is made of the client's machine-readable records which are to be analyzed. Procedures for analysis are then formulated and the economic and technical feasibility of developing a computer audit program is determined. The auditor may need assistance from EDP specialists in determining the technical feasibility of such programs. If it is found to be feasible to develop a program, the next step is to prepare system flowcharts and layouts.

The preparation of a system flowchart provides a broad view of the data processing required by the computer audit program. This chart indicates all the input and output files to be processed. An exact description of each file record is obtained for subsequent use and the format of the output is defined. Since the printed output becomes the audit working papers, it should be designed accordingly.

Auditors who have had some EDP training should be able to prepare system flowcharts and to design the necessary output records, though such tasks may require technical assistance

TABLE 12.1. Steps in preparing a computer program for audit use

STEPS	RESULTS	AUDITOR'S ROLE
1. Analysis of problem	Statement of objective	Preparation
2. Design of system to perform processing and provide information	System flowcharts Report layouts File designs Record layouts	Preparation or supervision of preparation
3. Planning of computer logic	Program flowcharts and/or decision tables	Review
4. Preparation of program		
(a) Coding in computer language	Coding sheets in source language Input deck keypunched from coding sheets	General cognizance
(b) Translation (assembly or compilation)	Source and object code listings Machine language program	General cognizance
(c) Debugging	Test data and test results	Preparation or review of test data and supervision of use
(d) Documentation	Run manual Computer operator instructions manual	Supervision and review
5. Input data preparation	Input data cards Master file Transaction file	Supervision or review
6. Running of program	Report or other output Error messages	Supervision and control

from EDP specialists. System flowcharts should be prepared either by the CPA or under his close supervision.

The planning of the specific computer logic requires some knowledge of computer programming. Therefore, the preparation of the program flowcharts and/or decision tables is usually performed by someone trained in computer programming. If technical specialists prepare the flowcharts and decision tables, the auditor should be able to review them critically to determine whether or not they contain the desired auditing procedures. This is usually not difficult for auditors with some EDP training, since the procedures involved in a computer program for audit use are generally not extensive or complex.

The coding and translation activities must be performed by persons trained to program and operate the computers. If adequate review has been made of the program flowchart logic, a general cognizance of these activities should be sufficient for the auditor.

The auditor should prepare or carefully review the test data for debugging and testing the program and should supervise its use. He should also supervise and review the preparation of the documentation for the program. All program documentation (flowcharts, record layouts, program listings) should be assembled in a program run manual and retained by the auditor. The auditor should control the program copy itself.

The input data may be client files. If so, the auditor should supervise the preparation of a copy and exercise control over the duplicate file until it is used. If new data must be prepared or files converted, the CPA should supervise preparation and review the results. The auditor should also be present to exercise supervision and control when his audit program is run.

Circumstances decide the person to do the detailed programming. If the auditor has no one on his staff competent in programming, he may (1) obtain programming assistance from the client or (2) contract for the program to be written by outside programmers.

The first alternative has the advantage of the programmer's familiarity with the installation. Of course, the programmer chosen should not be the one who wrote the program which processes the data to be tested by the audit program. The choice of a company programmer is especially appropriate where the client sees the possibility of using such a program for other than audit purposes. Such a choice is probably inappropriate, however, where there is only one programmer, or where there is inadequate internal control.

There are both individual programmers and programming concerns which contract to write programs. One CPA, for example, employs a person who does programming as a part-time job. Also, many computer service centers write programs besides providing data processing services. When contracting for outside writing of programs, the auditor should ensure agreement on the extent of debugging and documentation and on arrangements for later changes to alter or update the program.

The Programming Language

The auditor should keep in mind the characteristics of the different programming languages which can be used. Essentially, these languages are divided into two groups: the symbolic machine-oriented languages and the higher-order machine-independent languages, such as FORTRAN, PL/I, COBOL and Report Program Generators (RPG). Each type of language has its advantages: use of problem and procedure-oriented languages saves time for writing, debugging and altering programs and makes program conversion from computer to computer easier; use of machine-oriented symbolic coding saves running time for the programs and necessitates less storage for implementation.

A comparison of these advantages favors a higher-order language such as COBOL, FORTRAN, PL/I, or RPG for the coding of audit routines. Such coding is easier for the auditor to understand and easier to debug and alter. The disadvantage in running time is not significant for most audit routines. A more significant difficulty is the fact that most of these languages are not available for many small configurations. COBOL, for example, requires more primary and secondary storage than is available on approximately half of the business configurations. The RPG (Report Program Generator), however, is available for fairly small configurations and may be used instead of COBOL. FORTRAN is available for many computers which do not have COBOL compilers.

Although FORTRAN should not be overlooked as a possible language for coding audit routines, COBOL is usually the most appropriate for computers which do have COBOL compilers. RPG is probably most useful for those smaller business computers for which it is available. FORTRAN is designed as a language for writing computational problems; COBOL is designed as a business data processing language; RPG is designed especially for performing limited processing on input files and printing the results in a report format.

Evaluation of the use of computer programs for audit use

The auditor must always determine the economic advisability of using computer programs for performing audit procedures on computer-based records. He must estimate the time it would take to develop the programs and compare this to the time it would take to audit the records by other means. Since records on computer storage media can always be printed out, alternative means are available. Experience indicates that applications containing few records to be analyzed and requiring relatively little audit time do not lend themselves to computer procedures. Applications containing many records and requiring significant time for testing and analysis are usually more appropriate for computer audit programs. The whole problem is illustrated by the following two examples.

In auditing a medium-sized manufacturing company, the auditors developed computer audit programs for accounts receivable. Routines were developed to review the accounts receivable records, to select accounts for confirmation, to age the accounts, and so on. The auditors spent 150 hours developing and using the computer approach in each of the first two years.

An Un-economic Application

In previous years, they spent approximately 50 hours in accounts receivable year-end work, largely in confirmation of the receivables. Although there were 6,000 accounts, the auditors were able to verify 80 to 90 per cent of the dollar value of the company's accounts receivable with 50 to 75 confirmations.

It is doubtful that the computer programs used in the audit for accounts receivable can ever accomplish the audit work in fewer hours than were spent manually. Although the computer programs do contain certain innovations as to account selection and analysis of the file and although certain benefits have been derived from use of the computer programs, the application did not pay off. One reason arose from the small volume of confirmations and from the relatively small number of accounts comprising most of the dollar volume. The remaining accounts in the file needed very little work in the manual audit, and thus the audit program "overaudited" them. Another reason arose from the high start-up costs. Since this was the first application of a computer audit program for the client, the time requirements were quite high.

An Economic Application

Computer programs were written to review the entire perpetual inventory file of a company and to perform the following tests (usually performed on a sample basis) on all 11,000 items:

1. A check of cost versus market price conditions

2. A check of arithmetic extensions and accumulations

3. A comparison of item cost with standard cost criteria

4. A check of outstanding procurements for unusual items

5. A check against cycle inventory counts

By reviewing the entire file, the auditor was assured of revealing 100 per cent of the exceptions to his tests. Accordingly, he had excellent evidence from which to make an inference about the records examined.

The work performed for the first year, including the preparation of the computer programs, required 100 hours. In the previous year, 110 hours were required to perform the work manually. The time necessary to perform the same work in succeeding years was estimated at 10 hours.

The success of this application resulted from the fact that the audit tests to be performed were simple but time-consuming and the number of records involved was large. This justified the expense of writing an audit program. Once the program was written, the review of the entire file (though not required for reasonable audit assurance) was just as convenient as sampling. This application is described in a case study on page 197.

Summary

This chapter has discussed computer programs which are used to analyze data produced by the data processing system. Such a program processes client records according to auditing criteria embodied in the program to obtain information for the auditor's evaluation or for further examination.

The use of computer audit programs is probably advisable when the auditor needs an efficient means of analyzing large masses of machine-readable data and of selecting those items which require review.

The chapter has described three different methods for using computer programs for the evaluation of client machine-readable records:

1. Client programs tested by the auditor and run under his control to produce the analysis needed

2. Generalized computer audit routines

3. Special audit routines prepared under the supervision of the auditor and run under his control.

The use of these computer audit routines must be considered in the context of the economic advisability of a computer approach versus that of alternative methods. The use of generalized computer audit routines is probably the least expensive of the computer alternatives; the use of a tested, controlled client program is more expensive and the use of a routine written especially for an audit is the most expensive.

Case Study: Evaluating Inventory Records Using the Computer

This study illustrates the use of a computer program which was written to aid in the performance of year-end audit procedures for finished stock inventories in a medium-sized manufacturing company.

After reviewing and evaluating the system of internal control within the data processing area and after testing the client's computer programs for finished stock inventory, the auditors determined that the system of internal control was adequate. This discussion is confined to the audit work involving a computer program for testing and evaluating the finished stock inventory records.

Background

The company was a specialty metals manufacturer, with two divisions; steel and tungsten. The steel division manufactured hot and cold finished specialty steels which were distributed in the form of bars, rods, flats and rounds. The products of the tungsten division included metal-cutting and mining tools, tips and dies.

Aggregate finished goods inventories of the two divisions totalled about 11,000 items, representing about 18 per cent of total assets. These items were warehoused at the principal manufacturing plant and at eight sales offices throughout the United States. There was no physical product deterioration, but slow movement and obsolescence presented a continuing audit problem.

For financial reporting purposes, inventories were stated at the lower of cost or market on a last-in first-out (LIFO) basis. For internal data processing purposes, detail inventories were initially accumulated using variable standard costs, which approximated first-in first-out (FIFO) costs. The standard costs were revised annually. At year-end, the inventory was adjusted to full absorption LIFO cost. The detail inventories were priced and accumulated at both the old and the new standard prices, so as to reveal the amount of the pricing adjustment and to facilitate calculation of the current year's price index for the steel division LIFO calculation. The LIFO reserve for the tungsten division was calculated only on the tungsten content. Fixed costs were added to the inventories (valued at variable cost) to make reporting on a "full absorption" basis possible in accordance with generally accepted accounting principles.

All inventories other than the two finished goods inventories were physically counted at or near year-end. The latter were cycle-counted throughout the year.

Summary of system

The computer system consisted of a medium-scale business-oriented configuration and a Teletypewriter order-entry network. The perpetual finished stock records, maintained on magnetic tape, contained the following information:

1. *General information:* item code, description, standard cost, gram weight per piece, date of stock authorization

2. *Procurement information:* order date and order number for all procurements; supplier code for purchased procurements

3. *Inventory status and transaction information:* actual and available inventory quantities; unshipped quantity (material available); back order quantity (no material available); interdepartment transfers, receipts, and scrapping for the current month; date and quantity of the most recent physical adjustment

4. *Inventory control and sales information:* lead-time; set-up and order costs; reorder point quantity; economic order quantity; maximum stock; inventory on order; sales forecast; designations of discontinued, "slow-moving" and "dead" items; date of last sale; largest sale in current and preceding year; gross sales (amount and quantity) for the month and year to date.

Two inventory files were maintained: the perpetual inventory file and the historic inventory file. At the end of each month the historic inventory file was updated from the month-end perpetual inventory file. Month-end analysis resulted in various reports— of obsolete and dead stock, warehouse overstocks, activity analysis, distribution, and so on.

The computer programs

Two computer audit programs (INV-01 and INV-02) were developed to utilize the client's computer for the accumulation and pricing of finished goods inventories. The audit system is shown in Figure 12-1 (page 200). Program INV-01 was used to process the client's year-end perpetual inventory files (at both new and old standard costs) and the year-end historic inventory file. Each item selected by the program was assigned a code which identified the reason for its selection. This program performed the following tasks:

1. Reviewed and reported on an exception basis all items on the inventory files, as follows:

   (a) items in files with no new or old standard costs (exception codes 1 and 2)

(b) items for which the standard cost did not change (exception code 3)

(c) items for which the standard cost increased or decreased by more than 30 per cent (exception codes 4 and 5)

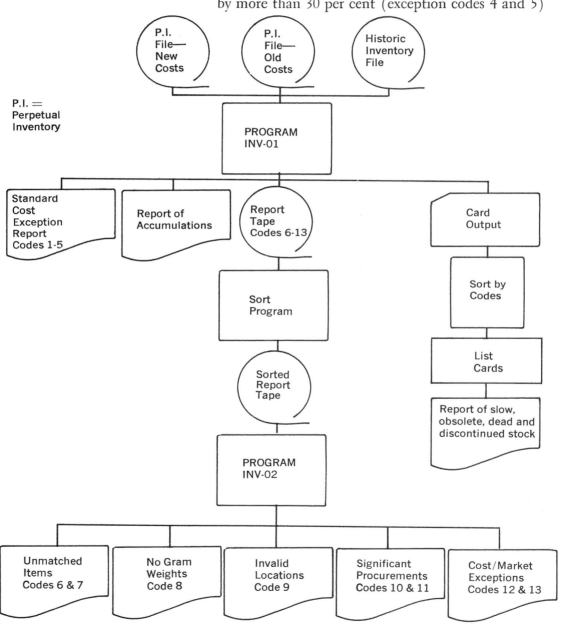

P.I. = Perpetual Inventory

FIGURE 12-1.   Systems flowchart for audit routines

(d) items appearing in new or old standard cost file, but not in both (exception codes 6 and 7)

(e) tungsten items with no gram weight (exception code 8)

(f) items stocked at invalid or fictitious locations (exception code 9)

(g) items with procurements outstanding classified as discontinued (exception code 10)

(h) items with procurements outstanding, for which procurements plus actual inventory exceed both the preceding six months' sales and the current back order (exception code 11)

(i) items for which the unit cost exceeds the unit market value (exception code 12)

(j) items for which there have been no sales in the current year (exception code 13)

2. Accumulated and reported the following data:

(a) number of items or records on the file

(b) total gram weight of tungsten products

(c) value of items classified as discontinued; the preceding twelve months' cost of sales of these items

(d) value of inventory in excess of the preceding twelve months' sales; cost of the twelve months' sales of these items

(e) market value and cost value of the inventory by major product category

(f) value of "slow-moving" and "dead" stocks; value by location of inventory with no physical adjustments in the current year

A Standard Cost Exception Report was made from this processing. It contained items with exception codes 1 through 5, indicating item code, description, exception code, inventory quantity and old and new standard costs where available. A listing of the various accumulations performed during the processing was also printed out.

The machine-readable output from program INV-01 included a magnetic tape containing the data on items with exception codes 6 through 13. This data included item code, description, exception code and inventory quantity. Inventory value, location, procurement quantity, procurement cost, cost of preceding six months' sales and unit market value were also included where applicable. The tape was sorted according to exception code; the client's sort program was used for this procedure but the sort control cards used were those maintained by the auditor. Audit computer program INV-02 was then used to process the sorted tape and to prepare reports of unmatched items, tungsten items with no gram weights, invalid locations, significant procurements and cost value in excess of market value.

During the INV-01 processing, cards were also punched for items for which there was no new standard cost and which conformed to the conditions listed below. These conditions relate to slow, dead, obsolete, missing, discontinued and unauthorized stock. A code was punched in each card identifying the reason for its selection. These codes were used in sorting the cards.

1. No inventory cycle counts made during the current year

2. Item "dead" at a particular location

3. Item "slow-moving" at a particular location

4. Item discontinued

5. Inventory quantity greater than the preceding twelve months' sales quantity

6. No "date stock authorized" in the record

The punched card output was sorted and the client's card-to-print utility program was then used to process the punched card output and to list the items.

Evaluation

Aspects of the evaluation of computer audit routines can be categorized under quantity of work, quality of work, management benefits, or incidental benefits. The comments below do not imply that the quality or quantity of work in preceding years was not adequate. Rather, they emphasize the fact that the use of the computer routines offered advantages over previous methods. When reviewing an inventory file, for instance, the auditor seldom requires a 100 per cent sample in order to obtain the assurance necessary to render an opinion. In this case, however, a 100 per cent sample did provide useful data beyond that obtainable from a smaller sample. Since it was obtained at virtually no additional cost, the 100 per cent sample was clearly one of the benefits of the computer audit routines.

Audit computer programs were used to review the entire perpetual inventory file. The following tests (traditionally performed on a sample basis) were performed on the entire file:

Quantity of Work

1. Checking of cost or market conditions

2. Checking of arithmetic extensions and accumulations

3. Review and comparison of standard costs

4. Checking that all items were accounted for in the inventories at both new and old standard cost

5. Checking of procurements outstanding

6. Checking of cycle inventory counts

Formerly, these procedures had been performed manually, on a sample basis, in approximately 110 man-hours. For the first year, the computer audit procedures (including the design and implementation of the audit computer programs) required 100 man-hours. The time required for applying the audit procedures in succeeding years was estimated at 10 hours.

The quality as well as the quantity of the cost or market test was improved. Formerly, such a test was performed by using catalogue prices adjusted for quantity and trade discounts. These prices were then compared on a sample basis to current invoices. When the test was performed by using an audit computer program, however, the program utilized actual experience by calculating market price for each item from the actual sales amount and sales quantity for the current year.

Quality of Work

The arithmetic check of accumulations, the comparison of standard costs, the test for gram weights and the check that items were contained in the inventory at both old and new standard price were all judged to be more reliable when the computer was used. The monotony of these procedures provided a possibility of error in the manual processing which was not present in the computer processing.

The information from the computer audit program on discontinued, slow-moving and "dead" stocks and on items in excess of one year's supply was helpful for evaluating "slow-moving and obsolete" inventory. When the client first installed the computer, the method of analyzing obsolete inventory was changed. Data from the computer audit program was useful to the auditor in making statistical analyses and comparisons as a basis for evaluating allowances for anticipated losses. Because of the change in reporting, past data was not applicable and new historical data had yet to be accumulated.

Management Oriented

Some of the procedures programmed into the audit computer program were specifically management-oriented: the item by item market versus cost data check, for example. Like many companies, this company had "loss-leaders" and items stocked merely to accommodate certain customers; management was generally aware of these items. In the current year, however, the audit routine disclosed items which were being sold at or below cost and of which management was unaware.

The information produced about purchase orders for discontinued stock was advantageous to management as one check on the effectiveness of the company's reordering policies. Information about outstanding procurements plus inventory in excess of the preceding six months' sales and current back orders was advantageous for the same reason.

Incidental Benefits

A byproduct of the project was the auditor's increased knowledge and understanding of the client's system. This was not advantageous from an audit viewpoint only; it also resulted in a more effective letter of recommendations from the auditor to management on points relating to the finished goods inventory.

CHAPTER 13

AUDITING ADVANCED DATA PROCESSING SYSTEMS

CHANGES AND IMPROVEMENTS in computer hardware and software have allowed the implementation of new, advanced systems concepts. Two such concepts important in business data processing are real-time response processing and integrated processing. Advanced systems employing these concepts are expected to have a significant impact on auditing methods, though the impact is expected to be less than that forecast in much of the EDP literature. As yet there are only a limited number of advanced systems in operation, and auditing experience has been minimal. This is partly because it takes from two to four years to design and implement such a system.

Since experience with auditing advanced systems has been so limited, much of the discussion in this chapter deals with potential problems and possible solutions; i.e., control problems perceived in the systems installed or being planned, and possible control and audit methods for handling these problems.

Definitions

The terms "on-line," "real-time"[1] and "integrated system" refer to concepts associated with advanced systems.

---

[1] The trend in data processing is towards single unhyphenated terms. These terms may also be found in the literature of data processing as "online" and "realtime."

On-Line

On-line pertains to peripheral equipment or devices connected to and in direct communication with the central processing unit of the computer. The term is also used to describe the connection of terminal equipment to a transmission line in a data communications system. On-line equipment includes a printer connected to the computer, a remote typewriter connected via a telephone line, a data collection device connected directly to a central processing unit, or a scale linked electronically to a central processing unit to record the weight of production completed by a department.

On-line processing implies that transactions are processed when recorded instead of accumulated in batches. Data may be recorded at a remote input terminal connected to the central processing unit by communication facilities. The processing usually requires a direct access (random access) file storage device.

Real-Time

Real-time refers to the time required for an action, activity, or decision to take place. When data processing is performed concurrently with a particular activity and the results of the processing are available soon enough to influence the course of the action being taken or the decision being made, the processing is said to be real-time processing. In business applications, the term is used to refer to fast-response systems in which the files are updated as soon as the transactions are recorded and in which outputs are provided immediately when they are requested. Real-time systems are always on-line.

The reservations systems used by the major airlines are good examples of real-time systems. Devices resembling typewriters are located at the reservations desks in airline terminals and at ticket offices. These devices are in direct communication with a central computer. Among other things, the central computer files contain a master record of each flight and the status of reservations for that flight. When a customer requests a seat on flight 123, the reservation clerk uses the typewriter device to inquire directly of the computer whether or not a seat is available. Within seconds the computer supplies the answer via the typewriter device. If a seat is available and accepted, the reservations clerk types in information about the customer, such as his name and traveling companions. All of this information is placed by the computer onto the master record for the flight.

An integrated data processing system is a system designed to minimize duplicate operations and duplicate records. The concept of such a system recognizes the interrelationship and interdependence of the economic functions of a business. In other systems, records are maintained according to organizational function (purchasing, accounts payable, sales, etc.); the integrated system is designed so that records for different functions with similar information are combined into a single comprehensive record. Some important characteristics of an integrated system for data processing are the following:

1. Once entered into the system, a single source document describing a transaction or providing other data initiates the updating of all records associated with the transaction or data item.

2. The parts of the system are interrelated and duplicate records are eliminated.

An integrated system need not be a real-time system, but many advanced integrated business systems have applications which operate on the basis of real-time response. A system may be fully integrated or partially integrated (i.e., with all or only part of the data processing operations and files of the organization integrated). An integrated system that contains and furnishes all the information needed by management for efficient organization and running of a business has been termed a "total system." An integrated set of data records in a data processing system has been termed the "data base" for the system.

Since it is extremely difficult to implement a fully integrated system, most integrated systems cover only a selected part of the activities of the organization. Typical of such a system is one which automatically performs all of the following steps, based on the entry of a sales order:

1. Finished goods inventory reduced (and, perhaps, a reorder triggered to start a purchase or production order process leading eventually to payment for materials, labor, etc.)

2. Order priced

3. Billing prepared

4. Accounts receivable updated

5. Sales analysis updated

6. Sales analysis compared with sales forecast; forecast revisions made, if necessary

7. Order costed

8. Cost of sales updated

Potential audit problems and possible solutions

Industrial experience with advanced data processing systems has been limited, but the characteristics (integrated, on-line, real-time) of the systems do suggest four problem areas:

1. Source documents

2. Authorizations

3. Audit trail

4. Control totals

Source Documents

A common feature in advanced systems is a point-of-origin device (sometimes termed a POD) for direct input of data. This may be a remote typewriter, a remote keyboard, or a remote visual display device. Experience to date indicates that direct input of data may change the form but not the substance of source documentation. Every direct input should be logged in order to provide a management inquiry trail and adequate managerial controls. This recording of input may occur at two points: (1) almost always at the computer facility and (2) usually also at the originating device (see Figure 13-1, page 209).

Information is usually recorded at the point-of-origin device as a by-product of a business transaction which has created a document. Examples are sales slips, invoices and passbook entries, all of which are auditable. In some applications, the input device prepares a locked log of all transactions entered through it.

The recording of all input at the computer center is usually necessary to provide for reconstruction of files in the event of loss or of extensive file degradation from erroneous processing. Therefore, the natural requirements of control and reconstruction usually provide source records for audit purposes, provided

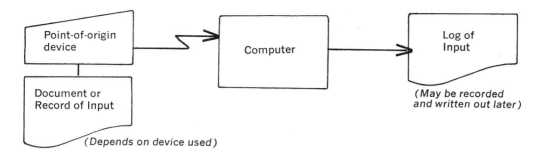

FIGURE 13-1. Logging of data entered through point-of-origin device

these records are retained for a sufficient period of time.

Retrieval of documents for audit tests may present a problem in an integrated system which operates on-line with random processing of source documents. Source documents are often entered into the system and filed in the order in which they are received, not matched and filed in the more conventional manner. Copies of a purchase order, a receiving report and an invoice, for instance, are normally matched to form an accounts payable voucher. In an integrated system, however, they may be processed separately and the matching routines performed by the computer. These source documents are time-consuming but not impossible to locate and they may be filed at locations some distance from where they were processed.

In systems using remote on-line input devices, the problem of authorization may be more complex than in traditional systems. Some type of source input record is usually produced; this source record, along with control over access to the device, provides control over authorizations. The control methods listed below illustrate the fact that the use of remote input devices and the elimination of traditional source documents need not remove the authorization phase of control over transactions:

Authorizations

1. Each user of a remote input device has his own key, code or card, which identifies him as an authorized user. The user code is entered on all source data logs and source documents produced by the device.

2. All inputs are checked for validity by the computer; all errors are reported to the person exercising the control function.

209

3. A listing, in meaningful form, of all inputs is sent back to the supervisor of the originating department for review and approval.

4. The input document produced by the remote device is the source document; approval of this document constitutes approval of the input.

A computer program containing a complex set of decision rules is a further aspect of authorization in advanced computer systems. A sale, for example, automatically causes an adjustment of the sales forecast. This forecast, when compared with inventory on hand and in process, may trigger a production order; this order may trigger raw material purchase orders, and so on. Authorization is programmed into the computer. Proper managerial control requires that the actions prescribed by such computer processing be subjected to human review before being carried out. The automatic authorization is controlled by this review.

The Audit Trail

A non-integrated system requires a separate document for each step in processing. Since a characteristic of an integrated system, however, is the updating of all related files from a single data input, much less documentation is required. The system is designed to perform automatically all processing required by the input (or by the results of the input), so intermediate authorization documents are not prepared. When an inventory requisition is processed against the inventory file and the expense file, for instance, the transaction may trigger automatically a purchase order and associated processing without employee intervention.

A designer could design a system without an audit trail. However, an organization with an integrated computer system cannot afford to lose control by establishing a system without adequate provisions for a management trail. In other words, the system designer is constrained by the requirements of customers, governmental agencies and outside auditors as well as management, even though it is apparent that the audit trail could be eliminated.

Control Totals

One of the most effective controls in data processing is the control total. It has been applied in batch totals, file totals, record counts, etc. It can also be used effectively in advanced systems.

Control totals may be accumulated for each type of source transaction entered as input and may then be traced to controls at other points in integrated processing to check whether or not all input transactions have reached the intermediate and final steps. A control total may be established for each remote input station and compared with a separately prepared control total of input from the station. Control totals may also be established by sorting and restructuring input and output for comparison with ledger controls and other control figures.

The effects of the source document controls, the authorization controls, the audit trail and the control totals in an advanced system is illustrated by the on-line savings and loan system described below.

Customer accounts for all branches are maintained on a central computer. A customer can make a deposit or withdrawal from any branch because each branch has access to the records of savings accounts for all branches. A customer presents a passbook and a deposit or withdrawal slip to the teller. Using an input/output device similar to a bookkeeping machine, the teller enters the account number, the transaction amount and the transaction code (and possibly other control information, such as last recorded balance). The data is transmitted to the computer, the customer account is updated, and the result is transmitted back to the I/O device where it is recorded. The device is also used for such inquiries as those regarding the status of an account. All processing is performed by the remote computer. Although the possibility of inadequate controls does exist, the visible trail may be improved (see Figure 13-2, page 212).

The audit of advanced systems

The preceding discussion has emphasized the facts that in an on-line integrated system the auditable source documentation does not usually disappear, provisions can be made for auditing authorizations, and the audit trail is usually still available. One audit problem, however, is expected to result from integration in the complex system. Since a single input triggers a number of data processing activities, the system is more difficult to understand and more complex to test for audit purposes. The processing of a particular application may be possible to trace in detail in a non-integrated environment, yet very difficult to trace when there are complex interrelationships. Programs interact not only with each other, but also with the control program in the operating system. The authorization procedure may provide for manual review, but the selection procedure may be imbedded in a complex set of computer routines.

The audit methods and approaches described in chapters 10-12 may also be applied to an integrated system. The auditor engaged in the examination of an advanced system, however, must usually have a greater knowledge of computers and computer-

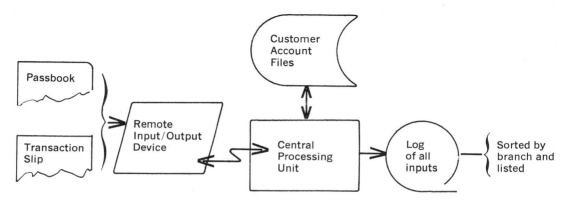

Controls at Input/Output Station

Transaction recorded and visible record of input created

Copy of input log kept in locked portion of machine

I/O device accumulates control totals mechanically

Output is in visible form for visual review

Customer receives record of processing for visual review

Erroneous input will lock machine and only supervisor can release it

Teller must reconcile I/O device input with computer control total and with transaction slips and cash

Controls at Computer Center

Input validation controls

Control totals established for each device

Log of input sorted down into customer order for each branch Control totals compared to control totals from input

Listing of exceptions for supervisory review

Periodic listing of account balances

FIGURE 13-2. Representative controls for on-line real-time savings and loan system

based systems than is necessary for most simpler systems. By considering the characteristics of the system being audited, the knowledgeable auditor can apply appropriate techniques. Some possible trends in the auditing of advanced systems include continuous monitoring and increased reliance on system testing and system controls.

Normal audit procedure usually includes tests of a sample of the processing performed during the audit period. For an advanced system employing remote input devices and integrated processing, it may be more effective to arrange for continuous monitoring of the system—either by a monitoring audit routine designed for this purpose or by tests performed at irregular intervals during the period.

The use of a monitoring audit program is a sophisticated technique. An audit routine is added to the set of programs controlling the data processing. Transactions entering the system are sampled at random intervals and the sample transaction is written on an audit tape or at an audit output terminal for use in testing. The system may be designed to record control information automatically on an input/output device under auditor control.

The use of on-line input/output devices may make it possible for the auditor to introduce random test transactions into the system during the period under audit in order to trace the system response. This procedure is similar to the procedure for test data and the precautions mentioned for test data may be applicable.

The limitations of test data method for system testing have been described in Chapter 11, where it is suggested that test data, though a useful audit technique, has a restricted applicability. Test data may be useful in advanced integrated systems, however, because it provides a method for testing the operation of an integrated set of programs which would be difficult to test manually.

The problems of test data preparation, described in Chapter 11, are increased in an advanced system. One approach is to rely partially on test data maintained by the client for his testing of the integrated system. In this case, the client procedures for documentation, change controls and test data preparation must be reviewed and the client test data checked for adequacy. After making appropriate additions to or deletions from the client test data, the auditor uses it to evaluate the operation of the set of routines performing the integrated processing. Of course, this is only one of several audit procedures used to evaluate the system.

Increased Reliance on System Controls

By nature, an advanced system is not usually a one-man operation. On the contrary, it is likely to require a substantial staff for programming, systems and operations. Therefore, organization controls associated with large systems can be applied (division of duties, supervisory control, rotation of operators, programming teams, program and tape library procedures, internal auditing, etc.). The auditor must test the operation of these controls to ensure that they have been operable during the audit period.

Research project

Auditing experience with advanced systems is still quite limited. However, the AICPA Advisory Committee on Auditing EDP Systems is constantly monitoring this area and will undertake research regarding the evaluation of auditing methods for advanced (and especially highly integrated) systems, as appropriate. When completed, the results of this research will supplement the material offered in this chapter.

CHAPTER 14

AUDITING DATA PROCESSING PERFORMED BY COMPUTER SERVICE CENTERS

COMPUTER SERVICE ORGANIZATIONS are available for the company which does not have enough data processing activity to justify the possession of a computer or which does not wish to invest the time and money necessary for establishing its own computer center and training its personnel in computer skills. Such service may be provided by an organization formed exclusively for that purpose, or by a division of an equipment manufacturer, or by a bank, CPA firm, or other service company.

Different services are offered by outside organizations. They may include (1) standard programs developed by the service center for specific functions (billing, etc.) (2) standard industry programs (customer and stock record accounting for the broker-age industry, for example) and (3) computer service tailored to the specific needs of the individual user, with programs prepared by the user or by the service organization. Some service centers also sell time on their equipment so that the user may operate his own programs with his own personnel. From an auditing and control viewpoint, it makes no difference whether the equipment belongs to the client or to a service center if the client operates his own programs with his own personnel. The audit and control programs discussed in this chapter, therefore, are applicable when the center provides processing services (not when the center merely rents a block of time on the EDP equipment).

Time-shared data processing, in which many users are connected directly to a central computer, is another form of computer service. This service, however, has some unique characteristics and is discussed in a separate section of the chapter.

Operations of a computer service center

The user delivers the input data to the computer center for processing. The input data may be either in the form of hard copy documents or in a machine-readable form such as punched cards prepared by the user. It is usually delivered to the service center manually or by mail, though in some cases it is forwarded by a telecommunication system. The amount of input can frequently be reduced by the use of the exception principle. For example, in a salaried payroll operation, where the great majority of employees are normally paid the same amount each period, only the changes to be made from the previous payroll need be reported in order for the payroll to be processed.

The permanent (master) files against which the input is to be processed are usually retained by the computer service center. A master file may be retained in tape, disk, or card format depending on the system and equipment being used. Changes in the master file data are often submitted as file maintenance adjustments and processed before the processing of the transactions.

Most computer service center processing is designed to provide the user with the final output document (invoice, payroll check, etc.) together with appropriate listings or registers. Occasionally, the end-product of the processing consists of punched cards or other machine-readable records, which must be processed further or printed at the user's office. Most centers require that a schedule of all processing to be performed and reports to be prepared be established in advance. Upon request, service centers usually provide special purpose reports, though these are often delayed because of scheduling and programming problems. The data stored in the master files is not commonly reproduced for the user's information unless absolutely necessary.

The responsibility for record retention usually rests with the user. The reports obtained from the service center, therefore, must contain all necessary historical data and the user must arrange for it to be stored. The service center usually retains only those records that are necessary for the reconstruction of files in the event of loss, destruction or significant error.

Responsibilities and controls

The role of the computer service center may vary from the operation of a program prepared by the user to the provision of a full data processing service. The trend is toward the latter arrangement because it requires fewer EDP skills of the user. In this case, the service center participates (and often takes the initiative) in the design of the system and accepts full responsibility for the programming and program testing as well as for the operation of the system. The user's participation is limited to establishing the requirements of the system and contributing toward its design. The user must also develop a sufficient knowledge of the system to enable him to provide the necessary input, to react to exceptions and differences reported, and to understand the output records.

In keeping with the service concept, the computer service center usually assumes full responsibility for hiring, training and supervising the personnel who program and operate the system. The user seldom has any voice in these matters; in fact, he is often uninformed about the qualifications of the personnel at the service center and has contact only with the account executive or other liaison personnel.

The user of a computer service center is often concerned about the security measures taken to protect the information held at the center. Some users are so sensitive in this regard that they furnish the service center with code numbers instead of names for customers or employees; they themselves retain responsibility for inserting the names on the output. Most users, however, have been able to satisfy themselves that the selected computer service center is a reputable and reliable business organization which employs adequate procedures for protecting information. If the security of any information is sufficiently critical, the user can deliver the input data, observe the processing and, at the completion of the processing, withdraw all transaction and master file data from the center. This safeguard is only necessary for extreme cases.

Another important aspect of security involves the provisions at the computer service center for master file reconstruction in the event of loss or destruction. Methods used for in-house installations (fireproof vaults, off-premises storage, etc.) apply equally well in service centers. The user is rightly concerned about these provisions and about the arrangements the center has made for back-up facilities. The question of back-up may be critical in cases where the service center obtains its computer time by off-shift rental of computers belonging to other organizations.

The audit trail is sometimes a problem. However, the management inquiry trail and other output provided by the service center usually furnishes adequate documentation of data processing. The user should make certain he retains sufficient printouts and other data for reconstruction of processing in the event of a computer center failure.

User Controls

The controls which ensure the orderly and supervised processing of data are the responsibility of the management of the computer service center. Though the user is seldom concerned with these controls, he generally establishes some overall input data controls (control totals, document counts, numbers of accounts, for instance) which enable him to check the completeness and accuracy of the service center's processing. He may also review the output documents and records completely or on a sampling basis, depending upon the nature and volume of the processing. The user may also undertake to test check manually some of the processing performed by the service center.

The user should make provisions to protect against a loss of source documents in transit to and from the service center. For example, if paid but unposted checks are transported to a service center for bank data processing, a microfilm copy should be kept at the sending bank. Another approach is for a copy of the source documents to be prepared for data processing purposes.

To ensure the timely and complete processing of all transactions, both the user and the service center usually review and screen the input data. The user corrects any errors or omissions he detects before the data is sent. Any erroneous data items detected by the service center's review or computer input validation (editing) routines are left unprocessed. They are listed and returned to the user.

The user may correct the data items and resubmit them with the next batch or, as in the case of payroll, he may have to process them manually if it is not practicable to wait until the next cycle of processing. If processing is performed manually, an adjustment must be prepared to update the master records at the next processing.

Audit problems

A company which uses a computer service center presents to the auditor, in addition to the usual audit problems of EDP systems, the complicating factor of an outside organization which enters into the company's scheme of processing, internal control and record retention. Some of the additional considerations, however, are two-sided, since the outside service center can represent a formalization and possible expansion of the controls afforded by division of duties. Deliberate manipulation of records is made unlikely by the separation of the persons in a position to perform such manipulation from those having custody of or access to the assets of the company. There are some exceptions to protection provided by this separation. An employee of a service center performing processing for a bank or a savings and loan institution may have limited asset access via his accounts. Suitable precautions should be taken in such cases. Errors in data processing are often more likely to be detected if a service center is used; this is because of the arm's-length relationship that exists between the employees of the user (who are responsible for the accuracy of the data) and the employees of the computer service center (who are performing the data processing).

Auditors have frequently concluded that, all things considered, the use of an outside computer service center (particularly for operations which can be subjected to overall controls and review—payroll preparation, accounts receivable processing, etc.) leads to improved internal control and diminished audit problems. Some auditors have concluded that, where the overall controls can be maintained effectively, neither the client nor the auditor need have great concern over the operations within the service center. It is maintained that there is a definite similarity between the computer service and the other services utilized by the client (telephone, electricity, mail), where, as long as the service is rendered, there is no need to question how it is done.

The above-mentioned concept is probably valid in many cases where a computer service center is utilized. Most data processing applications run by service centers are straightforward and well defined. Control totals and audit trails are usually adequate for audit purposes. Also, there are practical limitations which make it difficult for the auditor to satisfy himself directly about the operation and controls of the service center itself. First, the client is generally only one of many companies using the service center so that it may be difficult to obtain the co-operation of the service center's personnel. Second, the operations performed for the client may be quite simple, but the operations of the service center may be complex. In addition, questions may be raised about the ownership of the programs and records maintained at the service center. (This question should be clarified by the client before he contracts with the service center.) Thus, although the auditor inquires into a few aspects of the service center operations, he usually concentrates his attention on his client's controls.

Auditor activities

There are two tasks for the auditor whose client is utilizing a computer service center. The first is to advise his client about the adequate controls which should be established and maintained; the second is to test the operation of these controls.

Controls For Use With Service Center Processing

The controls to be established are the same as those used in a data processing installation. The absence of client control over the processing itself increases the significance of input controls and controls based on evaluation of output. The controls applied are generally as follows:

1. Control over data transmitted for processing; additional controls are necessary if the client performs data conversion

    (a) document count
    (b) transaction count
    (c) control totals

2. Control over master file changes

    (a) control printout of all changes
    (b) control count of master records
    (c) control totals for items in master records

3. Control over error correction and resubmissions

    (a) error printout identifying all errors

    (b) error log maintained by client

    (c) correction and resubmission review and approval procedure

4. Control over output

    (a) output distribution list

    (b) control tests on sample of output

5. Adequate management inquiry trail

    (a) transaction records

    (b) periodic printout of ledger balances

6. Adequate protection and security

    (a) client provision for copy of source documents transmitted

    (b) client provision for "worst case" file reconstruction

    (c) service center provision for routine reconstruction

    (d) security maintenance over client records kept at service center

A sample questionnaire useful for recording information about these controls is included at the end of this chapter.

Audit procedures include the following steps, which are directly related to the use of the service center computer:

Audit Procedures

1. Review client controls.

2. Check client controls against details processed by the service center.

3. Check client provisions for liaison with computer service center. Check that issuance of instructions and data to service center is restricted to authorized persons and that summary and control reports prepared at the center are delivered directly to the client personnel responsible for maintaining controls.

4. Inquire about operations at the computer center; observe supervision; record security procedures followed.

5. Check for accuracy a sample of transactions processed at

service center. Possibly introduce test data to check operations of controls, procedures and program steps or exception listings (see discussion below).

In addition to following these audit procedures, the auditor must perform his usual tests of the records and so on. If data volume and other economic considerations dictate, the auditor may arrange to use the service center computer to perform audit procedures such as those described in Chapter 12.

Observing Service Center Operations

If the service center maintains at the center records important for the audit, the auditor should try to observe the center's operations. The following control points are appropriate subjects of inquiry:

1. Security provisions over client data and files

2. Back-up and reconstruction provisions

3. Methods for handling important conditions, such as (a) unmatched transactions (no master file records), (b) control total or control count inconsistencies and (c) error corrections

At the same time, the auditor can obtain an idea of the adequacy of supervision at the center.

Using Test Data at Service Centers

The auditor must evaluate the adequacy of the controls which are supposed to exist at the computer service center. If he finds that the error printouts produced during processing are insufficient for this purpose, he may introduce some erroneous data with the regular input data. The problems of using such test data are discussed in Chapter 11.

Time-sharing computer service centers

In time sharing, a single, central computer system is used concurrently by several independent users. At least until now (mid-1967), its major use has been for scientific and mathematical processing. It is too soon to predict how extensively time sharing will be adopted for commercial processing.

A time-sharing service center is organized very differently from the service centers described above. Its characteristics usually include the following:

1. Each user has one or more input/output devices connected to the central computer facility by communication lines. The most common input/output (terminal) device is the teletypewriter. The facilities of a telephone company or Western Union are usually used for communication.

2. Each user sends data and instructions from his terminal as if he were the sole user.

3. The central computer accepts the data and instructions which arrive simultaneously from many users. By allotting each user a small but frequently repeated segment of computer time, it services all users concurrently. The computer can usually return the requested output immediately.

4. The user's data files are maintained at the central computer center. Instructions to the computer identify the files to be used. The system is designed to prevent one user from gaining unauthorized access to the files of another.

5. There is a set of programs for each user's processing. These may be standard programs serving a number of users or (more commonly) specific programs prepared for each user.

6. The data files, program files and input/output devices are all directly connected to the computer, so that processing can be performed at random as transactions or requests are entered.

The on-line processing method used in a time-sharing service is very different from the method of batching data and sending it to a service center for processing (described above). The user has immediate access to the computer either for processing transactions or for obtaining data from his files. Thus, in time sharing, the user may employ a service center and still have the advantage of the quick access and responsiveness which would be provided by an in-house computer.

Three factors inhibit the growth of time-sharing facilities: (1) the cost of communications, (2) the complexity of the time-sharing computer hardware and software and (3) the inadequacy for commercial processing purposes of most input/output devices.

Control Features   A time-sharing service center should establish controls and protections such as the following:

1. Protection against alteration or destruction of subscriber's programs

2. Control against unauthorized use of subscriber's proprietary programs

3. Control against unauthorized access to subscriber's files

4. Protection against loss or destruction of data files

5. Provision for file reconstruction

6. Provision for recovery from equipment failure

7. Control against inaccurate transmission of data between the computer and the subscriber's terminal device

The protection of the user's data and programs is a function of the hardware controls (see Chapter 4) and of the controls in the operating system programs. These latter programs recognize the initiation of an action at a user's terminal device; they then screen and control all communications, perform editing, assign priority sequence and bring into memory the appropriate user program. In some installations, the operating system programs remain in one computer while a second computer is used for executing user programs. The systems operation programs are usually very complex and are the responsibility of the computer center.

Checking features should be written into the user's programs or should form a part of the processing performed by the service center programs. These checks may include:

1. Control totals for batches of processing and for time periods

2. Transaction listings

3. Transaction numberings

4. Periodic file printouts and analyses

Again, it is important for the user to develop control totals for data being processed or stored in the center's files. These totals should be checked regularly against the comparable information furnished by the system during each processing routine. Another important control procedure involves test checks of the data processed at the service center; this provides a regular check of the system's accuracy.

When using a time-sharing computer service center, a company should ensure that the information required for audit purposes can be made available. This information should be obtainable from the user's files, from his terminal device, or directly from the computer service center. Data available from time-sharing or other real-time systems is often limited, since only current data (not historical data) is usually contained in the system files. If the requirements for an adequate management trail are met, however, the auditor should be able to perform most of his audit procedures by using data available from the user's files or obtainable through his terminal. This is particularly possible if an adequate system of control totals is maintained by the user.

A time-sharing computer service center (even more so than a normal center) presents problems for the auditor who wishes to review data processing thoroughly. A time-sharing system (particularly its internal programs) is highly complex. The internal program, which applies to all the users of the center, affects critically the accuracy of the data processing. Experience indicates that it is very impracticable for a user's auditor to obtain satisfaction about the computer center's time-sharing system by direct examination.

Some time-sharing computer centers have retained accounting firms to examine the systems and to offer opinions about the organization of the centers. Such examinations are major undertakings and should reassure the user and the auditor. Like any review, however, they provide assurance only for as long as the system remains unchanged and is operated in the authorized fashion. The internal controls most important to the auditor are the controls exercised by the client over input data and the control totals, record counts, etc., provided by both the user programs and the system programs. The audit trail of printouts in such a system should provide sufficient documentation for evaluating controls. Though the auditor is seldom able to audit the control programs of the time-sharing center, he can audit the processing performed by the user programs and can influence the controls which are included in them.

Records maintained at the service center may be tested by using printouts of the file or by running audit routines. When a

Audit Considerations

computer program is used for testing, it may be possible, or even necessary, to use the client's terminal devices.

QUESTIONNAIRE FOR EVALUATION OF CONTROLS FOR
PROCESSING PERFORMED BY AN INDEPENDENT DATA
PROCESSING SERVICE ORGANIZATION

General Information

1. *Background*

    1–1. Name of data processing service organization _____
    _____

    1–2. Address _____
    _____

    1–3. Name and title of person at service center responsible for client's jobs _____

    1–4. Major computer equipment available at service center
    _____

    1–5. Client applications being processed by service center

Application	*Frequency*
_____	_____
_____	_____
_____	_____
_____	_____

    1–6. Name and title of person in client organization responsible for liaison with service center _____
    _____

2. *General Review of Data Processing Service Center Operations*

    Yes No

    2–1. Have adequate provisions been made by the service center for back-up in case of equipment failure? ☐ ☐

2–2. Do service center personnel have access to client assets (charge accounts and bank accounts)? ☐ ☐

2–3. Does security over client records at service center appear adequate? ☐ ☐

2–4. Does service center have adequate insurance to protect client against substantial loss (lost data, lost files, errors in processing)? ☐ ☐

Controls for Each Application

101. *Control Over Input*

    101–1. Is the original or a copy kept of all source documents transmitted to the service center? ☐ ☐

    101–2. Is a control established for all data sent for processing? ☐ ☐
        Document numbering ☐
        Document count ☐
        Transaction count ☐
        Control totals (list below) ☐

    _____

    _____

    101–3. Do input controls in program appear adequate to detect incorrect input data? ☐ ☐

    101–4. Does client reconcile his input control figures with control figures furnished by the service center? ☐ ☐

102. *Control Over Master File Changes*

    102–1. Is a control printout provided for the client for all master file changes? ☐ ☐

    102–2. Is there a master file control record count or other control total provided for client to check for loss or non-processing of master file records? ☐ ☐

102–3. Does client check and reconcile this control figure? ☐ ☐

103. *Control Over Error Corrections and Resubmissions*

103–1. Is there an adequate error printout identifying all errors? ☐ ☐

103–2. Does client have adequate procedures for recording errors and controlling correction and resubmission? ☐ ☐

103–3. Do error procedures of both service center and client appear adequate for handling

(a) unmatched transactions? ☐ ☐
(b) control total or control count differences? ☐ ☐

104. *Control Over Output*

104–1. Are client procedures adequate for reviewing or testing output prior to distribution? ☐ ☐

104–2. Does client have adequate procedures for controlling distribution of output? ☐ ☐

105. *Adequacy of Management Trail*

105–1. Is there a listing of input data or any other satisfactory means for identifying transactions processed by the service center? ☐ ☐

105–2. Is there a periodic printout of ledger balances or a satisfactory alternative for providing this information? ☐ ☐

106. *Adequacy of Protection and Security*

106–1. Does service center appear to have adequate provisions for file reconstruction? ☐ ☐

106–2. Does client have provisions for "worst case" file reconstruction (that is, if all files at service center are destroyed)? ☐ ☐

106–3. Does client have complete documentation and copy of source program for all programs written specifically for him and for which full payment has been made (client ownership)? ☐ ☐

CHAPTER 15

THE TRAINING OF THE CPA FOR AUDITING EDP

THE AUDITOR SHOULD understand EDP for two reasons: (1) so that he can prepare a reliable evaluation of internal control in a computer-based data processing system and (2) so that he can utilize the computer in auditing if the characteristics of the system and the relative cost of the application make this procedure advisable. Since the computer is becoming omnipresent in all areas of information processing, there is a strong case for the position that all CPAs should have a good knowledge of EDP. A concurrent updating of audit staff computer expertise has often failed to accompany the rapid adoption of computer technology by client companies. In a 1966 survey by the Canadian Institute of Chartered Accountants, 34 per cent of a sample of Canada's largest companies stated that they were dissatisfied with the degree of computer "know-how" displayed by their auditors.

The need for EDP specialists

Not every auditor need be an expert in auditing EDP. A certain amount of specialization is advisable within most firms. The typical CPA needs to have a good general understanding of taxation, for example, but not every member of the audit staff needs to be an expert or specialize in that subject. The same is true for any specialized subject, including EDP.

The proficiency level required for auditing in an EDP environment depends somewhat on the complexity of the particular computer system. A firm performing audits involving complex systems, therefore, should have computer audit specialists with greater proficiency than is necessary in a firms that works with systems of average complexity. This concept is illustrated by

TABLE 15·1.   Recommended knowledge requirements

RECOMMENDED KNOWLEDGE REQUIREMENTS		1 Where client has a small card computer			2 Where client has a magnetic tape or random access system			3 Where client has a large integrated system		
		G	W	E	G	W	E	G	W	E
COMPUTER SYSTEMS	Main components									
	Tape & random access components									
	Hardware controls									
COMPUTER PROGRAMMING	Concepts of programming languages									
	Problem definition									
	Program testing & debugging									
	Program controls									
SYSTEMS DESIGN	Elements of systems design									
	Elements of feasibility studies									
	Controls outside the computer									
	Sequential system design									
	Random access system design									
COMPUTER AUDITING	Audit implications of computer processing									
	Evaluation of controls									
	Use of test decks									
	Use of computer as an audit tool									
	Audit of tape & random access systems									
APPLICATIONS	Management science techniques									

KNOWLEDGE LEVELS: G—GENERAL KNOWLEDGE   W—GOOD WORKING KNOWLEDGE   E—EXPERT KNOWLEDGE
(as defined by the Uniform Final Examination Syllabus)

Table 15.1 (page 232), which summarizes the knowledge requirements recommended by a special committee of the Canadian Institute of Chartered Accountants for its members.

What the auditor should know about EDP

The topics described in this section comprise the relevant body of knowledge for CPAs having field work or immediate supervisory responsibility in audits involving a computer. These topics are as follows:

1. EDP equipment and its capabilities

2. Characteristics of computer-based systems

3. Fundamentals of computer programming

4. Computer center operations

5. Organization and management of the data processing function

6. EDP documentation

7. Controls in EDP systems

8. Auditing techniques not using the computer

9. Auditing techniques using the computer

Study of these topics should provide any CPA with a general understanding of EDP. This discussion, however, emphasizes the greater depth of training necessary for those CPAs who are responsible for computer audits.

The auditor should have a general understanding of computer equipment. He should be familiar with the uses and capabilities of the central processor and the peripheral equipment, but need not be concerned with details such as internal circuit design.

EDP Equipment and Its Capabilities

The auditor should have a broad knowledge of file organization, process flow and system design. He should also understand the various methods for safeguarding computer files and the problems of including management or audit trails. He should

Characteristics of Computer-Based Data Processing Systems

have the ability to analyze and design an information system of modest complexity.

Fundamentals of Computer Programming

Though the auditor need not be a programmer, he should understand what programming entails. Elementary training in programming is often helpful in this respect and also provides an awareness of the capabilities of the computer. The auditor should have the ability to prepare specifications for and supervise preparation of a computer program.

Computer Center Operations

The auditor should understand the use of software in the operation of the computer. Though he does not generally operate the computer himself, he should understand the operator's role and should be able to supervise the running of computer audit programs.

Organization and Management of the Data Processing Function

Typical duties and different patterns of organization, supervision and division of duties should be understood by the auditor. He should also understand the application of management principles to the data processing function.

EDP Documentation

A knowledge of good documentation practices is necessary. The auditor should be able to follow system flowcharts, record layouts and error listings. Though he generally does not need to be able to decipher detailed symbolic coding or assembly printouts, he should understand their use in documentation.

Controls in EDP Systems

The auditor should be familiar with the controls used in EDP systems (data conversion controls, input controls, hardware controls, processing controls, output controls, operating controls, file and program controls, etc.). He should know the types of errors usually encountered and the methods for detecting, handling and correcting them.

Auditing Techniques Not Using the Computer

The auditor must understand fully the audit procedures that do not make use of the computer and must know how to obtain the records necessary for implementing these procedures.

The auditor should be able to recognize situations in which the computer can be used effectively for conducting the audit. He should be able to plan and supervise the development and use of techniques such as test data, controlled processing and audit computer programs.

The Common Body of Knowledge study recommendations for the beginning CPA

The Common Body of Knowledge study[1] was directed toward the CPA just entering the profession. The recommendations quoted below reflect the need for every CPA entering the profession to have a good general knowledge of computers.

"1. *The beginning CPA should have basic knowledge of at least one computer system.* This implies a knowledge of the functions of the component parts, of the general capabilities of the system, and of the more universal terms associated with the computer.
2. *He should be able to chart or diagram an information system of modest complexity.* This means that he should be able to comprehend the procedural steps in a system and utilize basic diagram symbols that describe the system clearly and precisely.
3. *He should have a working knowledge of at least one computer language.* We recommend no specific language, but there are several relatively universal languages that would serve better than those with more limited applicability. With an understanding of a programming language together with his overall knowledge of information systems, *the beginning CPA should be in a position to design a simple information system, program it, and proceed to debugging and testing.*" [2] (Emphasis added)

Of interest is the emphasis on the importance of obtaining knowledge through specific training (for example, obtaining a

[1] Robert H. Roy and James H. MacNeill, *Horizons for a Profession*, American Institute of Certified Public Accountants, 1966. (Approved by Council, 1969)
[2] *Ibid.*, p. 213.

knowledge of programming through the study of one higher-order language). By contrast, the discussion in this chapter stresses the importance of gaining an understanding of programming in general. However, this general knowledge can usually be best obtained by studying a specific language.

Sources of training for the CPA

The following sources of training are available:

1. Courses given by computer manufacturers

2. Courses given by colleges and universities

3. Courses given at local technical schools

4. Self-study and programmed learning

5. On-the-job training

6. AICPA Professional Development courses

7. Seminar programs

The desirability of learning-by-doing is a significant factor in the evaluation of training sources. It is a great advantage for a trainee to have the opportunity of writing, assembling, debugging and running a simple program. Though this "hands-on" method requires access to a computer, it is generally to be preferred.

Courses by Computer Manufacturers

Computer manufacturers are the major source of computer training today. They usually offer general orientation courses as well as courses in programming and operating particular machines. In general, the content of the courses and the quality of instruction has been very good. However the courses are not designed for the CPA, enrollment is restricted, and the equipment of particular manufacturers is emphasized.

Courses by Colleges And Universities

The colleges and universities have responded slowly to the need for training in electronic data processing. Since 1965, however, the number of courses offered has increased, and it is expected to continue increasing to satisfy the needs of the business community. Many colleges and universities have equipment available (at least on a limited basis) for use in connection with the courses; many offer evening courses in adult education programs.

Courses are offered in most metropolitan areas by technical schools. At least one computer manufacturer has established technical institutes for the purpose of providing local computer training. Any evaluation of this training source should consider the availability of equipment for student use, the qualifications of instructors, the content of courses as shown by outlines, and the comments and recommendations of persons who have completed the training. Plans underway for accreditation of such schools were not complete at this writing. When they are, the accreditation status of a school should also be considered.

Courses at Local Technical Schools

The general principles of electronic data processing and many elements of programming can be learned through self-instruction, and there are a number of programmed self-study courses available. Several manufacturers use the programmed learning method extensively. Home-study computer courses are offered by several home-study institutions. A major drawback of self-instruction, however, involves the lack of "hands-on" experience and the difficulty of asking questions.

Self-Instruction and Programmed Learning

Most qualified business data processing personnel have been trained on the job. Most have completed manufacturer courses and/or introductory courses at colleges and universities, but the major part of their expertise has been achieved through on-the-job experience. This method is economical for the practicing CPA only under certain circumstances. Staff members, for example, may be trained on the job by arrangement with a local installation. Some CPAs have benefited from the cooperation of a client moving into a new EDP installation.

On-The-Job Training

As of mid 1970, the Professional Development Division of the AICPA offered courses in Computer Concepts—featuring "hands on" experience on the computer, and "Control and Audit of EDP Systems." In addition, more specialized courses such as "System Flowcharting," "Program Flowcharting and

Professional Development Courses Offered By the AICPA

Decision Tables," "Selection of an EDP Service Center" and Evaluation, Selection and Installation of EDP Systems and Generalized Retrieval Languages were also offered. Plans for additional EDP oriented courses are constantly under development.

Seminar Programs   Many organizations such as the American Management Association offer seminars on computer data processing topics. The Association for Computing Machinery (ACM) offers a number of seminars on advanced topics. The CPA need not be a member of these organizations to attend their programs.

Summary

The CPA who performs audits in an EDP environment should have an adequate understanding of computers. Since most CPAs did not receive instruction in EDP as part of their academic training, other sources of training have become necessary. A general knowledge of EDP is appropriate for most CPAs, whether or not they perform audits for organizations using computers. The problems of developing proficiency and of keeping up in the EDP field have caused many accounting firms to hire non-accountant computer specialists.

To date, manufacturers have provided most of the computer training, though colleges and universities are responding to the need. In addition, the AICPA is expanding the number and depth of the Professional Development Division courses in EDP.

238

AN OVERVIEW OF COMPUTER DATA PROCESSING

THE PURPOSE OF this appendix is (1) to assist the auditor whose understanding of computer data processing is limited or (2) to act as a "refresher" survey for the auditor who needs to review. The material offered here outlines the elements of computer data processing in order to provide a review of its terminology and major concepts. For study in greater depth, other materials must be used.

Definition of a computer

The term "computer" can be applied logically to any calculating device. In common usage, however, the term refers specifically to the electronic computer. (Early writers in the computer field frequently referred to the "automatic computer" in order to differentiate it from other calculating devices.) The computer has certain differentiating characteristics, as follows:

1. *Electronics.* The computer relies largely on electronic elements (transistors, resistors, diodes, etc.) rather than on mechanical operations. The use of electronic elements makes possible much faster operation than is possible with mechanical devices.

2. *Internal storage.* The computer has internal storage (fre-

239

quently called memory) for storing both the program and the data being processed by the program.

3. *Stored program.* Prior to its execution, the program of instructions which specifies the sequence of operations is put into the internal memory. This program makes the computer "automatic," since the entire set of steps to be taken is determined in advance and human intervention is seldom required during execution.

4. *Branching capability.* A distinguishing feature of the computer is its ability to check the types of data being processed or the results of computations against previously defined conditions, and then to select from alternative sets of processing instructions or to modify instructions in the stored program.

In other words, a computer is an electronic device capable of solving problems. A stored program of instructions directs the computer in accepting data, in performing prescribed operations and in supplying the results of these operations as output.

The two main types of computers are the digital and the analog. The digital computer operates essentially by counting; all quantities are expressed as numbers. The analog computer operates by measuring; for example, quantities may be expressed as voltages which are read from meters. Computers which combine features from both the analog and the digital are called hybrid computers. Most electronic computers are digital and in this review the term "computer" refers only to the digital computer.

Digital computers may be categorized according to orientation: (1) business data processing, (2) scientific and engineering computation, (3) process control. There is a trend, however, toward making general purpose computers, so that these distinctions do not always hold. Computers may be designed with any or all of the characteristics summarized below.

1. Business data processing usually involves the processing of large numbers of records with relatively little computation for each record. A large volume of output in the form of updated records, reports, checks, invoices and other business documents must be produced. The computer oriented toward business data processing is therefore designed for high-speed input and output and high-speed sorting; it also has instruc-

tions to facilitate the conversion of stored data into report format.

2. Scientific and engineering computation involves extensive internal computation with relatively little input or output. The computer designed for scientific computation, therefore, is capable of high-speed internal processing but has limited input and output facilities.

3. Process control involves frequent inputs of data from the process being controlled, tests of the data and computations to adjust the process controls. Since the computer must usually service several controls, the hardware is designed to accept and process many concurrent or simultaneous inputs. Such a computer is used to monitor the measuring devices and adjust the controls in an oil refinery or chemical plant, for example.

Elements of a computer data processing system

Five basic elements make up a computer data processing system: hardware, software, user-written programs, procedures and personnel. Operating procedures (including documentation) and personnel are discussed in Chapters 2, 3 and 8. This appendix therefore contains discussions of hardware, software and user-prepared programs.

Computer hardware consists of devices which can perform one or more of the following functions: data preparation; input to the computer; computation, control and primary storage; secondary (auxiliary) storage; and output from the computer. "On-line" (or online) equipment is connected directly to the computer; "off-line" (or offline) equipment is used separately and is not connected directly. The relationships between these functions are shown in Figure A-1, page 242.

Hardware

Software consists of programs and routines provided to facilitate the use of the computer. The term can be used to include application programs or routines written for a specific installation, but it is more commonly used to refer only to the general pro-

Software

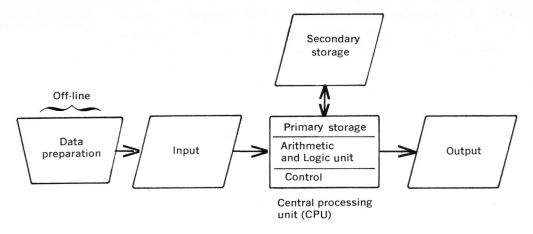

FIGURE A-1.   Functions in a computer configuration

gramming and operating aids which are usually furnished by the manufacturer. These aids include programs for such tasks as making printouts of machine-readable records, sorting records, organizing and maintaining files, assembling or compiling programs and scheduling jobs through the computer. Software is as important as hardware, since it makes possible the fullest and most effective use of the computer's capabilities. Some manufacturers charge separately for software and services. This practice of separate pricing is known as "unbundling."

User Programs   Although the computer manufacturer does supply generalized programs for some common tasks, the user must write most of the programs he needs himself. A program consists of a set of instructions for performing a data processing task. A complete data processing application usually requires a number of programs.

Equipment in a computer configuration

The full complement of equipment in a computer configuration depends on the amount and type of processing being performed and on the types of equipment available for use with the particular computer. Most systems have one or more pieces of equipment for each of the five equipment functions described earlier in this chapter. The different types of equipment are summarized in Table A.1, page 243.

242

The central processing unit (CPU) is the "computer" part of the computer system. It contains an arithmetic unit for computation, a control unit and the primary storage (or internal memory) for the program being used and the data being processed. The CPU has a control console for the operator. This may be a panel on the CPU cabinet or a separate console with a typewriter or visual display device (see Figure A-2, page 244).

Equipment for Computation and Control

Secondary storage (mass or auxiliary storage) is used to hold the programs not currently in use and the data files (see Figure A-3, page 244). Magnetic tape is the most popular reusable magnet-

Equipment for Secondary Storage

Equipment for Each Computer Data Processing Function   *TABLE A.1*

FUNCTION	TYPE OF EQUIPMENT USED
Data preparation	Key-driven card punch Key-driven card verifier Paper tape punch Magnetic tape encoder Magnetic ink enscriber Optical character enscriber Data collection devices (with keyboard, plastic card sensor, etc.) which transcribe onto a machine-sensible medium Devices which prepare cards, paper tape or optical tape as by-products of another operation Conversion devices (such as paper tape to magnetic tape converter or paper tape to punched card converter)
Input	Card reader Magnetic tape unit Paper tape reader Magnetic-ink character reader Optical scanner Console typewriter On-line data collection devices
Computation, control and primary storage	Central processing unit (CPU)
Secondary storage	Storage devices using magnetic tape, magnetic disk, magnetic drum, or magnetic strip
Output	Printer Card punch Paper tape punch Console typewriter Visual display (CRT) Graph plotter Audio response unit

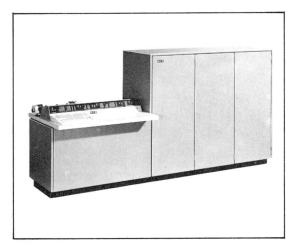
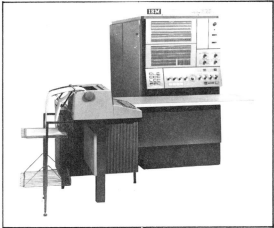

FIGURE A-2. Central processing unit with control panel on cabinet (left) and with separate console typewriter (right)

Storage Media

Magnetic tape

Magnetic disk

Magnetic drum

Magnetic strip.

Storage Holder

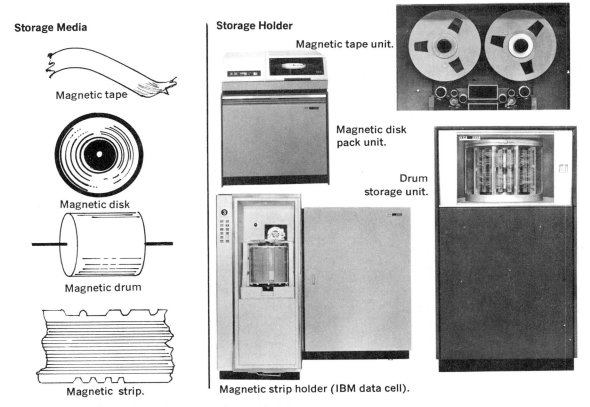

Magnetic tape unit.

Magnetic disk pack unit.

Drum storage unit.

Magnetic strip holder (IBM data cell).

FIGURE A-3. Secondary storage media and holders

ically-encodable storage media. In small commercial systems punched cards are used for file storage. Table A.2 (below) lists the storage capacities and transfer rates of magnetic file storage devices.

The most commonly used input device is the punched card reader. Paper tape readers must be used when input data has been punched onto paper tape by an add punch, a cash register attachment, or a typewriter attachment. Magnetic character readers are most often used for check processing in banks. Optical scanners are increasingly popular, especially for reading ticket data (gasoline charge tickets and airline tickets, for example). Figure A-4 (page 246) shows the various input devices.

Input Devices

The printer heads the list of output devices (see Figure A-5, page 247). Output data must be in a form readable by personnel (unless it is to be used for further processing); the line printer performs this task. The cathode ray tube (CRT) display device is expected to become more popular for systems in which many persons at remote locations must interrogate the computer or view records in the file. Table A.3 (page 248) shows typical speeds for common input and output units.

Output Devices

Since punched cards are the most common input medium, the data preparation equipment in an EDP system will usually include keypunches. It may also include other card handling equipment, such as sorters, collators, interpreters and repro-

Equipment Data Preparation

Storage Capacities of Secondary Storage Devices   *TABLE A.2*

DEVICE	TOTAL CAPACITY	RANGE OF TRANSFER RATES
Magnetic tape	1-20 million characters per tape	15,000-350,000 characters per second
Magnetic disk pack	1-7 million characters per pack	100,000-225,000 characters per second
Magnetic drum	1-4 million characters per drum	275,000-1,200,000 characters per second
Magnetic strip	10-400 million characters per handler	25,000-45,000 characters per second

Input Medium

Punched card

Magnetic tape on reel

Paper tape on reel or roll

Document
(such as check)

Document

Operator typewriting

Input Device

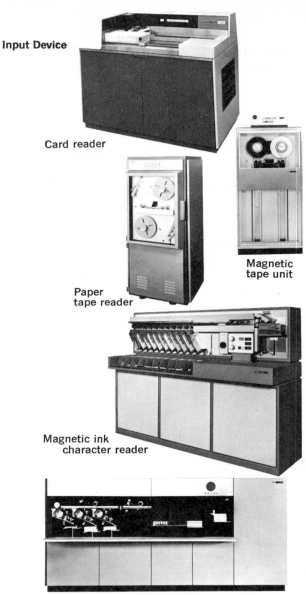

Card reader

Magnetic
tape unit

Paper
tape reader

Magnetic ink
character reader

Optical scanner

Console
typewriter

FIGURE A-4. Input devices

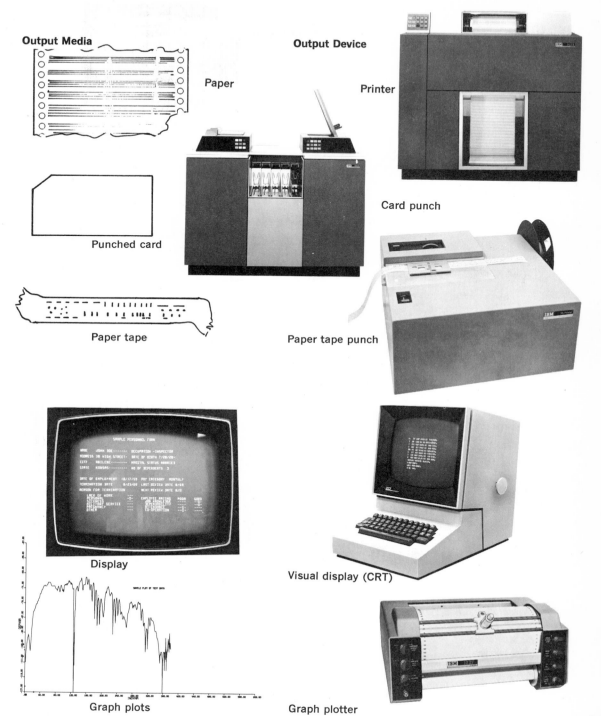

Output Media

Paper

Punched card

Paper tape

Display

Graph plots

Output Device

Printer

Card punch

Paper tape punch

Visual display (CRT)

Graph plotter

FIGURE A-5. Output devices and media

247

Typical Speeds for Input/Output Devices

| DEVICE | UNIT OF MEASUREMENT | TYPICAL RATES | | |
		LOW	MEDIUM	HIGH
Card reader	Cards per minute	300	600	1200
Paper tape reader	Characters per second	350	500	1000
Magnetic ink reader	Documents per minute	750	1200	1600
Printer	Lines per minute	300	600	1100
Card punch	Cards per minute	100	300	500
Paper tape punch	Characters per second	20	100	150

ducers. Data preparation, however, is time-consuming and expensive, and there is a trend toward reduction or elimination of this step. This can be done either by encoding data in machine-readable markings on the source document or by creating a machine-readable by-product while making the source document. Direct read-in of data from on-line input devices (teller window machines, for example) also eliminates the data preparation step. (See Figure A-6, page 249).

Typical computer system configurations

A computer system may range in size from a small configuration with a monthly rental of less than $1,000 per month to a large-scale system with a monthly rental of over $100,000. Four configurations—three small systems (card, magnetic tape and magnetic disk) and a medium-scale system—are discussed here to describe the equipment and cost range of a typical system. The discussions do not treat data preparation or the use of off-line equipment.

Small System—Card   In this type of system, the transaction files, the master files and the programs not in use are stored on punched cards. Processing is of the batch type and uses sequentially organized data and files. In addition to computations, many card-handling operations (sorting, merging, etc.) must be performed. These operations are usually performed by off-line sorters and collators, but some manufacturers offer a multi-function card handler which is

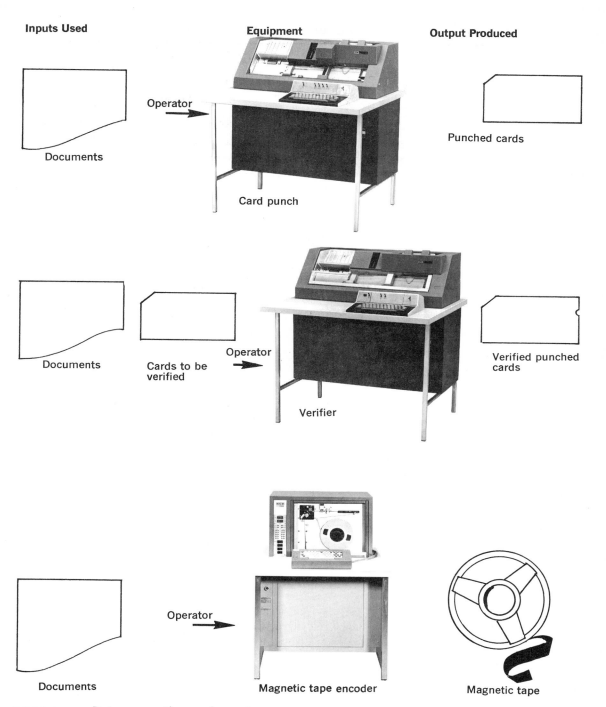

Inputs Used　　　　　　**Equipment**　　　　　　**Output Produced**

Operator

Documents

Card punch

Punched cards

Documents　　Cards to be verified

Operator

Verifier

Verified punched cards

Documents

Operator

Magnetic tape encoder

Magnetic tape

FIGURE A-6.　Data preparation equipment

249

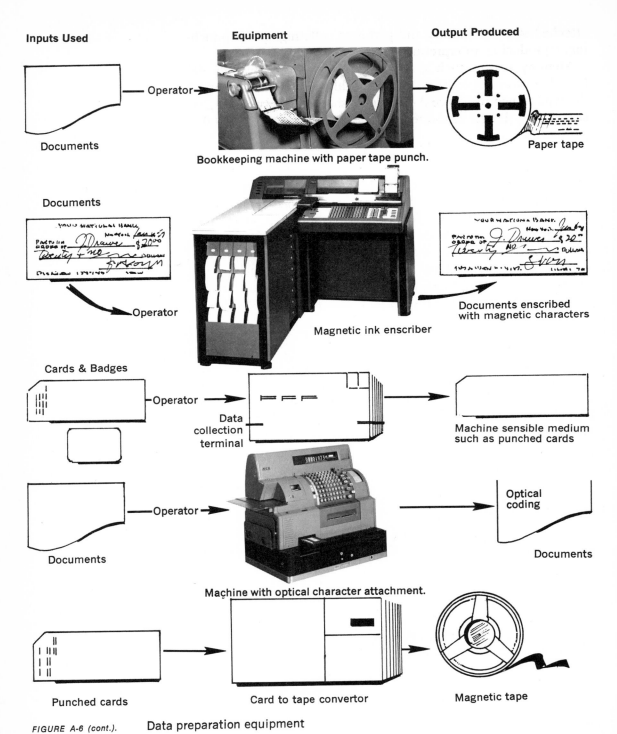

Inputs Used   **Equipment**   **Output Produced**

Documents

—Operator—→

Bookkeeping machine with paper tape punch.

Paper tape

Documents

—Operator

Magnetic ink enscriber

Documents enscribed
with magnetic characters

Cards & Badges

—Operator—→

Data
collection
terminal

Machine sensible medium
such as punched cards

Documents

—Operator—→

Machine with optical character attachment.

Optical
coding

Documents

Punched cards

Card to tape convertor

Magnetic tape

FIGURE A-6 (cont.).   Data preparation equipment

250

attached to the computer and performs collating, group punching, reproducing, interpreting, etc.

Memory size in such a system is small—probably only 4K (4,000) character positions. The monthly rental for a system of the type shown in Figure A-7 (below) should be between $1,200 and $2,500. Larger card-oriented systems may cost up to $4,000 per month.

Punched card files limit the speed and versatility of a system. Magnetic tape file storage is a great improvement. However, transactions to be processed must be sorted into the same order as the magnetic tape file they will be used to update—a requirement which takes three or four magnetic tape drives. Memory size in a small tape system is usually sufficient to store 8K characters. The monthly rental for a system of the type diagrammed in Figure A-8 (page 252) should be between $4,000 and $6,000.

Small System— Magnetic Tape

Removable disk pack storage is an alternative to tape storage. To ensure satisfactory file protection and reconstruction arrangements, it is desirable to have at least two disk storage units or to have magnetic tapes also. The monthly rental for a system of the type shown in Figure A-9 (page 253) should be between $4,000 and $6,000 per month. It should be noted that the cost of a disk pack is approximately $500, while the cost of a reel of magnetic tape is approximately $30.

Small System— Magnetic Disk

As a system expands in size, a faster central processor and faster peripheral equipment are chosen and the number of attached units is increased. A configuration like the one shown in

Medium-Scale Business System

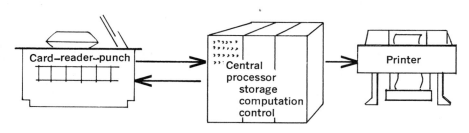

FIGURE A-7.   Small card-oriented system

251

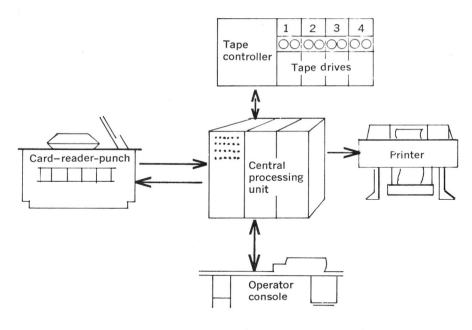

Small magnetic tape-oriented system

Figure A-10 (page 254) should cost between $5,000 and $8,000 per month. Memory size is sufficient to store from 16K to 32K characters.

Types of data processing

The major data processing jobs in a business are the updating of the master files and the preparation of business documents. Computer file terminology is similar to manual file terminology. A file consists of all records of a given type; each record consists of one or more data items associated with a record-keeping unit.

ELEMENT	DESCRIPTION	EXAMPLES
File	All records of given type	Payroll file containing all payroll records
Record	All data items associated with record-keeping unit	Record containing all payroll data for an individual
Item or field	Single unit of data	Payroll identification number, pay-to-date, etc.

A master file corresponds closely to a ledger and contains the up-to-date records maintained by the organization. Transactions are recorded and accumulated on a detail file—a procedure analogous to the maintaining of an accounting journal. The transactions on this file are used for the basic task of updating the master records. For this activity there are two possible methods: (1) batch processing (periodic processing of item batches) and (2) on-line processing (immediate processing of unbatched items). Items in a batch may be in sequential order or random order. File storage devices offer one of two types of access: (1) sequential access (punched cards, magnetic tape) or (2) direct access (magnetic disk, magnetic strips). Thus, the file devices partly determine the processing method to be used.

DEVICE	PROCESSING APPROACH
Sequential access	Batch — sequential
Direct access	Batch — sequential — random On-line (random)

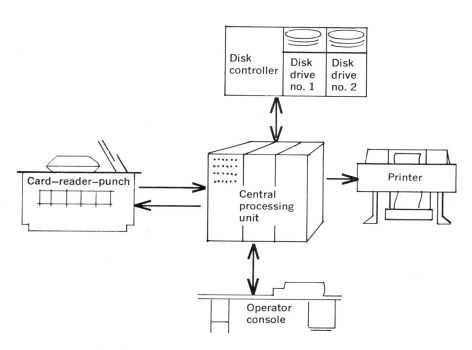

FIGURE A-9.   Small magnetic disk-oriented system

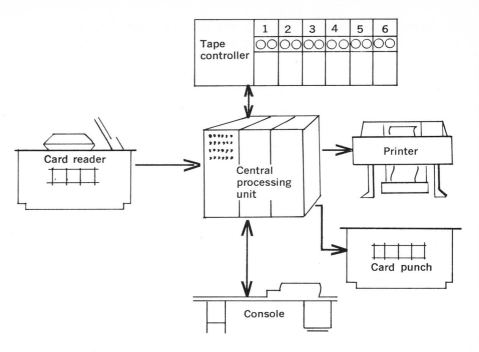

Note from the table that batch processing can be used with direct access devices as well as with sequential access devices.

Batch Processing with Sequential Access File Storage

Sequential access batch processing is usually used wherever records are maintained on punched cards or magnetic tape. Where batch-sequential processing is used with a sequential access file storage device, the entire master file is put through the computer at each updating (see Figure A-11, page 255). For this reason, it is desirable to allow the transactions to accumulate into large batches between each processing in order to reduce the frequency of processing. The user sorts the transactions into the same sequence as in the master file so that each record on the master file needs to be read only once. The time taken to read a record represents a fixed time cost each time the file is processed, whether or not the record is updated. The variable processing time to process a transaction may overlap, at least in part, the fixed time element for reading the record. The nature of many processing applications is such that batching and sequencing requirements are not actually restrictions. Batch processing is ideal for payroll and accounts payable, for example. Besides, it is faster and cheaper to process by batch.

A direct access file storage device can select and update a particular record without having to read all the other records too. The most popular direct (or random) access file device is the disk file. When using such a device, it is not necessary to batch the data, but in many cases speed and cost advantages make batching (sequential or nonsequential) appropriate. Processing with a magnetic disk, for instance, may be completed faster if the input data is sequenced to minimize the mechanical movement of the disk as it locates records. (See Figure A-12, page 256.)

Where applications involve relatively few transactions compared to the number of file records, however, the saving in direct access seek time is too small to justify the extra sorting time that would be necessary, so the transactions may be left in random order in the batch.

Batch Processing with Direct Access File Storage

In certain applications (production control, for example) records must always be kept up to date. Transactions are not batched

On-Line Processing

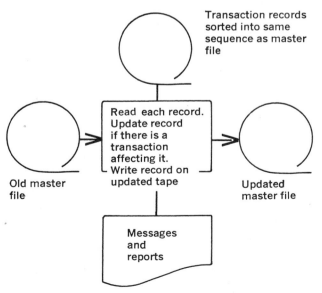

Transaction records sorted into same sequence as master file

Read each record. Update record if there is a transaction affecting it. Write record on updated tape

Old master file

Updated master file

Messages and reports

FIGURE A-11.   Batch-sequential data processing using sequential access storage (magnetic tape)

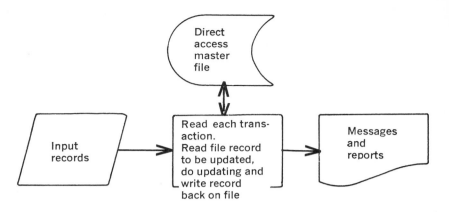

Data processing using direct access storage

but are processed randomly as received. This on-line processing requires direct access storage devices such as magnetic disks.

The on-line real-time system is an advanced type of on-line system in which transactions and inquiries are recorded and processed as soon as they are received. The results of the processing of a transaction are achieved so fast that they can themselves influence the transaction. Each point of origin of transactions is connected to the computer by a device which can send data and receive responses. Information is stored in direct access files. On-line real-time systems presently include airline reservation systems, savings and loan deposit accounting systems, stock market information systems, local and state law enforcement intelligence systems, hotel accounting and reservations systems and patient service record systems in hospitals.

Programming a computer

Figure A-13 (page 257) shows the sequence of steps necessary for computer data processing.

Steps in Preparing A Program

Steps 3 (planning computer logic) and 4 (preparing program) in Figure A-13 involve the preparation of a computer program.

Step 3 usually makes use of a program flowchart and/or a decision table, both of which show the processing step sequences and the decisions on which the selection of a sequence is based.

Steps

1. Analysis of problem.

2. Design of a system to provide the information.

3. Planning of the computer logic.

4. Program preparation.

5. Documentation.

6. Input data preparation.

7. Running of program.

8. Use of the output.

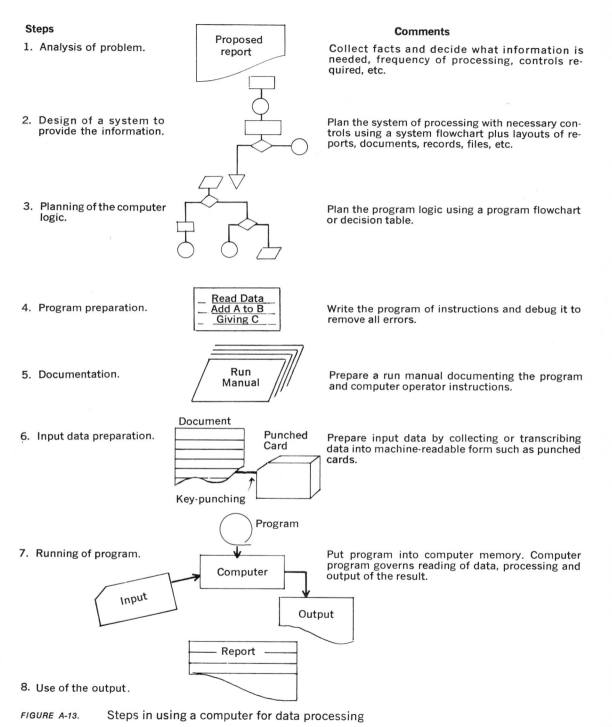

Comments

Collect facts and decide what information is needed, frequency of processing, controls required, etc.

Plan the system of processing with necessary controls using a system flowchart plus layouts of reports, documents, records, files, etc.

Plan the program logic using a program flowchart or decision table.

Write the program of instructions and debug it to remove all errors.

Prepare a run manual documenting the program and computer operator instructions.

Prepare input data by collecting or transcribing data into machine-readable form such as punched cards.

Put program into computer memory. Computer program governs reading of data, processing and output of the result.

FIGURE A-13. Steps in using a computer for data processing

The program flowchart is a basic part of the documentation supporting a program; without it, it is difficult to follow the logic behind each detailed program step. The standard flowchart symbols established by the American National Standards Institute are shown in Appendix C. The use of program flowcharts and decision tables is illustrated in Appendix B, which contains an example of documentation.

Step 4 involves the writing of detailed instructions for directing the computer. The level of the language used governs the form of the instructions and the extent of their detail. There are essentially four language levels:

1. Machine language (absolute)

2. Symbolic language

3. Symbolic language with macro-instructions

4. Procedure and problem-oriented language (higher order)

Machine language is required by the computer, in which it is represented in binary form. For operator purposes, notations such as octal, hexadecimal and binary coded character are used. The other language levels are written in a form more convenient for the programmer and must be translated into the absolute machine language form (see Figure A-14, below). Conversion is performed by special translator programs (called assemblers and compilers) which are usually furnished by the manufacturer. Assembly programs convert from symbolic language to machine language; compiler programs convert from procedure or problem-oriented language to machine language. A program coded in symbolic form is known as a source program; a program coded in machine language is known as an object program.

Symbolic coding is essentially machine-oriented, since one

Machine language in binary as stored in the computer	0101100000100000000010000111 0000 0101101000100000000010000111 0001 010100000010000000001000011110010
Symbolic assembly language	L 2,A A 2,B ST 2,C
Procedure-oriented language (COBOL)	ADD A AND B GIVING C.

FIGURE A-14.   Coding of steps to perform C = A + B in machine, symbolic and procedure-oriented languages

symbolic instruction is generally translated into one machine-language instruction. The programmer utilizes symbolic operation codes (for example, the code for addition might be ADD or A) and memory locations are referenced by symbolic names instead of actual location numbers. When the assembly program converts these symbolic codings into absolute instructions, it also performs simple checks to detect errors in coding. Steps for using a symbolic programming system are shown in Figure A-15 (page 260).

Since many computer operations are programmed in the same way, it is wasteful for the programmer to have to rewrite the same set of detailed instructions each time the operation is to be performed. To improve programmer efficiency, most computer manufacturers provide symbolic programming languages with "macro" instructions. "Macros" are names given to sets of coded instructions for performing often-used operations. By including a macro-instruction in a program, the programmer generally avoids a great deal of detailed coding. During the translation process, the assembly program interprets the macro name as a specification calling for a set of instructions rather than as a simple one-for-one translation. Accordingly, the set of instructions is copied from the assembly program library and inserted in the object program being assembled.

A procedure- or problem-oriented language is machine-independent and is usually written with little or no reference to the computer on which it is to be translated and run. Each computer must have a unique compiler program for translation. The programmer uses descriptive English words and common mathematical notion to describe processing steps. Examples of these languages are (1) FORTRAN (FORmula TRANslator—an algebraic language), (2) COBOL (COmmon Business Oriented Language) and (3) PL/I (Programming Language, version 1— a combined algebraic and business language).

Report program generators (RPG) are of special interest to the business user. The generators accept programs written in a problem-oriented set of specifications and produce a complete machine-language program. They are especially suitable for the preparation of simple printed reports.

Each of these levels of programming has its advantages and disadvantages. Lower-level languages are generally more efficient in terms of running time. Higher-level languages are easier to use, reduce programming time and can be used with different

1. Flowcharting the program logic

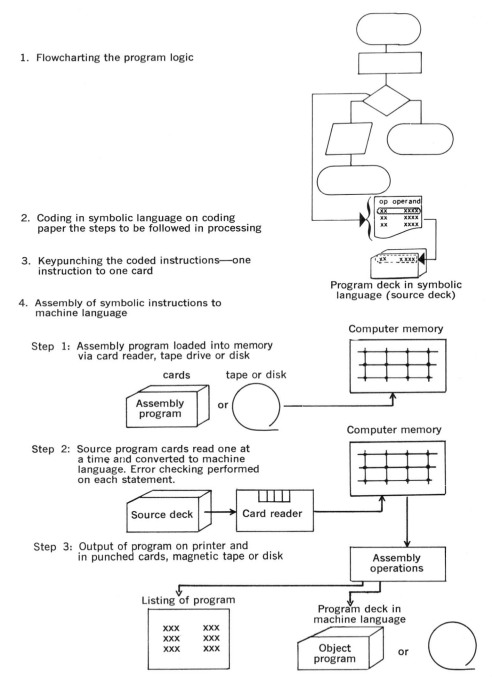

2. Coding in symbolic language on coding paper the steps to be followed in processing

3. Keypunching the coded instructions—one instruction to one card

4. Assembly of symbolic instructions to machine language

Program deck in symbolic language (source deck)

Step 1: Assembly program loaded into memory via card reader, tape drive or disk

Computer memory

cards   tape or disk

Assembly program   or

Step 2: Source program cards read one at a time and converted to machine language. Error checking performed on each statement.

Computer memory

Source deck → Card reader

Step 3: Output of program on printer and in punched cards, magnetic tape or disk

Assembly operations

Listing of program

xxx	xxx
xxx	xxx
xxx	xxx

Program deck in machine language

Object program   or

Store program on cards or tape until needed.

FIGURE A-15.   Preparing a program using a symbolic assembly system

computers. Documentation is improved with the use of higher-order coding. Programs written in a language such as COBOL are partially self-documenting because of the use of English phrases and sentences in the coding. In general, the trend is toward the use of higher-order languages. Depending on the efficiency of the compiler, the improvement of programming effectiveness is usually a more significant factor than the gaining of machine running time. In some cases there is virtually no difference in running time. Throughput time for programs involving little computation for each input item, for example, is not altered by a less efficient coding of the computational steps. A compiler language is usually preferred for once-used or infrequently used programs. For often-used programs, the choice depends on the cost advantages and disadvantages mentioned above.

In addition to the programming languages and the related assemblers and compilers, computer software furnished by the manufacturer usually includes a wide variety of support programs such as the following:

Support Programs

1. Tape utility programs:

    Programs to convert data on magnetic tape onto cards
    Programs to convert data on cards onto magnetic tape
    Programs to print data from magnetic tape

2. Disk utility programs:

    Programs to clear disks
    Programs to reorganize disks (to fill in locations left blank by the deletion of items, for instance)

3. Sort and merge programs (tape or disk)

4. File management programs

5. Simulator programs:

    These programs allow one computer to simulate the performance of another computer. Thus, a user can run old programs on a new computer without rewriting them or he can test the programs for a new computer before he has access to it.

6. Subroutines:

Short routines with wide application can be pre-written to be inserted in larger programs. Manufacturers generally provide subroutines for such common tasks as (a) calculating square roots, (b) generating random numbers and (c) multiplying and dividing (for computers which do not have hardware equipment for multiplication and division).

Operating Systems

An operating system (also referred to as a supervisor routine, an executive routine, or a monitor) is a set of routines which manages the running of other programs. Such a system schedules and loads jobs, gives instructions to the operator, keeps records, handles input/output and error conditions and performs many operator tasks. As a computer system becomes more complex, its operating system becomes more necessary for efficient operation.

AN EXAMPLE OF DOCUMENTATION

THE PROGRAM ILLUSTRATED (see page 267) is a simple one and therefore results in uncomplicated documentation. The program run book documents a program which took the general ledgers (on punched cards) of several subsidiary companies and combined them into a single general ledger which was printed out.

The parts of the run manual (see Chapter 3) are as follows:

SECTION	EXAMPLE DOCUMENTATION
Problem Definition	Problem statement
System Description	System flowchart Punched card layout Printer layout
Program Description	Decision table Program flowchart Symbolic coding Assembly printout
Operating Instructions	Operating instructions
Listing of Controls	Not shown
Acceptance Record	Keypunch worksheet for test data

Comments on the example

The example illustrates the use of computers for performing year-end accounting tasks. It is an uncomplicated example so that the reader can follow all the necessary steps for solving a data processing problem. A company with six subsidiary companies, each of which had approximately 1,000 general ledger accounts, kept these records on punched cards. A combined trial balance had to be prepared at year-end for use by the auditors. This was a time-consuming clerical job. A savings in time and labor was achieved by taking the final general ledger balance-forward cards for each company, sorting them together by account number and printing a combined trial balance on the computer. The following comments explain the steps taken in preparing the program (see Appendix A) and include explanations of various features of the resulting documentation.

Analysis of Problem

The first step was the preparation of the problem definition. The problem statement for this program (see page 267) is a brief but complete description including input and output. In this case, the only input consisted of punched cards and the output was a printed report.

System Design

The next step was the design of the system, for which a systems flowchart was prepared (see page 268). (A system flowchart is a pictorial description of the flow of information through the system, but it does not indicate the computer program steps which are needed to perform the processing.) The flowchart conformed to the standard flowchart symbols and conventions explained in Appendix C. Layouts were also prepared to show the form of the input and the desired form of the output (see pages 269-270).

Planning the Program Logic

A decision table (see page 271) and a program flowchart were used to assist in the planning of the program logic.

Decision tables, which are used less frequently than flowcharts, show conditions and actions in a clear and uniform fashion and therefore help to ensure that program logic will provide full coverage for all possible combinations of conditions. In the upper half of the table, each rule (there are five in this program) involves a different combination of conditions. The lower half of the table describes the action or actions to be taken during the running of the program in response to each combination of conditions.

The program flowchart (see pages 272-275) indicates the processing steps, arithmetic calculations, decision points and input/output functions which must be prepared in order to instruct the computer in executing the required processing tasks. As a cross-check that the logic is complete, it is useful to take each rule on the decision table and trace it through the flowchart to see if the flowchart shows the appropriate actions.

The detailed program steps were coded with the aid of the decision table and the program flowchart. This particular program was coded in a symbolic assembly language called AUTO-CODER. The source language instructions were written on coding sheets with one line of coding for each computer instruction (see pages 276-280). The numbers along the top line of each coding sheet indicate the card columns in which the information is to be punched. One card was punched for each line on the sheets, so that the source language card deck contained 118 cards. The numbers and comments which appear in columns 46-72 of some lines are explanatory comments to aid documentation. In line 03 on page 276, the number 1/23 means that this particular line of coding performs the function described in page 1, block 23, of the program flowchart. Such cross-references facilitate the future checking of program logic and coding. Lines 10 and 11 on page 280 contain another type of explanation which can be used on coding forms to clarify coding logic. The instruction on line 10 reserves a 6-character location in which the program can store an account number. This instruction is explained by the comment which begins in column 46 of line 10. Since the comment is longer than the space available on line 10, it is continued on line 11. The asterisk in column 6 on line 11 indicates that the line contains an explanatory comment rather than a computer instruction. This line will have no effect on the program, but it will be printed out every time the source deck is listed.

When the source deck had been keypunched and verified, it was assembled to produce a machine-language object deck. The program listing which was obtained from the assembly process became part of the permanent program documentation. This listing (see pages 281-283) shows each symbolic source language instruction and the corresponding machine-language instruction produced by the assembler. It was very useful during the testing and checking of the new program.

Debugging   The next step consisted of testing the new program and "debugging" any errors thus detected. Test cases were prepared to test four of the five rules contained in the decision table. (The fifth rule covers the last card condition; there was no need to test for this condition since the test deck naturally had a last card.) A keypunch worksheet (see page 286) was prepared for the test cases, and their expected results were calculated in advance. These manual calculations were compared later with the output produced by the test case processing (see page 287). Since the program output agreed with the pre-computed output, the program could be considered ready for use in producing the combined trial balance.

Documentation   All of the forms and documents used in designing and implementing the combined trial balance program became part of the program documentation. In addition, it was necessary to prepare a set of instructions for the computer operator to follow when running the program (see page 284). Such instructions must always be fairly detailed so that the operator need not seek assistance. If changes are made in the program, change records should be filled out and attached to the documentation. There were no control features in this simple program, so a listing of controls was not prepared.

RUN MANUAL

COMBINED TRIAL BALANCE PROGRAM MO73

DATE 12/20/67 PAGE _____
REFERENCE # MO73
PREPARED BY D.L. Adams
REVIEWED BY _____

PROBLEM STATEMENT COMBINED TRIAL BALANCE PROGRAM

PROBLEM: TO PREPARE A COMBINED TRIAL BALANCE FROM THE SUBSIDIARY COMPANY GENERAL LEDGER BALANCE FORWARD CARDS PRODUCED WHEN THE FINAL DECEMBER 31 GENERAL LEDGER (PREAUDIT) WAS PREPARED FOR EACH COMPANY.

FORMULAS: NONE

DESCRIPTION OF INPUT: GENERAL LEDGER YEAR-END BALANCE FORWARD CARDS (LAYOUT ATTACHED)

DESCRIPTION OF OUTPUT: PRINTOUT OF COMBINED TRIAL BALANCE (LAYOUT ATTACHED).

FLOWCHART WORKSHEET **COMBINED TRIAL BALANCE PROGRAM**

CHECK ONE:
SYSTEM (✔)
MACRO ( )
MICRO ( )

DATE 12/20/67 PAGE _____
REFERENCE # M073
PREPARED BY D.L. Adams
REVIEWED BY _____

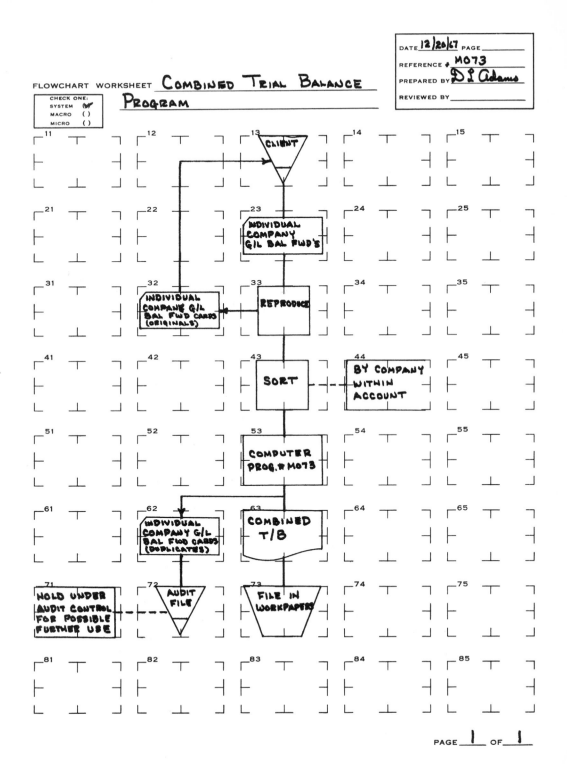

- CLIENT
- INDIVIDUAL COMPANY G/L BAL FWD'S
- INDIVIDUAL COMPANY G/L BAL FWD CARDS (ORIGINALS)
- REPRODUCE
- SORT — BY COMPANY WITHIN ACCOUNT
- COMPUTER PROG. # M073
- INDIVIDUAL COMPANY G/L BAL FWD CARDS (DUPLICATES)
- COMBINED T/B
- HOLD UNDER AUDIT CONTROL FOR POSSIBLE FURTHER USE
- AUDIT FILE
- FILE IN WORKPAPERS

268

PUNCHED CARD LAYOUT __COMBINED TRIAL BALANCE__
__PROGRAM__ _____

1. __GENERAL LEDGER YEAR-END BALANCE FORWARD CARDS__

ACCOUNT #	COMPANY CODE	DATE 123167	TYPE (BAL FWD)	AMOUNT $	$	NOTE: X PUNCH (11 ZONE) IN COLUMN 30 DENOTES A CREDIT AMOUNT

```
99999 9 999999 99999 99999 99999999 9  99999999999999999999999999999999999999999999999999
1 2 3 4 5 6 7 8 9 10 11 12 13 14 15 16 17 18 19 20 21 22 23 24 25 26 27 28 29 30 31 ... 80
```

2. _____

```
99999 99999 99999 99999 99999 99999 99999 99999 99999 99999 99999 99999 99999 99999 99999 999
1 2 3 4 5 6 7 8 ... 80
```

3. _____

```
99999 99999 99999 99999 99999 99999 99999 99999 99999 99999 99999 99999 99999 99999 99999 999
1 2 3 4 5 6 7 8 ... 80
```

4. _____

```
99999 99999 99999 99999 99999 99999 99999 99999 99999 99999 99999 99999 99999 99999 99999 999
1 2 3 4 5 6 7 8 ... 80
```

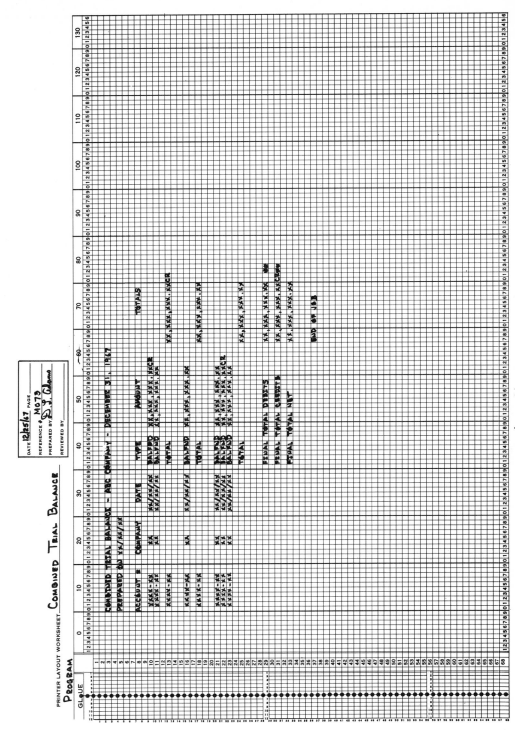

DATE	12/25/67	PAGE
REFERENCE #	M073	
PREPARED BY	D. J. Adams	
REVIEWED BY		

DECISION TABLE **COMBINED TRIAL BALANCE PROGRAM**

STUB	ENTRY																			
CONDITION:	RULE NUMBER																			
	1	2	3	4	5	6	7	8	9	10	11	12	13	14	15	16	17	18	19	20
LAST CARD PROCESSED	Y	N	N	N	N															
ACCOUNT # = ACCOUNT # IN PRIOR RECORD		Y	Y	N	N															
AMOUNT IS A CREDIT		Y	N	Y	N															
Y = YES																				
N = NO																				

ACTION:	RULE NUMBER																			
	1	2	3	4	5	6	7	8	9	10	11	12	13	14	15	16	17	18	19	20
WRITE ACCOUNT TOTAL	X			X	X															
CLEAR ACCOUNT TOTAL				X	X															
STORE ACCOUNT #		X	X	X	X															
WRITE A DETAIL LINE		X	X	X	X															
ADD AMOUNT TO TOTAL		X	X	X	X															
ADD AMOUNT TO DEBIT			X		X															
ADD AMOUNT TO CREDIT		X		X																
READ A CARD		X	X	X	X															
WRITE A DEBIT TOTAL	X																			
WRITE A CREDIT TOTAL	X																			
WRITE NET TOTAL	X																			
WRITE END OF JOB	X																			
HALT	X																			

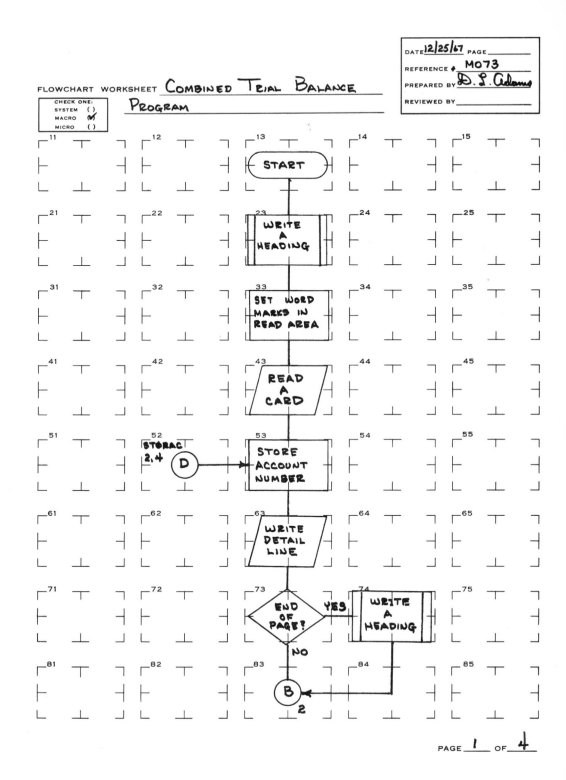

FLOWCHART WORKSHEET   COMBINED TRIAL BALANCE PROGRAM

DATE 12/25/67   PAGE _____
REFERENCE # M073
PREPARED BY D. L. Adams
REVIEWED BY _____

CHECK ONE:
SYSTEM ( )
MACRO (✓)
MICRO ( )

START

WRITE A HEADING

SET WORD MARKS IN READ AREA

READ A CARD

STORAG 2,4   D →   STORE ACCOUNT NUMBER

WRITE DETAIL LINE

END OF PAGE?   YES →   WRITE A HEADING

NO

B 2

272

FLOWCHART WORKSHEET COMBINED TRIAL BALANCE PROGRAM

CHECK ONE:
SYSTEM ( )
MACRO ✓
MICRO ( )

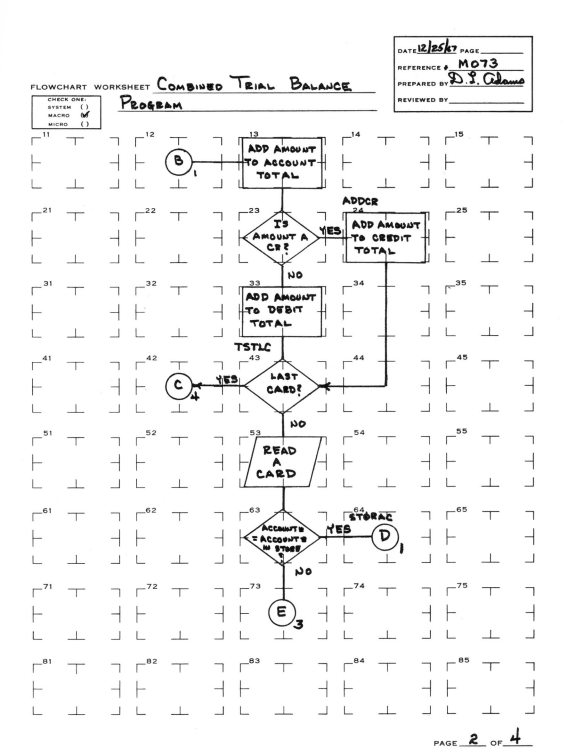

COMBINED TRIAL BALANCE
PROGRAM

CHECK ONE:
SYSTEM ( )
MACRO (✓)
MICRO ( )

DATE 12/25/67 PAGE _____
REFERENCE # M073
PREPARED BY D.S. Adams
REVIEWED BY _____

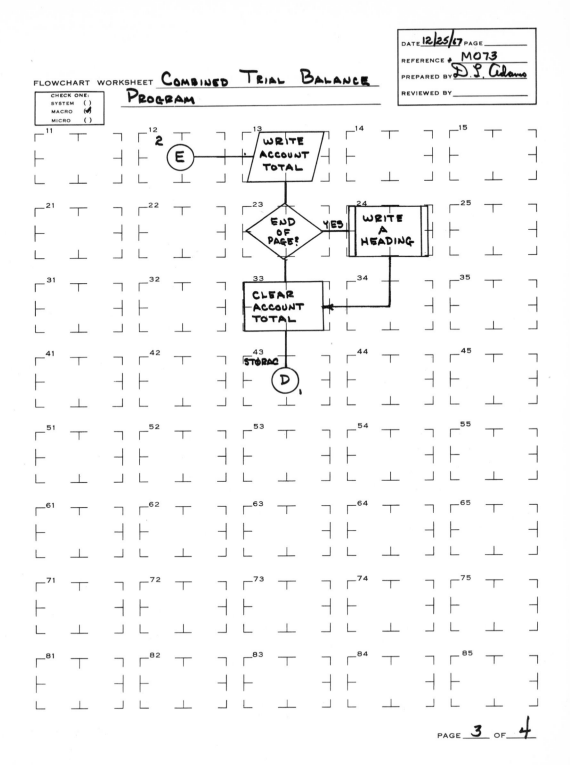

FLOWCHART WORKSHEET COMBINED TRIAL BALANCE
PROGRAM

DATE 12/25/67   PAGE _____
REFERENCE # M073
PREPARED BY D. J. Adams
REVIEWED BY _____

CHECK ONE:
SYSTEM ( )
MACRO (✓)
MICRO ( )

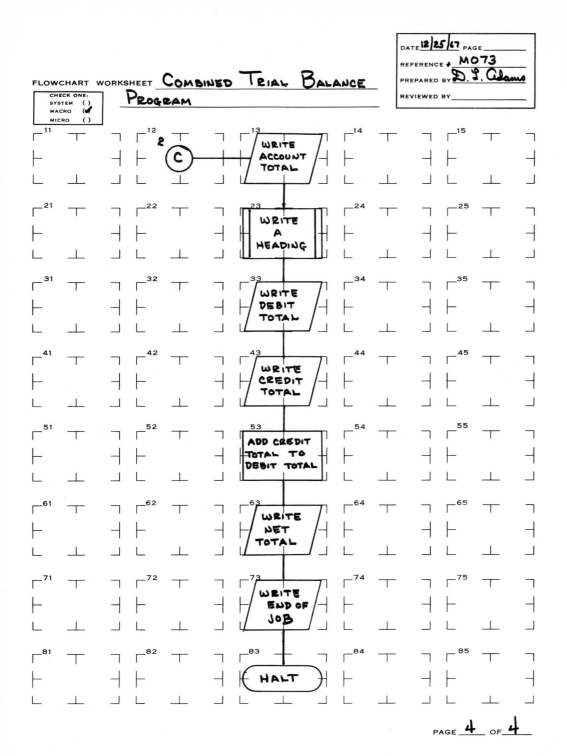

11	12	13 WRITE ACCOUNT TOTAL	14
	2 ©——		15
21	22	23 WRITE A HEADING	24
			25
31	32	33 WRITE DEBIT TOTAL	34
			35
41	42	43 WRITE CREDIT TOTAL	44
			45
51	52	53 ADD CREDIT TOTAL TO DEBIT TOTAL	54
			55
61	62	63 WRITE NET TOTAL	64
			65
71	72	73 WRITE END OF JOB	74
			75
81	82	83 HALT	84
			85

IBM

Program **COMBINED TRIAL BALANCE PROGRAM**

Programmed by *D. I. Adams*

Date 12/25/67

INTERNATIONAL BUSINESS MACHINES CORPORATION

AUTOCODER CODING SHEET

IBM 1401-1410-1440-1460

Identification M073 (76–80)

Line	Label	Operation	OPERAND
0 1		JOB	COMBINED TRIAL BALANCE PROGRAM
0 2		CTL	5511
0 3	START	B	WRTHDR
0 4		SW	1,7 1/23
0 5		SW	9,15 1/33
0 6		SW	21,21
0 7		R	
0 8	STORAG	MCW	6,ACTSTR 1/43
0 9		MCW	6,217 1/53
1 0		MCW	@-@,215 1/63 SETUP A/C NUMBER
1 1		MCW	4,214
1 2		MCS	8,225
1 3		MCW	14,238 SETUP COMPANY
1 4		MCW	@/@,236 SETUP DATE
1 5		MCS	12,235
1 6		MCW	@/@,233
1 7		MCS	10,232
1 8		MCW	@BALFWD@,246
1 9		MLCWA	EDIT1,263 SETUP TYPE
2 0		MCE	30,263 SETUP AMOUNT
2 1		W	
2 2		CS	
2 3		CS	
2 4		BCV	WRTHDR 1/73
2 5		A	30,ACTTOT 2/13

IBM

Program _____

Programmed by _D. I. Odom_

Date __12/25/67__

INTERNATIONAL BUSINESS MACHINES CORPORATION

AUTOCODER CODING SHEET

IBM 1401-1410-1440-1460

Line	Label	Operation	Operand
0 1		BM	ADDCR,30 2/23
0 2		A	30,DETOT 2/33
0 3		B	TSTLC
0 4	ADDCR	A	30,CETOT 2/24
0 5	TSTLC	BLC	ENDJOB 2/43
0 6		R	2/53
0 7		C	6,ACTSTR 2/63
0 8		BE	STORAC 2/64
0 9		MCW	6,217 3/13 SETUP A/C NUMBER
1 0		MCW	C-C,215
1 1		MCW	4,214
1 2		MCW	CTOTAL@,245 SETUP TYPE
1 3		MLCWA	EDIT1,281 SETUP TOTAL
1 4		MCE	ACTTOT,281
1 5		CC	J
1 6		W	
1 7		CS	
1 8		CS	
1 9		CC	K
2 0		BCV	NETADR 3/23
2 1		S	ACTTOT 3/33
2 2		B	STORAC 3/49
2 3	ENDJOB	MCW	6,217 4/13 SETUP A/C NUMBER
2 4		MCW	C-C,215
2 5		MCW	4,214

277

IBM

Program _____

Programmed by _D. L. Adams_

Date 12/25/67

Line	Label	Operation	OPERAND
0 1		MCW	@TOTAL@,245 SETUP TYPE
0 2		MLCWA	EDIT1,281 SETUP TOTAL
0 3		MCE	ACTTOT,281
0 4		W	
0 5		CS	
0 6		CS	
0 7		B	WRTHDR
0 8		MCW	@FINAL TOTAL DEBITS@,250 4/33
0 9		MLCWA	EDIT1,281
1 0		MCE	DRTOT,281
1 1		MCW	@##@,283
1 2		W	
1 3		CS	
1 4		CS	
1 5		CC	J
1 6		MCW	@FINAL TOTAL CREDITS@,259 4/43
1 7		MLCWA	EDIT1,281
1 8		MCE	CRTOT,281
1 9		MCW	@##@,283
2 0		W	
2 1		CS	
2 2		CS	
2 3		CC	J
2 4		A	CRTOT,DRTOT 4/53
2 5		MCW	@FINAL TOTAL NET@,255 4/63

278

IBM

Program _____
Programmed by **P.J. Adams**
Date **12/25/67**

INTERNATIONAL BUSINESS MACHINES CORPORATION
AUTOCODER CODING SHEET
IBM 1401-1410-1440-1460

Line	Label	Operation	OPERAND
0 1		MCW	AEDIT1,281
0 2		MCE	DETOT,281
0 3		W	
0 4		CS	
0 5		CS	
0 6		CC	L
0 7		MCW	@END OF JOB@,278
0 8		W	4/73
0 9	HALT	H	9999,9999
1 0		B	HALT 4/83
1 1	*		
1 2	*WRITE HEADING SUBROUTINE		
1 3	*		
1 4	WRTHDR	SBR	HDEX+3
1 5		CC	1
1 6		MCW	@COMBINED TRIAL BALANCE -@,233
1 7		MCW	@ABC COMPANY - DECEMBER 31, 1967@,265
1 8		W	
1 9		CS	
2 0		CS	
2 1		CC	J
2 2		MCW	@PREPARED ON / / @,229
2 3		W	
2 4		CS	
2 5		CS	

279

IBM

Program: D. S. Adams

Programmed by: D. S. Adams

Date: 12/25/67

INTERNATIONAL BUSINESS MACHINES CORPORATION

AUTOCODER CODING SHEET

IBM 1401-1410-1440-1460

Line	Label	Operation	Operand
0.1		CC	K
0.2		MCW	@ACCOUNT * COMPANY, DATE TYPE@,245
0.3		MCW	@AMOUNT@,258
0.4		MCW	@TOTAL@,278
0.5		CS	
0.6		CS	
0.7		CC	J
0.8			
0.9	HDREXT	B	000
1.0	ACTSTR	DCW	*6 STORAGE AREA FOR ACCOUNT
1.1	*		NUMBER OF PRIOR CARD
1.2	EDITI	DCW	@ , , O. CR@ EDIT MASK FOR 10 CHARACTER
1.3	*		DOLLAR AMOUNTS
1.4	ACTTOT	DCW	*10 ACCOUNT TOTAL ACCUMULATOR
1.5	DBTOT	DCW	*10 DEBIT TOTAL ACCUMULATOR
1.6	CRTOT	DCW	*10 CREDIT TOTAL ACCUMULATOR
1.7		NOP	
1.8		END	START
1.9			
2.0			
2.1			
2.2			
2.3			
2.4			
2.5			

SEQ	PG	LIN	LABEL	OP	OPERANDS	CT	ADDR	INSTRUCTION	FLAG
001	01	01		JOB	COMBINED TRIAL BALANCE PROGRAM				
002	01	02		CTL	5511				
003	01	03	START	B	WRTHDR	4	0333	B 751	
004	01	04		SW	1,7	7	0337	, 001 007	
005	01	05		SW	9,15	7	0344	, 009 015	
006	01	06		SW	21,21	7	0351	, 021 021	
007	01	07		R		1	0358	1	
008	01	08	STORAC	MCW	6,ACTSTR	7	0359	M 006 820	
009	01	09		MCW	6,217	7	0366	M 006 217	
010	01	10		MCW	@-@,215	7	0373	M 871 217	
011	01	11		MCW	4,214	7	0380	, 004 217	
012	01	12		MCS	8,225	7	0387	Z 008 225	
013	01	13		MCW	14,238	7	0394	M 014 238	
014	01	14		MCW	@/@,236	7	0401	M 872 236	
015	01	15		MCS	12,235	7	0408	Z 012 235	
016	01	16		MCW	@/@,233	7	0415	M 872 233	
017	01	17		MCS	10,232	7	0422	Z 010 232	
018	01	18		MCW	@BALFWD@,246	7	0429	M 873 246	
019	01	19		MLCWA	EDIT1,263	7	0436	L 826 263	
020	01	20		MCE	30,263	7	0443	E 030 263	
021	01	21		W		1	0450	2	
022	01	22		CS		1	0451	/	
023	01	23		CS		1	0452	/	
024	01	24		BCV	WRTHDR	5	0453	B 751 @	
025	01	25		A	30,ACTTOT	7	0458	A 030 841	
026	02	01		BM	ADDCR,30	8	0465	V 484 030 K	
027	02	02		A	30,DRTOT	7	0473	A 030 851	
028	02	03		B	TSTLC	4	0480	B 491	
029	02	04	ADDCR	A	30,CRTOT	7	0484	A 030 861	
030	02	05	TSTLC	BLC	ENDJOB	5	0491	B 574 A	
031	02	06		R		1	0496	1	
032	02	07		C	6,ACTSTR	7	0497	C 006 820	
033	02	08		BE	STORAC	5	0504	B 359 S	
034	02	09		MCW	6,217	7	0509	M 006 217	
035	02	10		MCW	@-@,215	7	0516	M 871 215	
036	02	11		MCW	4,214	7	0523	M 004 214	
037	02	12		MCW	@TOTAL@,245	7	0530	M 879 245	
038	02	13		MLCWA	EDIT1,281	7	0537	L 826 281	
039	02	14		MCE	ACTTOT,281	7	0544	E 841 281	
040	02	15		CC	J	2	0551	F J	
041	02	16		W		1	0553	2	
042	02	17		CS		1	0554	/	
043	02	18		CS		1	0555	/	
044	02	19		CC	K	2	0556	F K	
045	02	20		BCV	WRTHDR	5	0558	B 751 @	
046	02	21		S	ACTTOT	7	0563	S 841 841	
047	02	22		B	STORAC	4	0570	B 359	
048	02	23	ENDJOB	MCW	6,217	7	0574	M 006 217	
049	02	24		MCW	@-@,215	7	0581	M 871 215	
050	02	25		MCW	4,214	7	0588	M 004 214	
051	03	01		MCW	@TOTAL@,245	7	0595	M 879 245	
052	03	02		MLCWA	EDIT1,281	7	0602	L 826 281	
053	03	03		MCE	ACTTOT,281	7	0609	E 841 281	

SEQ	PG	LIN	LABEL	OP	OPERANDS	CT	ADDR	INSTRUCTION	FLAG
054	03	04		W		1	0616	2	
055	03	05		CS		1	0617	/	
056	03	06		CS		1	0618	/	
057	03	07		B	WRTHDR	4	0619	B 751	
058	03	08		MCW	@FINAL TOTAL DEBITS@,258	7	0623	M 884 258	
059	03	09		MLCWA	EDIT1,281	7	0630	L 826 281	
060	03	10		MCE	DRTOT,281	7	0637	E 851 281	
061	03	11		MCW	@$$@,283	7	0644	M 902 283	
062	03	12		W		1	0651	2	
063	03	13		CS		1	0652	/	
064	03	14		CS		1	0653	/	
065	03	15		CC	J	2	0654	F J	
066	03	16		MCW	@FINAL TOTAL CREDITS@,259	7	0656	, 904 259	
067	03	17		MLCWA	EDIT1,281	7	0673	L 826 281	
068	03	18		MCE	CRTOT,281	7	0680	E 861 281	
069	03	19		MCW	@**@,283	7	0687	M 902 283	
070	03	20		W		1	0694	2	
071	03	21		CS		1	0695	/	
072	03	22		CS		1	0696	/	
073	03	23		CC	J	2	0697	F J	
074	03	24		A	CRTOT,DRTOT	7	0699	A 861 851	
075	03	25		MCW	@FINAL TOTAL NET@,255	7	0706	M 923 255	
076	04	01		MLCWA	EDIT1,281	7	0713	L 826 281	
077	04	02		MCE	DRTOT,281	7	0720	E 851 281	
078	04	03		W		1	0727	2	
079	04	04		CS		1	0728	/	
080	04	05		CS		1	0729	/	
081	04	06		CC	L	2	0730	F L	
082	04	07		MCW	@END OF JOB@,276	7	0732	M 938 276	
083	04	08		W		1	0739	2	
084	04	09	HALT	H	9999,9999	7	0740	. W9W W9W	
085	04	10		B	HALT	4	0747	B 740	
086	04	11	*						
087	04	12	*WRITE HEADING SUBROUTINE						
088	04	13	*						
089	04	14	WRTHDR	SBR	HDREXT+3	4	0751	H 819	
090	04	15		CC	1	2	0755	F 1	
091	04	16		MCW	@COMBINED TRIAL BALANCE -@,233	7	0757	M 948 233	
092	04	17		MCW	@ABC COMPANY - DECEMBER 31, 19	7	0764	M 972 265	
092	04	17			6/@,265				
093	04	18		W		1	0771	2	
094	04	19		CS		1	0772	/	
095	04	20		CS		1	0773	/	
096	04	21		CC	J	2	0774	F J	
097	04	22		MCW	@PREPARED ON / / @,229	7	0776	M ←03 229	
098	04	23		W		1	0783	2	
099	04	24		CS		1	0784	/	
100	04	25		CS		1	0785	/	
101	05	01		CC	K	2	0786	F K	
102	05	02		MCW	@ACCOUNT # COMPANY DATE	7	0788	M ←23 245	
102	05	02			TYPE@,245				
103	05	03		MCW	@AMOUNT@,258	7	0795	M ←59 258	
104	05	04		MCW	@TOTAL@,278	7	0802	M 879 278	
105	05	05		W		1	0809	2	
106	05	06		CS		1	0810	/	

```
SEQ PG LIN LABEL   OP    OPERANDS                           CT  ADDR INSTRUCTION FLAG

107 05 07          CS                                        1  0811 /
108 05 08          CC    J                                   2  0812 F J
109 05 09 HDREXT   B     000                                 4  0816 B 000
110 05 10 ACTSTR   DCW   #6                                  6  0820
111 05 11 *
112 05 12 EDIT1    DCW   @   ,    ,   0.    CR@             15  0826
113 05 13 *
114 05 14 ACTTOT   DCW   #10                               10  0841
115 05 15 DRTOT    DCW   #10                               10  0851
116 05 16 CRTOT    DCW   #10                               10  0861
117                      @-@                                 1  0871
118                      @/@                                 1  0872
119                      @BALFWD@                            6  0873
120                      @TOTAL@                             5  0879
121                      @FINAL TOTAL DEBITS@               18  0884
122                      @**@                                2  0902
123                      @FINAL TOTAL CREDITS@              19  0904
124                      @FINAL TOTAL NET@                  15  0923
125                      @END OF JOB@                       10  0938
126                      @COMBINED TRIAL BALANCE -@         24  0948
127                      @ABC COMPANY - DECEMBER 31, 19     31  0972
127                      67@
128                      @PREPARED ON    /  /  @            20  1003
129                      @ACCOUNT #    COMPANY     DATE     36  1023
130                      @AC
130                      @AMOUNT@                            6  1059
131 05 17          NOP                                       1  1060 N
132 05 18          END   START                                  / 333 080
```

283

Operating Instructions
Combined Trial Balance Program MO73
December 27, 1967

Program Description

The program prepares a combined trial balance from punched card trial balance cards of the subsidiary companies. The balance cards have been reproduced from the company files and sorted into account number order.

Card Layout

The card layout for the ledger balance-forward cards is:

1. General ledger year-end balance-forward cards

Account no.	Date	Type	Amount	Note: X30 means credit
	12 31/66	Bal. Fwd.		

Company code

Setup

The input for the run consists of the program cards followed by the ledger balance-forward cards which have been sorted off-line into account-number order. There is no sentinel card for the data.

The printer is used for output. Two-part paper—100 to 132

column—is required, either blank or lined. There is no special form.

UNIT	USED FOR
Reader	Input of program and data
Printer	Output
Punch	Not used
Sense Switches	Not used

The program deck will be furnished by a representative of the auditing firm of . . . . The data cards are duplicate balance-forward cards from the subsidiary company general-ledger runs.

Error Messages and Halts

There are no error messages as the program contains no provision for the detection of an error in the sorting of the input deck. Such an error will be detected only by an examination of the output where a mis-sort will cause an account number to appear more than once.

The program comes to an orderly halt after sensing the last card. A message "END of JOB" is printed as the last line of the report. The Halt command has 999 as the A and B addresses.

Restart

The starting location for the program is location 333.

Output

Both copies of the output plus the program and data decks will be picked up by a representative of the auditing firm of . . . .

COMBINED TRIAL BALANCE PROGRAM

DATE 1/4/68 PAGE _____
REFERENCE # M073
PREPARED BY D. L. Adams
REVIEWED BY _____

COLUMNS SKIPPED: 15 - 20, 31 - 80

FIELD NAME	ACCOUNT#	COMPANY CODE	DATE	AMOUNT		
CARD COLUMNS	1 - 6	7 - 8	9 - 14	21 - 30		
CHARACTER COUNT	6	2	6	10		
ALPHA OR NUMERIC	N	N	N	N		
TEST BLOCK OR RULE #						
	111111	01	123167	0000002000		
	111111	02	"	0000098000		
	222222	01	"	0008000000		
	222222	03	"	0007000000		
	333333	01	"	0006000000		
	333333	02	"	0006000001		
	444444	01	"	0000099999		
	444444	02	"	0000000001		

COMBINED TRIAL BALANCE - ABC COMPANY - DECEMBER 31, 1967

PREPARED ON 01/10/68

ACCOUNT #	COMPANY	DATE	TYPE	AMOUNT	TOTALS
1111-11	01	12/31/67	BALFWD	20.00	
1111-11	02	12/31/67	BALFWD	980.00	
			TOTAL		1,000.00
2222-22	01	12/31/67	BALFWD	80,000.00	
2222-22	03	12/31/67	BALFWD	70,000.00CR	
			TOTAL		10,000.00
3333-33	01	12/31/67	BALFWD	60,000.00	
3333-33	02	12/31/67	BALFWD	60,000.01CR	
			TOTAL		.01CR
4444-44	01	12/31/67	BALFWD	999.99CR	
4444-44	02	12/31/67	BALFWD	.01CR	
			TOTAL		1,000.00CR

FINAL TOTAL DEBITS   141,000.00 **

FINAL TOTAL CREDITS   151,000.01CR**

FINAL TOTAL NET   9,999.99

END OF JOB

287

STANDARD FLOWCHART SYMBOLS FOR INFORMATION PROCESSING

FLOWCHARTS ARE symbolic diagrams of operation sequence and data flow in information processing. Though the same set of symbols is used for both, it is convenient to separate flowcharts into two types:

1. A system flowchart describes the data flow and the operations for a data processing system.

2. A program flowchart describes the sequence of operations and decisions for a particular program. It is sometimes referred to as a block or logic diagram.

Flowcharting is also applicable for manual and electromechanical processing, but the greater complexity of computer systems makes the use of flowcharting for computer processing especially widespread. Flowcharts must be written so as to communicate effectively to others besides the writer. This need is best met if there is agreement on a standard set of flowchart symbols.

In the United States, groups desiring to develop industry-wide standards usually work through the American National Standards Institute (formerly the United States of America Standards Institute). This is a voluntary association with representation from manufacturers, consumers and the general public. A sectional

289

committee of the ANSI, Computers and Information Processing (X3), is responsible for developing data processing standards; a subcommittee for problem definition and analysis (X3.6) has developed a standard set of flowchart symbols. The first ANSI flowchart standards were approved in 1965 but were not published because of conflicts with a proposed international standard. A revised set of standard flowchart symbols were approved and published in June of 1966 (see Figure C-1, page 291). Though not published, the early efforts received wide acceptance in the period from 1964-1966. To prevent confusion a description of the changes made in 1966 is included in this appendix.

A complete set of definitions and specifications for the ANSI flowchart symbols (standard X3.5-1966) may be purchased from the American National Standards Institute, 1430 Broadway, New York, New York 10018.

A note on individual differences

Flowcharts are sufficiently creative so that no two people draw them exactly alike. Clarity of presentation can be achieved more easily if the ANSI standards are used.

Since the standards are new, the CPA should expect documentation prior to mid-1967 to vary. Some installations may even ignore ANSI flowchart standards. Though the auditor must therefore be willing to accept variances, he will find future system reviews easier if standards are generally accepted.

Description of use

Flowcharts normally read from left to right and from top to bottom. Arrowheads are often included on the flowlines for clarity's sake; they are required if the flow is in other than the normal direction.

When a symbol is to be identified for reference purposes, a notation is placed above the symbol to the right or left of the vertical bisector or inside the symbol separated by a horizontal

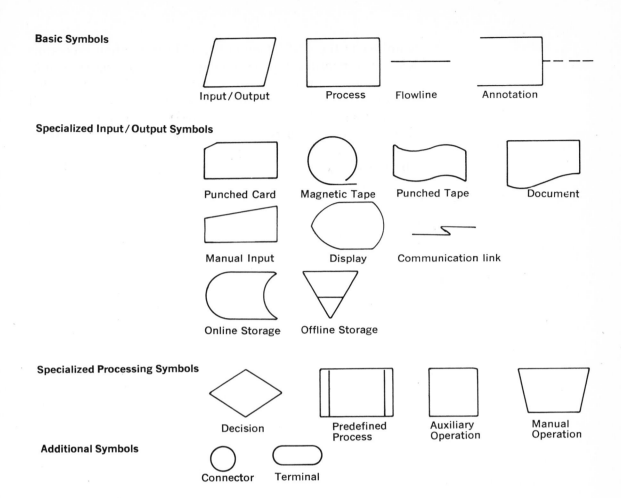

Basic Symbols

Input/Output   Process   Flowline   Annotation

Specialized Input/Output Symbols

Punched Card   Magnetic Tape   Punched Tape   Document

Manual Input   Display   Communication link

Online Storage   Offline Storage

Specialized Processing Symbols

Decision   Predefined Process   Auxiliary Operation   Manual Operation

Additional Symbols

Connector   Terminal

FIGURE C-1.   Summary of flowchart symbols

stripe (see Figure C-2, page 292). Athough ANSI flowchart standards specify a standard usage for symbol identification, the symbol identifier and striping code can be written so as to reflect other information important for the reader (the department involved, for example).

Each of the standard symbols is described in Figure C-3 (page 292) together with an example of its use. Where both a general symbol and a specialized symbol are available, either may be used. If there is no specialized symbol, the general symbol must be used. A short description of the document, file or process

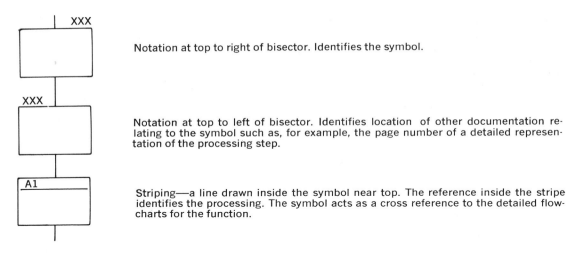

FIGURE C-2.   Identification notation

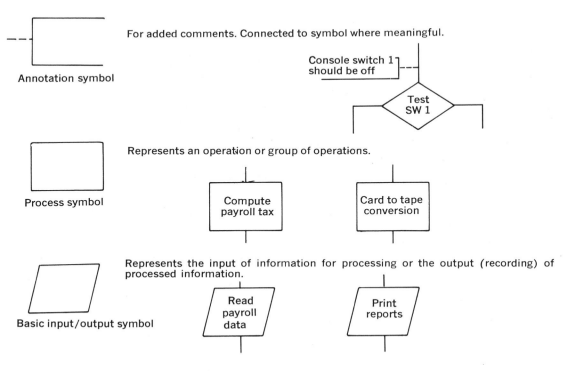

FIGURE C-3.   Standard symbols

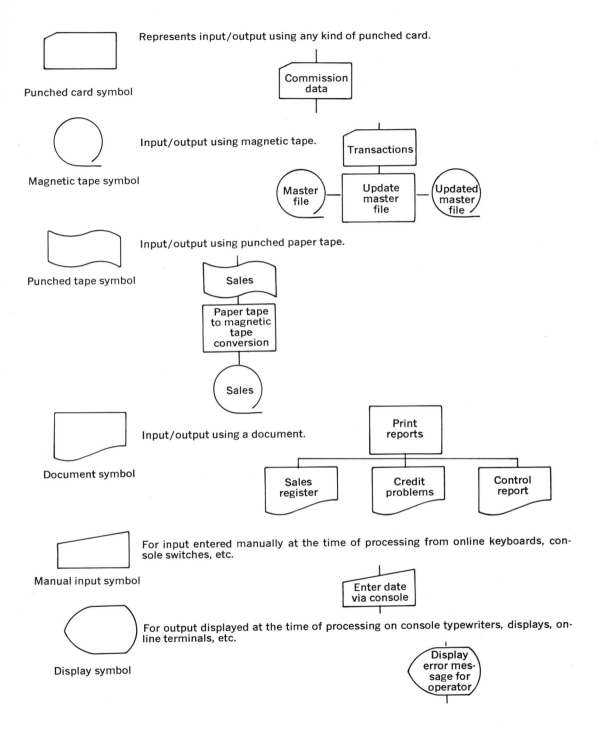

Represents input/output using any kind of punched card.

Punched card symbol

Commission
data

Input/output using magnetic tape.

Magnetic tape symbol

Transactions

Master
file — Update
master
file — Updated
master
file

Input/output using punched paper tape.

Punched tape symbol

Sales

Paper tape
to magnetic
tape
conversion

Sales

Input/output using a document.

Document symbol

Print
reports

Sales
register   Credit
problems   Control
report

For input entered manually at the time of processing from online keyboards, console switches, etc.

Manual input symbol

Enter date
via console

For output displayed at the time of processing on console typewriters, displays, online terminals, etc.

Display symbol

Display
error mes-
sage for
operator

FIGURE C-3 (cont.). Standard symbols

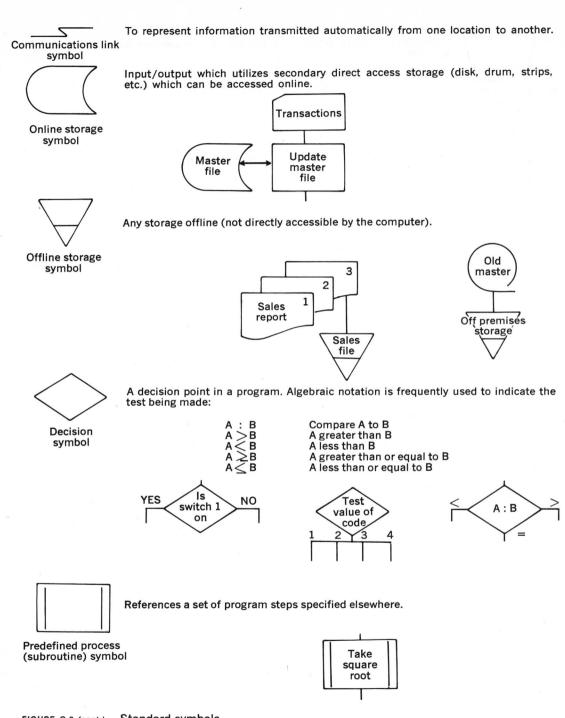

Communications link symbol
To represent information transmitted automatically from one location to another.

Online storage symbol
Input/output which utilizes secondary direct access storage (disk, drum, strips, etc.) which can be accessed online.

Transactions

Master file ↔ Update master file

Offline storage symbol
Any storage offline (not directly accessible by the computer).

Sales report

3
2
1

Sales file

Old master

Off premises storage

Decision symbol
A decision point in a program. Algebraic notation is frequently used to indicate the test being made:

A : B — Compare A to B
A > B — A greater than B
A < B — A less than B
A ≥ B — A greater than or equal to B
A ≤ B — A less than or equal to B

YES — Is switch 1 on — NO

Test value of code
1   2   3   4

< A : B >
=

Predefined process (subroutine) symbol
References a set of program steps specified elsewhere.

Take square root

FIGURE C-3 (cont.). Standard symbols

294

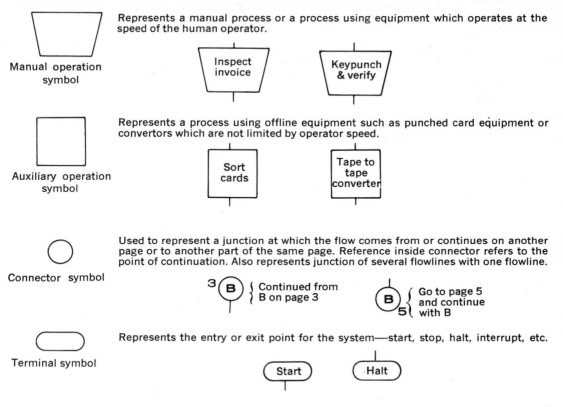

Manual operation symbol

Represents a manual process or a process using equipment which operates at the speed of the human operator.

Inspect invoice

Keypunch & verify

Auxiliary operation symbol

Represents a process using offline equipment such as punched card equipment or convertors which are not limited by operator speed.

Sort cards

Tape to tape converter

Connector symbol

Used to represent a junction at which the flow comes from or continues on another page or to another part of the same page. Reference inside connector refers to the point of continuation. Also represents junction of several flowlines with one flowline.

3 **B** { Continued from B on page 3

B { Go to page 5 5 { and continue with B

Terminal symbol

Represents the entry or exit point for the system—start, stop, halt, interrupt, etc.

Start

·Halt

FIGURE C-3 (cont.). Standard symbols

involved is usually written inside the symbol. If additional description or explanation is required, the annotation symbol should be used.

Symbols prior to 1966

Before 1964, each manufacturer prepared his own symbols. One manufacturer's decision symbol was an oval, another's was a diamond. The work of the American Standards group was reflected by the 1964 adoption by most manufacturers of revised templates. Since there were some confusing differences between the 1964 symbols and the final ANSI standards of 1966, the differences between a typical 1964-66 template and a standard 1966 template are shown in Figure C-4 (page 296).

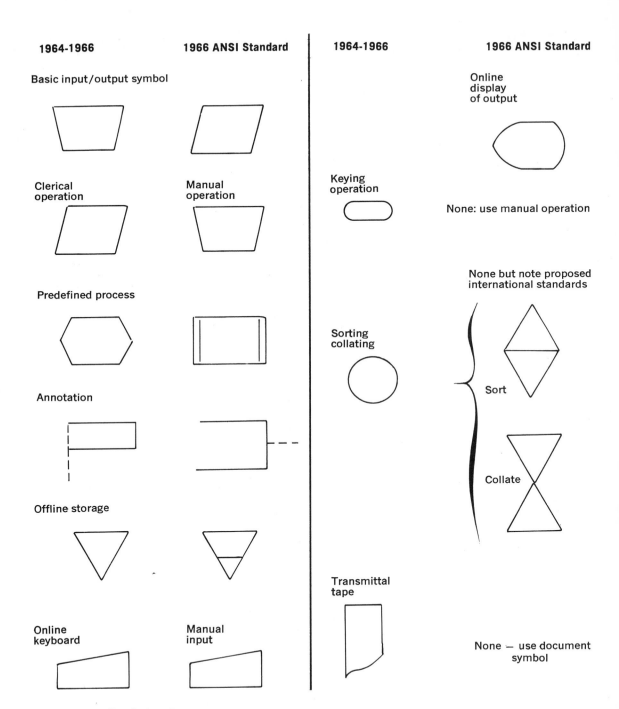

1964-1966	1966 ANSI Standard
Basic input/output symbol	
Clerical operation	**Manual operation**
Predefined process	
Annotation	
Offline storage	
Online keyboard	**Manual input**

1964-1966	1966 ANSI Standard
	Online display of output
Keying operation	None: use manual operation
Sorting collating	None but note proposed international standards Sort Collate
Transmittal tape	None — use document symbol

FIGURE C-4. Symbols prior to 1966

296

International symbols

The reader may have noted in Figure C-3 (page 292) the omission of some commonly used symbols. These are the international standard flowchart symbols (see Figure C-5 below), which have now been adopted and which form a supplement to the ANSI standard symbols.

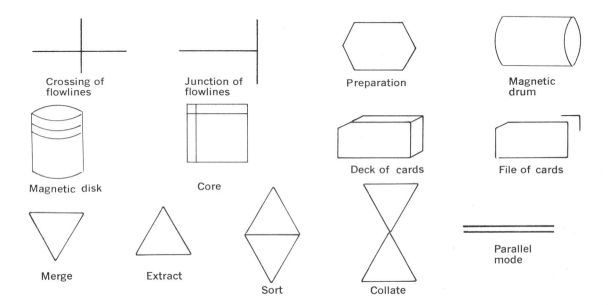

FIGURE C-5. International symbols

GLOSSARY

THIS GLOSSARY CONTAINS selected terms used in the book, plus other terms important to the auditor's understanding of EDP.

There are two published glossaries which have substantial official status or industry support. These are:

1. *IFIP/ICC Vocabulary of Information Processing,* IFIP/-ICC (International Federation for Information Processing and International Computation Centre), North-Holland Publishing Company, Amsterdam, 1966.

2. *American Standard Vocabulary for Information Processing,* American National Standards Institute, ANSI Standard X3.12-1966, New York, 1966.

Neither of these was entirely suitable for the purpose of this book. Almost 90 per cent of the entries in this glossary are taken from or adapted from the glossary contained in *AUERBACH Computer Notebook for Accountants,*[1] which is one of the most readable glossaries available. The IFIP/ICC and ANSI vocabularies were used in the writing of the definitions for this glossary.

The glossary is arranged in natural order (for example, "abso-

---

[1] *AUERBACH Computer Notebook for Accountants* is a looseleaf reference service, which is updated monthly and contains summaries of computer systems, performance comparison charts, and special reports for accountants. It is published by AUERBACH Info, Inc., Philadelphia, and is available from the American Institute of Certified Public Accountants.

lute coding" rather than "coding, absolute"). In the case of terms with two or more meanings, the meanings are numbered sequentially, with the most common or the most general one listed first. The formal definitions are often followed by examples and comments which clarify the meaning, usage and significance of each term defined in the glossary.

Several different types of cross-references are used. Their meanings are as follows:

1. *same as* indicates that the referenced term has the same meaning as the term containing the reference and that the referenced term is the preferred one.

2. *synonymous with* indicates that the referenced term has the same meaning as the term containing the reference and that the term containing the reference is the preferred one.

3. *contrast with* indicates that the referenced term is a related term that has a meaning significantly different from that of the term containing the reference.

4. *see also* indicates that the referenced term is a related term whose definition provides additional background or clarification.

5. *see* indicates that the referenced term is an alternative or qualified form of the term containing the reference.

absolute coding. Coding that uses machine instructions and absolute addresses; can therefore be executed directly by a computer without prior translation to a different form; contrast with **symbolic coding**.

access mode. A technique used to obtain a specific record from, or to place a specific record into, a specific file; see **random access** and **serial access**.

acronym. A word formed from the initial letter or letters of each word in a name or phrase; for example, ALGOL from ALGOrithmic Language, COBOL from COmmon Business Oriented Language.

activity. The degree of frequency with which individual records in a file are used, modified, or referred to; for example, an "activity factor" of 0.10 (or 10 per cent) denotes that an average of one out of every ten master-file records is referenced or affected by a transaction during a run.

ADP (Automatic Data Processing). Data processing performed largely by automatic means; that is, by a system of electronic or electrical machines that require little human assistance or intervention.

alphameric. Same as **alphanumeric**.

alphanumeric. Pertaining to a character set that includes both alphabetic characters (letters) and numeric characters (digits). Note: Most alphanumeric character sets also contain special characters (dollar signs, commas, etc.).

ASCII (American Standard Code for Information Interchange. A 7-bit (or 8-bit compatible) ANSI standard code adopted to facilitate the interchange of data among various types of data processing and data communications equipment.

assemble. To prepare a machine-language program from a program written in symbolic coding by substituting absolute operation codes for symbolic operation codes and absolute or relocatable addresses for symbolic addresses; for example, the symbolic instruction ADD TAX might be assembled into the machine instruction 24 1365, where 24 is the operation code for addition and 1365 is the address of the storage location labeled TAX; contrast with **compile** and **generate**.

assembler. A computer program that assembles programs written in symbolic coding to produce machine-language programs. Note: Assemblers are an important part of the basic software for most computers and can greatly reduce the human effort required to prepare programs.

audit trail. A means for identifying the actions taken in processing input data or in preparing an output such that data on a source document can be traced forward to an output (a report, for example) and an output can be traced back to the source items from which it is derived. Note: The audit trail can also be termed an inquiry trail or a management trail because it is used as a reference trail for internal operations and management as well as for audit tests.

auxiliary storage. Storage that supplements a computer's primary internal storage. Note: In general, auxiliary storage has a much larger capacity but a longer access time than primary storage. Synonymous with **mass storage**; same as **secondary storage**.

back-up. Pertaining to equipment or procedures that are available for use in the event of failure or overloading of normally used equipment or procedures. Note: The provision of adequate back-up facilities is an important factor in the design of all data processing systems—especially real-time systems, where a system failure may bring the total operations of a business to a virtual standstill.

batch processing. A technique in which items to be processed are collected into groups (batched) to permit convenient and efficient processing. Note: The records of all transactions affecting a particular master file are accumulated over a period of time (one day, for example), then arranged in sequence and processed against the master file; most business applications are of the batch processing type.

batch total. A sum of a set of items which is used to check the accuracy of operations on a particular batch of records.

batch control ticket. A document accompanying a batch of transaction documents that records such information as batch number, control totals and routing.

BCD (Binary Coded Decimal). Pertaining to a method of representing each of the decimal digits 0 through 9 by a distinct group of binary digits; for example, in the "8-4-2-1" BCD notation, which is used in numerous digital computers, the decimal number 39 is represented as 0011 1001 (whereas in pure binary notation it is represented as 100111).

binary. Pertaining to the number system with a radix of two, or to a characteristic or property involving a choice or condition in which there are two possibilities; for example, the binary numeral 1101 means

$$(1 \times 2^3) + (1 \times 2^2) + (0 \times 2^1) + (1 \times 2^0),$$

which is equivalent to decimal 13. Note: The binary number system is widely used in digital computers since most computer components (such as vacuum tubes, transistors, flip-flops and magnetic cores) are essentially binary in that they have two stable states.

bit. A binary digit; a digit (0 or 1) in the representation of a number in binary notation.

block. A group of words, characters, or digits that are held in one section of an input/output medium and handled as a unit; for example, the data recorded on a punched card, or the data recorded between two interblock gaps on a magnetic tape.

block diagram. See **program flowchart**.

blocking. Combining two or more records into one block, usually to increase the efficiency of computer input/output operations; for example, the effective data transfer rates of most magnetic tape units can be greatly increased if the need for frequent tape stops and starts is reduced by combining multiple short records into long blocks.

boundary protection. Same as **storage protection**.

branch. (1) An instruction that may cause a departure from the normal sequence of executing instructions, depending on the results of an operation, the contents of a register, or the setting of an indicator; (2) A set of instructions executed between two successive conditional transfer instructions.

breakpoint. A specified point in a program at which the program may be interrupted by manual intervention or by a monitor routine. Note: Breakpoints are usually used as aids in testing and debugging programs; they facilitate the halting of a computer or the triggering of a printout at a particular point so that specific conditions can be examined.

buffer. A storage device used to compensate for differences in the rates of flow of data or in the times of occurrence of events when transmitting data from one device to another; for example, a buffer holding the characters to print one line is associated with most line printers to compensate for the difference between the high speed at which the computer transmits data to the printer and the relatively low speed of the printing operation itself.

bug. A mistake in the design of a program or computer system, or an equipment fault.

byte. A group of adjacent bits operated on as a unit and usually shorter than a word. Note: In a number of important and current computer systems, this term stands specifically for a group of eight adjacent bits that can represent one alphanumeric character or two decimal digits.

card field. A group of columns (or parts of columns) whose punchings represent one item on a punched card; for example, a three-column field might hold an item representing an order quantity whose value ranges from 000 to 999.

central processor. The unit of a computer system that includes the circuits controlling the interpretation and execution of instructions; synonymous with **CPU (central processing unit)** and **main frame**.

check bit. A binary check digit. Note: A parity check usually involves the appending of a check bit of appropriate value to an array of bits.

check digit. A digit associated with a word or part of a word for the purpose of checking for the absence of certain classes of errors; see **residue check**.

check problem. A problem whose correct results are known, used to determine whether a computer and/or a program are operating correctly.

COBOL (COmmon Business Oriented Language). A procedure-oriented language developed to facilitate preparation and interchange of programs which perform business data processing functions. Note: Designed in 1959 by a committee representing the US Government and several computer manufacturers, COBOL has evolved through several versions (for example, COBOL-60, COBOL-61, COBOL-61 Extended, COBOL-65); every COBOL source program has four divisions whose names and functions are as follows: (1) Identification Division, which identifies the source program and the output of a compilation, (2) Environment Division, which specifies those aspects of a data processing problem that are dependent upon the physical characteristics of a particular computer, (3) Data Division, which describes the data that the object program is to accept as input, manipulate, create, or produce as output and (4) Procedure Division, which specifies the procedures to be performed by the object program by means of English-like statements such as "SUBTRACT

TAX FROM GROSS-PAY GIVING NET-PAY" or "PER-
FORM PROC-A THRU PROC-B UNTIL X IS GREATER
THAN Y."

coding. (1) An ordered list or lists of the successive instructions which direct a computer to perform a particular process;
(2) the act of preparing a coding.

compile. To prepare a machine-language program (or a program expressed in symbolic coding) from a program written
in another programming language (usually a procedure-oriented language such as COBOL or FORTRAN); the compilation process usually involves examining and making use
of the overall structure of the program, and/or generating
more than one object program instruction for each source
program statement; contrast with **assemble** and **generate**.

compiler. A computer program that compiles. Note: Compilers are an important part of the basic software for most
computers, permitting the use of procedure-oriented languages
that can greatly reduce the human effort required to prepare
computer programs; however, the computer time required to
perform the compilation process may be excessive and the
object programs produced by the compiler usually require
more execution time and more storage space than programs
written in machine-language or symbolic coding.

console. A computer part used for communication between operators or maintenance engineers and the computer, usually
by means of displays and manual controls.

console operator. A computer operator.

console run book. A book containing computer operator instructions for a run.

constant-ratio code. A code in which all of the valid characters have the same number of 1 bits, thereby facilitating the
performance of a validity check; for example, in the "4-of-8"
code, frequently used in data communications, each of the
valid characters is represented by a combination of four 1 bits
and four 0 bits.

control clerk. A person having responsibility for performing
duties associated with the control over data processing operations. Note: Such duties usually include the checking of con-

trol totals, the checking of run-to-run controls, the checking of output before distribution, etc.

control program. A routine, usually contained within an operating system, that aids in controlling the operations and managing the resources of a computer system.

control punch. A punch in a card column that indicates the action to be taken in processing the card; an 11($-$) or 12($+$) punch is often used for this purpose.

converter. A device that converts data from one form to another in order to make it available or acceptable to another device; for example, a "card-to-tape" converter that transcribes data from punched cards to magnetic tape so that the data can be read into a computer system at high speed.

CPU (Central Processing Unit). Same as **central processor.**

CRT. Cathode ray tube display device.

crossfooting test. A programmed check on computer processing in which individual items used in arriving at result items are totaled and the total is compared to an independently derived result total; for example, a total net pay figure reached by subtracting a deduction item total from a gross pay total can be compared with a total net pay figure developed by other program steps.

data base. Data items that must be stored in order to meet the information processing and retrieval needs of an organization. Note: The term implies an integrated file used by many processing applications as opposed to an individual data file for a particular application.

debug. To trace and eliminate mistakes in a program or faults in equipment. Note: The process is often assisted by a diagnostic routine.

decision table. A table listing all the contingencies to be considered in the description of a problem, together with the corresponding actions to be taken. Note: A decision table permits complex decision-making criteria to be expressed in a concise and logical format; it is sometimes used in place of flowcharts for problem definition and documentation; compilers have been written to convert decision tables into programs than can be executed by computers.

deck. A collection of punched cards, usually bearing data for a particular run.

desk checking. A manual checking process in which representative data items used for detecting errors in program logic are traced through the program before the latter is checked on the computer.

detail file. A file containing relatively transient information; for example, records of individual transactions that occurred during a particular period of time; synonymous with **transaction** file; contrast with **master file**.

diagnostic routine. A routine designed to perform diagnostic functions; see also **dump, postmortem routine, snapshot** and **trace routine** (commonly-used types of diagnostic routines).

direct access. See **random access**.

documentation. Preparation of documents during programming that describe the program and document its preparation, its approval and any subsequent changes; usually assembled in a run manual.

double-punch blank-column check. A check performed on some card-processing equipment and on some older computer input/output units wired to detect a double punch (or an absence of punches) in a card column which should be numeric (that is, contain one punch).

dual read. The use of two separate reading stations to read the same record; results of the two operations are compared to detect reading errors.

dump. (1) To copy the contents of a set of storage locations, usually from an internal storage device (such as core storage) to an external storage medium (such as magnetic tape) and usually for diagnostic or rerun purposes; (2) Data that results from the process defined in (1); see also **postmortem routine, selective dump, snapshot**.

EAM (Electrical Accounting Machine). Pertaining to predominantly electromechanical data processing equipment, such as keypunches, collators, mechanical sorters and tabulators. Note: EAM equipment is still widely used in lieu of, or in support of, electronic digital computers; the computers themselves are classified "EDP equipment" rather than "EAM equipment."

EBCDIC (Extended Binary Coded Decimal Interchange Code). An 8-bit code that represents an extension of the 6-bit "BCD" code widely used in computers of the first and second generations. Note: EBCDIC can represent up to 256 distinct characters and is the principal code used in many current computers.

echo check. A check upon the accuracy of a data transfer operation in which data received (usually by an output device) is transmitted back to its source (usually a control unit) and compared with the original data; for example, an echo check on an output operation usually can verify that the proper print hammers or punch pins were actuated at the proper moments, though it cannot ensure that the proper marks were actually recorded on the output medium.

edit. To modify the form or format of data; may involve the rearrangement, addition (for example, insertion of dollar signs and decimal points) and deletion (for example, suppression of leading zeros) of data, code translation and the control of layouts for printing (for example, provision of headings and page numbers).

emulator. A device, usually used in conjunction with special routines, that enables a computer to execute, without prior translation, machine-language programs written for another computer of dissimilar design. Note: Emulation is an important technique for achieving program compatibility between certain current computers and earlier computers produced by the same or different manufacturers; an emulator usually contains, in a read-only storage unit, logic that interprets and simulates the functions of each instruction in the original computer's programs; functions such as input/output operations that cannot be handled conveniently by the stored logic are performed by special associated routines.

error correcting code. An error detecting code that uses additional code elements (additional bits, for example) such that if a certain type of error occurs the mutilated representation can be analyzed and corrected. Note: An erroneous correction may result if there occurs an error that the code has not been designed to correct.

error detecting code. A code in which each representation or a character conforms to specific rules of construction, so that if certain types of errors occur the mutilated representation will not conform to the rules of construction; thus, the presence of errors can be detected without reference to the original message. Note: Each of the most common types of error detecting codes appends a parity bit to each array of bits and utilizes a parity check. Synonymous with **self-checking code.**

executive routine. A routine designed to organize and regulate the flow of work in a computer system by initiating and controlling the execution of other programs; a principal component of most operating systems; synonymous with **supervisory routine** and "supervisor."

external label. An identifying label attached to the outside of a file media holder; for example, a paper sticker attached to the side of a reel containing a magnetic tape file.

field. (1) In a punched card, a group of columns whose punchings represent one item; (2) A subdivision of a computer word or instruction (for example, a group of bit positions within an instruction that hold an address); (3) A subdivision of a record; that is, an item.

file. A collection of related records, usually (but not necessarily) arranged in sequence according to a key contained in each record. Note: A record, in turn, is a collection of related items; an item is an arbitrary quantity of data that is treated as a unit; in payroll processing, an employee's pay rate forms an item, a set of all items relating to a particular employee forms a record and the complete set of employee records forms a file.

file label. A label identifying a file. Note: An internal label is recorded as the first or last record of a file and is machine-readable; an external label is attached to the outside of the file holder and is not machine-readable.

file maintenance. The updating of files to reflect the effects of non-periodic changes by adding, altering, or deleting data; for example, the addition of new programs to a program library on magnetic tape.

file processing. The periodic updating of master files to reflect the effects of current data, often transaction data contained in detail files; for example, a weekly payroll run updating the payroll master file.

file protection ring. A removable plastic or metal ring, the presence or absence (depending on the computer manufacturer) of which prevents an employee from writing on a magnetic tape and thereby prevents the accidental destruction of a magnetic tape file. Note: The most common method involves the insertion of the ring to allow writing and the removal of the ring to prevent writing.

fixed-length record. A record that always contains the same number of characters. Note: Restriction to a fixed length may be deliberate in order to simplify and speed processing, or it may be dictated by the characteristics of the equipment used; contrast with **variable-length record**.

flowchart. A diagram showing by means of symbols and interconnecting lines (1) the structure and general sequence of operations of a program (program flowchart) or (2) a system of processing (system flowchart).

FORTRAN (FORmula TRANslating system). A procedure-oriented language designed to facilitate the preparation of computer programs that perform mathematical computations. Note: Designed by IBM in the 1950's to use symbols and expressions similar to those of algebra, FORTRAN was not originally intended to be a common language; however, it has evolved through several basic versions (FORTRAN I, FORTRAN II, FORTRAN IV, etc.) and numerous dialects, has become largely machine-independent and has recently been approved as a USA Standard programming language in two versions (FORTRAN and Basic FORTRAN); FORTRAN is now by far the most widely used procedure-oriented language in the U.S. and is being employed effectively in certain business as well as scientific applications; the essential element of the FORTRAN language is the assignment statement, for example: "$Z = X + Y$ causes the current values of the variables X and Y to be added together and their sum to replace the previous value of the variable Z."

frame. A set of bit positions extending across a magnetic tape perpendicular to its edge and capable of encoding one character; synonymous with **row**.

generate. To use a generator to prepare a machine-language program from a set of specifications.

generator. A computer program designed to construct other specialized programs; for example, a report program generator or a generator of data transcription routines. Note: Basing its decisions upon parameters supplied to it, a generator usually selects from among various alternatives the method most suitable for performing a specified task; it then adjusts the details of the selected method to produce a program matched to the characteristics of the data to be handled.

hard copy. Documentation containing data printed by data processing equipment in a form suitable for permanent retention (printed reports, listings and logs). Note: Volatile output, by contrast, is data such as that displayed on the screen of a cathode ray tube.

header label. A machine-readable record at the beginning of a file containing data identifying the file and data used in file control.

housekeeping. Pertaining to operations in a program or computer system that do not contribute directly to the solution of users' problems, but that are necessary in order to maintain control of the processing.

hole count. An error control procedure used in many card readers and card punches; in a card reader, for example, the holes in each column or row are counted when the card is read at the first read station; a second count is made at a second read station; when the two counts are compared, any difference indicates a read error.

IDP (Integrated Data Processing). Data processing by a system that coordinates a number of previously unconnected processes in order to improve overall efficiency by reducing or eliminating redundant data entry or processing operations; for example, a system in which data describing orders, production and purchases is entered into a single processing scheme that combines the functions of scheduling, invoicing, inventory control, etc.

interblock gap. The distance on a magnetic tape between the end of one block and the beginning of the next. Note: Within this distance the tape can be stopped and brought up to normal speed again; since, therefore, the tape speed may be changing, no reading or writing is permitted in the gap. Synonymous with **interrecord gap** and **record gap**, though the use of these two terms is not recommended because of the important distinction between blocks and records.

interlock. A protective facility that prevents one device or operation from interfering with another; for example, the locking of a console typewriter's keys to prevent manual entry of data while the computer is transferring data to the typewriter.

interrecord gap. Same as **interblock gap.**

interrupt. A signal, condition, or event that causes an interruption; for example, the completion of an input or output operation, the detection of incorrect parity, or the attempt to execute an illegal instruction or to write in a protected location.

interruption. A temporary suspension of the execution of a sequence of instructions, resulting from the occurrence of a prescribed event or condition. Note: An interrupt usually triggers an unconditional transfer to a predetermined location, where a special routine (usually part of an operating system) determines the cause of the interruption, takes appropriate action and then returns control to the point where the program was interrupted (or, in some cases, to another program of higher priority); effective interruption facilities are a vital factor in computers that are to operate in multiprogramming or realtime mode.

I/O. Same as **input/output.**

IOCS (Input/Output Control System). A standard routine or set of routines designed to initiate and control the input and output processes of a computer system, thereby making it unnecessary for users to prepare detailed coding for these processes.

key. One or more characters associated with a particular item or record and used to identify that item or record, especially in sorting or collating operations. Note: A key may or may not be attached to the record or item it identifies. Contrast **label** and **tag.**

label. A name attached to or written beside the entity it identifies; for example, a key attached to an item or record, or a name written beside a statement on a coding sheet.

lateral parity check. Same as **row parity check**.

limit test. A programmed check for errors in input data or processing. Note: For this test, a data item is compared with a test amount larger (or smaller) than the data item should be if it is correct; if the checked item is larger (or smaller) than the test amount, an error is indicated.

library routine. A tested routine maintained in a program library (as opposed to a routine written especially for a particular job).

log. A record of the operations of data processing equipment; each job or run, the time it required, operator actions and other pertinent data are listed.

logic diagram. Same as **program flowchart**.

longitudinal parity check. A parity check performed on the bits in each track of magnetic tape or punched tape. Note: For this check, the parity bits generated for each of the tracks are recorded simultaneously, at the end of each block, in the form of a "longitudinal check character" which is regenerated and checked when the block is read. Synonymous with **track parity check**.

loop. A sequence of instructions that can be executed repetitively, usually with modified addresses or modified data values. Note: Each repetition is called a cycle; cycling continues until a specified criterion is satisfied (for example, until a counter reaches a predetermined value); the use of loops greatly facilitates the coding of any iterative process.

macro instruction. An instruction, written in a machine-oriented language, that has no equivalent operation in the computer and is replaced in the object program by a predetermined set of machine instructions. Note: Macro instruction facilities can ease the task of coding in a machine-oriented language by precluding the need for detailed coding of input and output operations, blocking, format control, error checks, etc.

manual input. (1) The entry of data into a device by manual means at the time of processing; (2) Data entered into a device by manual means at the time of processing; for example, data entered by means of a keyboard, or by setting switches, dials, or levers.

master file. A file containing relatively permanent information which is used as a source of reference and is generally updated periodically; contrast with **detail file.**

memory layout. A diagram showing the assignment of internal storage locations for various purposes (storage of input or output record, storage of constants, etc.)

merge. To form a single sequenced file by combining two or more similarly sequenced files. Note: Merging may be performed manually, by a collator, or by a computer system for which a merge routine is available; the repeated merging, splitting and remerging of strings of records can be employed to arrange them in sequence; this process, known as a merging sort, is frequently used as the basis for sorting operations on computer systems.

modulo N check. Same as **residue check.**

monitor routine. (1) A routine designed to indicate the progress of work in a computer system; (2) Formerly, same as **executive routine.**

multiprogramming. A technique for handling two or more independent programs simultaneously by overlapping or interleaving their execution. Note: This overlapping or interleaving is usually controlled by an executive routine that attempts to optimize the overall performance of the computer system in accordance with the priority requirements of the various jobs.

object language. A language that is the output from a translation process; contrast with **source language.**

object program. A program expressed in an object language; for example, a machine-language program that can be directly executed by a particular computer.

OCR (optical character recognition). The automatic machine-reading of graphic characters by the use of devices sensitive to light.

off-line (or **offline**). Pertaining to equipment or devices that are not in direct communication with the central processor of a computer system. Note: Off-line devices cannot be controlled by a computer except through human intervention. Contrast with **on-line**.

on-line (or **online**). Pertaining to equipment or devices that are in direct communication with the central processor of a computer system. Note: On-line devices are usually under the direct control of the computer with which they are in communication. Contrast with **off-line**.

operating system. An organized collection of routines and procedures for operating a computer. Note: These routines and procedures normally perform some or all of the following functions: (1) scheduling, loading, initiating and supervising the execution of programs, (2) allocating storage, input/output units and other facilities of the computer system, (3) initiating and controlling input/output operations, (4) handling errors and restarts, (5) coordinating communications between the human operator and the computer system, (6) maintaining a log of system operations and (7) controlling operations in a multiprogramming, multiprocessing, or time-sharing mode; among the facilities frequently included within an operating system are an executive routine, a scheduler, an IOCS, utility routines and monitor routines.

optical character recognition. See **OCR**.

parity bit. A bit (binary digit) appended to an array of bits to make the sum of all the "1" bits in the array either always even (even parity) or always odd (odd parity); for example:

	Even Parity			Odd Parity		
	0	1	1	0	1	1
	0	1	0	0	1	0
Data bits	0	1	0	0	1	0
	0	1	1	0	1	1
	0	1	1	0	1	1
	1	1	0	1	1	0
Parity bit	1	0	1	0	1	0

parity check. A check that tests whether the number of "1" bits in an array is either even (even parity check) or odd

(odd parity check); see also **row parity check** and **longitudinal parity check**.

pass. One complete cycle of input, processing and output in the execution of a computer program; for example, a one-pass compiler reads the source program, compiles it and writes the object program without intermediate input/output operations or human intervention.

patch. To correct or modify a program in a rough or expedient way by adding new sections of coding.

peripheral equipment. The input/output units and auxiliary storage units of a computer system. Note: The central processor and its associated storage and control units are the only parts of a computer system which are not considered peripheral equipment.

postmortem routine. A diagnostic routine, often a dump, that is used after a program has failed to operate as intended.

preventive maintenance. Maintenance carried out to keep equipment in proper operating condition and to prevent faults from occurring during subsequent operations.

program compatibility. A characteristic enabling one computer system to execute programs written for another computer system and to obtain identical results. Note: Program compatibility can be achieved between two computer systems with similar instruction repertoires and facilities, or, by the use of emulators, simulators, translators, or coding in a common language, between dissimilar computers.

programmed check. A check that is carried out by a series of instructions in a program.

programmer. A person who devises programs. Note: The term "programmer" is most suitably applied to a person who is mainly involved in formulating programs, particularly at the level of flowchart preparation; a person mainly involved in the definition of problems is called an analyst, while a person mainly involved in converting programs into coding suitable for entry into a computer system is called a coder; in many organizations, all three of these functions are performed by programmers.

program flowchart. A flowchart diagramming the processing steps and logic of a computer program; contrast with **system flowchart**.

programming language. An unambiguous language used to express programs for a computer.

random access. Pertaining to a storage device whose access time is not significantly affected by the location of the data to be accessed. Note: Any item of data stored online can be accessed within a relatively short time (usually less than one second); same as **direct access**; contrast with **serial access**.

real-time (or **realtime**). (1) Pertaining to the time during which a physical process actually takes place; (2) Pertaining to a mode of operation in which the moments of occurrence of certain events in a system must satisfy restrictions determined by the moments of occurrence of events in some other independent system; for example, realtime operation is essential in computers associated with process control systems, message switching systems and reservation systems.

record. A collection of related items of data. Note: In payroll processing, for example, an employee's pay rate forms an item, a set of all the items relating to a particular employee forms a record and a complete set of employee records forms a file; see also **fixed-length record** and **variable-length record**.

record count. A count of the number of records in a file or the number of records processed by a program. Note: Such a count is used in error control to detect the non-processing of records.

record gap. Same as **interblock gap**.

record layout. A diagram showing the size, position and composition of data items making up a record. Note: Such a diagram is prepared during the preparation of a program.

record mark. A special character used in some computers either to limit the number of characters in a data transfer operation or to separate blocked records on tape.

redundancy check. A check based on the transfer of more bits or characters than the minimum number required to express the message itself, the added bits or characters having been inserted systematically for checking purposes. Note: The most common type of redundancy check is a parity check.

report file. A file containing records which constitute a report of the transactions and/or results of a data processing job.

report program generator (RPG). A generator designed to construct programs that perform routine report-writing functions, such as programs that accept input data from punched cards or magnetic tape and produce printed reports, often with headings and subtotals.

rerun. To make another attempt to complete a job by executing all or part of the process again with the same or corrected inputs.

rerun point. A point in a program where its execution can be re-established after an equipment failure or some other interruption. Note: Sufficient data is recorded at a rerun point to permit a restart from that point in the event of a subsequent interruption; thus, the provision of rerun points at reasonable intervals can save computer time by making it unnecessary to rerun a program from the beginning whenever a run is interrupted.

residue check. A check of numeric data or arithmetic operations in which each number, A, is divided by the modulus, N, and the remainder, B, accompanies A as a check digit or digits; for example, in a modulo 4 check, B will be either 0, 1, 2, or 3; if the remainder formed when A is divided by 4 does not equal B, an error is indicated. Note: The well-known arithmetic method of "casting out nines" is a modulo 9 check. Synonymous with **modulo N check**; see also **check digit**.

restart. To re-establish the execution of a program whose execution has been interrupted by using data recorded at a rerun point.

routine. A set of instructions arranged in correct sequence that causes a computer to perform a particular process. Note: In this context, the term "routine" is somewhat more precise than the more general (and more commonly used) term "program."

row parity check. A parity check performed on the bits in each row of a magnetic tape or punched tape; synonymous with **lateral parity check**.

run. The performance of a specific computer process using a given set of data; that is, the execution of one routine or of several routines which are linked to form one operating unit.

run manual. A manual documenting the processing system, program logic, controls, program changes and operating instructions associated with a computer run.

secondary storage. Synonymous with **auxiliary storage**.

selective dump. A dump of the contents of a set of storage locations specified by the user; for example, of the storage locations occupied by a particular program and/or its data.

self-checking code. Same as **error detecting code**.

self-checking number. A numeral that contains redundant information (such as an appended check digit) permitting it to be checked for accuracy after it has been transferred from one medium or device to another (for example, by means of a residue check); see **check digit**.

sense switch. A hardware switch on some types of computers which can be set by an operator and whose position can be sensed by a program instruction. Note: Such a switch can be used for programs which have alternate processing paths that are selected by the operator through the switch setting.

sentinel. A character or symbol that signals a particular condition, such as the end of a file.

sequential processing. Same as **batch processing**.

serial access. Pertaining to a storage device in which there is a sequential relationship between the access times to successive locations, as in the case of magnetic tape; contrast with **random access**.

snapshot. A dynamic dump of the contents of specified storage locations and/or registers that is performed at specified points or times during the running of a program.

software. A collection of programs and routines associated with a computer (including assemblers, compilers, utility routines and operating systems) that facilitates the programming and operation of the computer; contrast with **hardware**.

sort. To arrange items in sequence or to segregate items into groups according to a criterion of their keys or to definite rules. Note: Often the keys are groups of numbers or letters, such as account numbers or employee names, and the sorting operation involves arranging the items so that the keys of successive items are in numerical or alphabetical sequence; sorting is one of the most common data processing operations; it may be performed manually by a punched card sorter, or by a computer system for which a sort routine is available.

source document. A document from which data is extracted; for example, a document that contains typed or handwritten data to be keypunched.

source language. A language that is an input to a translation process; contrast with **object language**.

source program. A program written in a source language (for example, a program written in COBOL, FORTRAN, or symbolic coding for input to a compiler or assembler).

stacker. A part of a machine where punched cards or other documents are deposited after passing through the machine; also known as "pockets".

storage dump. Same as **dump**.

storage protection. Protection against unauthorized writing in and/or reading from all or part of a storage device. Note: This protection may be implemented by the use of manually set switches or automatic hardware facilities, usually in connection with an operating system; effective storage protection is a vital factor in multiprogramming and time-sharing systems both for ensuring privacy and for preventing concurrently operating programs from interfering with one another.

subroutine. A routine that can be used by a second routine in order to perform processing required by the latter. Note: A great deal of coding effort can be saved through the judicious use of subroutines to handle tasks encountered repetitively, such as the control of input/output operations, the evaluation of mathematical functions and the checking and recovering of errors.

summation check. A check in which the sum of a group of digits is formed (usually without regard to overflow) and compared to a previously computed value called the "check sum."

supervisory routine. Same as **executive routine**.

symbolic address. An address that is expressed in symbols convenient for the programmer but that must be translated, usually by an assembler, into absolute symbols before it can be interpreted by a computer; the storage location holding an employee's gross pay, for example, may be assigned the symbolic address GPAY.

symbolic coding. Coding that uses machine instructions with symbolic addresses. Note: The input to most assemblers is expressed in symbolic coding; mnemonic operation codes are usually employed in addition to symbolic addresses to further simplify the coding process; a two-address instruction that subtracts an employee's taxes from his gross pay, for example, might be written SUB TAX GPAY. Contrast with **absolute coding**.

synchronization check. A check that determines whether a particular event or condition occurs at the correct moment; for instance, whether the print hammers in a drum printer are activated at the moments when the appropriate character slugs on the drum are in correct position.

system. A set (or arrangement) of entities that forms (or is considered) an organized whole. Note: This term is very general and is applied to both hardware and software entities; therefore, it is meaningful only when carefully qualified, as, for example, in the following: computer system, management information system, number system, operating system, etc.

system analysis. The examination of an activity, procedure, method, technique, or business to determine what changes should be made and how they should be accomplished.

system configuration. (1) A specific set of equipment units interconnected and programmed to operate as a system; (2) The rules, concerning the interconnection of available equipment units, that collectively define the range of possible configurations in a particular computer system.

system flowchart. A flowchart diagramming the flow of work, documents and operations in a data processing application.

tag. One or more characters attached to a particular item or record and used to identify that item or record. Note: The tag may be removed from the item or record by a simple operation, but it then loses its significance. Contrast with **key**.

telecommunications. The transmission of signals over a long distance—by radio or telegraph, for example.

test routine. A routine designed to test whether or not a computer is operating correctly.

throughput. The total amount of useful work performed by a data processing system during a given period of time.

time-sharing. (1) The use of a given device by a number of other devices, programs, or human users one at a time and in rapid succession; (2) A technique or system for furnishing computing services to multiple users simultaneously, providing rapid responses to each. Note: Time-sharing computer systems usually employ multiprogramming and/or multiprocessing techniques and are often capable of serving users at remote locations via data communications networks.

trace routine. A diagnostic routine designed to check or demonstrate the operation of a program. Note: The output of such a routine usually includes some or all of the instructions (and their immediate results) in the program being checked, arranged in the sequence in which they are executed.

track. The part of a data storage medium that influences or is influenced by one head; for example, the ring-shaped portion of the surface of a drum associated with one nonmovable head, or one of several (most commonly 7 or 9) divisions running parallel to the edges of a magnetic tape.

track parity check. Same as **longitudinal parity check**.

trailer record. A record that follows another record or group of records and contains data pertinent to that record or group of records.

transaction code. One or more characters that form part of a record and signify the type of transaction represented by that record; in inventory control, for example, a transaction code may signify deliveries to stock, disbursements from stock, orders, etc.

transaction file. Same as **detail file**.

translator. A device or computer program that performs translations from one language or code to another; for example, an assembler or compiler.

322

trap. An unprogrammed jump to a particular location, activated automatically upon the occurrence of a particular condition; for example, upon an attempt to execute an instruction that is not in the computer's instruction repertoire. Note: The point where the jump occurs is recorded, so that normal execution of the program can be resumed after the faulty condition has been corrected.

troubleshoot. Same as **debug**.

unit record. (1) A record similar in form and content to other records but physically separate; for example, a record on a punched card; (2) pertaining to equipment or techniques for dealing with unit records as described in (1), especially to punched card equipment.

utility routine. A standard routine that assists in the operation of a computer by performing a frequently required process such as sorting, merging, report program generation, data transcription, file maintenance, etc. Note: Utility routines are important components of the software supplied by the manufacturers of most computers.

validity check. A hardware check that determines whether or not a particular character is a legitimate member of the permissible character set.

variable-length record. A record that may contain a variable number of characters; contrast with **fixed-length record**.

verifier. A machine used to verify the accuracy of a data transcription operation. Note: The most commonly used type of verifier checks the accuracy of keypunch operations by manually rekeying data and comparing the results with the keypunched data.

verify. To determine whether or not a data transcription or data transfer operation is accomplished accurately.

word. A group of bits or characters treated as a unit and capable of being stored in one storage location.

working storage. A storage section set aside by a programmer for use in the development of processing results, for storing constants, for temporarily storing results needed later in the program sequence, and so on.

QUESTIONNAIRE FOR EVALUATION OF INTERNAL CONTROL IN ELECTRONIC DATA PROCESSING

THIS APPENDIX CONTAINS a model questionnaire for obtaining information on internal control in an electronic data processing installation.

The questionnaire is divided into two major parts:

1. Questions relating to the operation of the electronic data processing installation

2. Questions relating to an individual data processing application.

This division reflects the fact that the organization, the policies and the procedures of the installation provide an environment in which individual applications are run. This environment must be understood before the controls associated with individual applications can be evaluated.

The review of a computer processing application should be carried out in the context of the entire processing cycle, including both computer and non-computer processing and controls. The firm's internal review questionnaire (or other method used to obtain information) should cover the non-computer procedures and controls; the application questionnaire is structured to provide only the added questions related to computer processing.

The number of questions to be included in a review questionnaire depends somewhat on how broadly the auditor views his audit assignment—whether he looks at items affecting operational efficiency as well as items directly affecting the audit. The control significance of the response to a particular question often, however, depends on the characteristics of the system being evaluated and the total picture of internal control. Each question in the model is coded A, B or C according to its general control significance. This code is only an indicator to aid the auditor; he must evaluate the significance in each particular case.

CODE	IN GENERAL, QUESTION RELATES TO:
A	Control element which may affect the auditor's evaluation of internal control
B	Control element which tends to affect data processing safeguards but is, however, not likely to affect audit procedures
C	Element affecting operational effectiveness or efficiency

The questions are arranged here so that reference can be made to the appropriate chapter in this book if background information is desired. For this reason there are no detailed explanations accompanying the questions.

All yes-or-no questions are worded so that "yes" is a favorable response and "no" indicates that further investigation or evaluation is required. The auditor may also wish to expand and clarify his answers by adding comments.

PART I: QUESTIONNAIRE FOR OPERATION OF THE ELECTRONIC DATA PROCESSING INSTALLATION

1. *Background*

    1–1. Where is the computer located? _____

    1–2. Give a brief description of equipment _____
_____

        (a) Manufacturer and model number of computer (this can be obtained from a copy of the manufacturer's invoice) _____

        (b) Internal memory size _____

(c) File storage devices
     Magnetic tape (no. units _____) ☐
     Disk (no. drives _____) ☐
     Other (describe) ☐

_____

_____

_____

(d) Input/output devices
     Card reader ☐
     Card punch ☐
     Printer ☐
     Other (list) ☐

_____

_____

_____

1–3. Applications

     Cash ☐
     Receivables ☐
     Inventory ☐
     Property, plant and equipment ☐
     Payables ☐
     Sales ☐
     Payroll ☐
     Cost and expenses ☐
     Other (list major ones below) ☐

_____

_____

_____

2. *Organization (Chapter 2)*

2–1. Prepare or obtain an organization chart of the EDP organization. Determine position titles, job descriptions and names of persons in these positions.

2–2. Is there a segregation of duties such that:

(a) The functions and duties of system

design and programming are separate from computer operation? ☐ ☐ A

(b) Programmers do not operate the computer for regular processing runs? ☐ ☐ A

(c) Computer operators are restricted from access to data and program information not necessary for performing their assigned task? ☐ ☐ B

(d) The employees in data processing are separated from all duties relating to the initiation of transactions and initiation of requests for changes to the master files? ☐ ☐ A

2–3. Are the operators assigned to individual application runs rotated periodically? ☐ ☐ A

2–4. Are the computer operators required to take vacations? ☐ ☐ B

2–5. Is supervision of operators sufficient to verify operator's adherence to prescribed operating procedures? ☐ ☐ B

3. *The Control Function (Chapter 2)*

3–1. Is there a person or group charged with responsibility for the control function in the data processing department? Obtain description of duties. These duties will normally include:

(a) Control over receipt of input data and recording of control information? ☐ ☐

(b) Reconciliation of control information (batch control with computer control totals, run-to-run controls, etc.)? ☐ ☐

(c) Control over distribution of output? ☐ ☐

(d) Control over errors to ensure that they are reported, corrected and reprocessed? □ □

(e) Review of console logs, error listings and other evidence of error detection and control? □ □

3–2. Is the person or group responsible for control over processing by the data processing department independent from the person or group responsible for the operation of the equipment? □ □ A

3–3. If there is an internal auditing group, does it perform EDP control activities related to:

(a) Review or audit? □ □ A

(b) Day-to-day control activities? □ □ A

If "yes" note the nature and extent of these activities.

3–4. Are master file changes or changes in program data factors authorized in writing by initiating departments? □ □ A

3–5. Are departments that initiate changes in master file data or program data factors furnished with notices or a register showing changes actually made? (Examples of such changes are changes in pay rates, selling prices, credit limits and commission tables.) □ □ A

4. *Control Over the Console (Chapter 2)*

4–1. Are provisions adequate to prevent unauthorized entry of program changes and/or data through the console? The following questions reflect the types of controls which may be used.

(a) Are adequate machine operation logs being maintained? For each run, these should include information covering the run identification, operator, start and stop time, error halts and delays, and details of reruns. Idle time, down time, program testing, etc., should also be logged.

☐ ☐ B

(b) Is there an independent examination of computer logs to check the operator performance and machine efficiency? If "yes,"

☐ ☐ B

    (1) How often _____
    (2) By whom _____
    (3) How carried out _____
    _____
    _____
    _____

(c) If the computer has a typewriter console, is there an independent examination of the console printouts to detect operator problems and unauthorized intervention?

☐ ☐ B

    (1) How often _____
    (2) By whom _____
    (3) How performed _____
    _____
    _____
    _____

5. *Management Practices (Chapter 2)*

5–1. Is there a written plan for future changes to be made to the system?

☐ ☐ C

5–2. Is approval for each application supported by a study of cost and benefit?

☐ ☐ C

5–3. Is a schedule of implementation prepared showing actual versus planned progress?

☐ ☐ C

Yes No

5–4. Is there a systems and procedures manual for the activities of the installation? ☐ ☐ C

6. *Documentation (Chapter 3)*

6–1. Is a run manual prepared for each computer run? ☐ ☐ C

6–2. Are operator instructions prepared for each run? ☐ ☐ C

6–3. Are documentation practices adequate? ☐ ☐ C
Does the normal documentation for an application include the following?

	Yes	No
Problem statement	☐	☐
System flowchart	☐	☐
Record layouts	☐	☐
Program flowcharts	☐	☐
Program listing	☐	☐
Test data	☐	☐
Operator instructions	☐	☐
Summary of controls	☐	☐
Approval and change record	☐	☐

6–4. Is there supervisory review of documentation to ensure that it is adequate? ☐ ☐ B

6–5. Is documentation kept up to date? ☐ ☐ C

7. *Program Revisions (Chapters 3 & 7)*

7–1. Is each program revision authorized by a request for change properly approved by management or supervisory personnel? ☐ ☐ B
(a) Who authorizes? _____
(b) How evidenced? _____

7–2. Are program changes, together with their effective dates, documented in a manner which preserves an accurate chronological record of the system? ☐ ☐ C

7–3. Are program revisions tested in the same manner as new programs? ☐ ☐ B

8. *Hardware Controls (Chapter 4)*

Unless there is evidence of hardware-based processing difficulties, the auditor can usually rely on the hardware. No review is ordinarily required for audit purposes.

9. *Control Over Input and Output Data (Chapter 5)*

Although the control over input and output data must be exercised for each application, general questions regarding these controls may be used to ascertain policy regarding the use of control procedures.

9–1. Are initiating departments required to establish independent control over data submitted for processing (through the use of batch totals, document counts, or otherwise)? ☐ ☐ A

9–2. Is a schedule maintained of the reports and documents to be produced by the EDP system? ☐ ☐ B

9–3. Are output reports and documents reviewed before distribution to ascertain the reasonableness of the output? ☐ ☐ A

9–4. Are there adequate procedures for control over the distribution of reports? ☐ ☐ B

10. *Programmed Control Over Processing (Chapter 6)*

Programmed controls must be evaluated in terms of each application.

11. *Controlling Error Investigations (Chapter 5)*

11–1. Are all error corrections reviewed and approved by persons who are independent of the data processing department? ☐ ☐ A

		Yes	No	
11–2.	Are records maintained of errors occurring in the EDP system?	☐	☐	C
11–3.	Are these error records periodically reviewed by someone independent of data processing?	☐	☐	C

12. *Physical Safeguards Over Files (Chapter 7)*

		Yes	No	
12–1.	Are important computer programs, essential documentation, records and files kept in fire-proof storage?	☐	☐	C
12–2.	Are copies of important programs, essential documentation, records and files stored in off-premises locations?	☐	☐	C

13. *Procedural Controls for Safeguarding Files (Chapter 7)*

		Yes	No	
13–1.	Are external labels used on all files?	☐	☐	B
13–2.	Are internal labels used on all magnetic tape files?	☐	☐	B
13–3.	Are file header labels checked by programs using the files?	☐	☐	B
13–4.	Are file protection rings used on all magnetic tape files to be preserved?	☐	☐	B
13–5.	Is the responsibility for issuing and storing magnetic tape or portable disk packs assigned to a tape librarian, either as a full-time or part-time duty?	☐	☐	C

14. *Capability for File Reconstruction (Chapter 7)*

		Yes	No	
14–1.	Are there provisions for the use of alternative facilities in the event of fire or other lengthy interruption?	☐	☐	C
14–2.	Is there adequate data processing insurance (other than fire coverage)?	☐	☐	B
14–3.	Are data processing personnel covered by fidelity insurance?	☐	☐	B

Part II. Questionnaire for Individual Applications

The questions in this section are expected to supplement an internal review questionnaire or any other information-obtaining method. They should enable the auditor to obtain information on whether or not various control techniques have been used in the computer processing phase of a particular application.

The questionnaire is organized around the following control points:

1. Adequacy of control over input data

      (a) Verification of correctness of input data
      (b) Control over transmittal of data for processing
      (c) Validity tests and other tests of input data

2. Adequacy of control over processing

      (a) Control for completeness of processing
      (b) Checks for correctness of processing
      (c) Handling of rejects
      (d) Management trail or audit trail

3. Adequacy of control over programs and data files

      (a) Documentation
      (b) Control over changes to master files
      (c) Back-up procedures

The questions are numbered from 101 to distinguish them from questions in the general questionnaire. In cases where a control can be implemented by two or more methods, the related question is followed by a check-list of common control procedures. For each application (or run) related to the audit, the auditor should obtain information sufficient for answering all the relevant questions.

A data processing control review sheet may be used as a means of describing the input, processing and output controls for a particular application (see Figure E-1, page 335). It may be used in place of or in addition to questions 101 and 102. The use of the control review sheet is illustrated in Chapter 10 (see Figure 10-3, page 143).

101. *Control Over Input and Output for an Application (Chapter 5)*

      101–1. Are there adequate controls over the

DATA PROCESSING CONTROL REVIEW SHEET

Prepared by_____ Date____

Reviewed by_____ Date____

APPLICATION _____

RUN NO. AND RUN NAME	DESCRIPTION OF CONTROL FIELD OR CONTROL ITEM	TYPE OF CONTROL	CONTROLS ESTABLISHED BY				CONTROLS VERIFIED BY			
			DEPARTMENT SENDING DATA	DATA PROCESSING DEPARTMENT CONTROL SECTION	COMPUTER PROGRAM	PRECEDING RUN (RUN-TO-RUN)	COMPUTER PROGRAM		DATA PROCESSING DEPARTMENT CONTROL SECTION	USER OR OTHER OUTSIDE DEPARTMENT
							CONTROL INFORMATION OUTPUT	EXCEPTION OUTPUT ONLY		

FIGURE E-1.   Sample questionnaire for processing control review

creation of data and its conversion
to machine-readable form? ☐ ☐ A

   (a) Procedural controls ☐
   (b) Mechanical or visual
      verification ☐
   (c) Check digit ☐

101–2. Is there adequate control over transmittal and input of data to detect
loss or nonprocessing? Note data
field controlled. ☐ ☐ A

Field

   (a) Financial control totals ———
   (b) Hash control totals ————
   (c) Document counts ———
   (d) Sequential numbering of
      input documents ———
   (e) Other ———

101–3. Are the input control totals and run-
to-run control totals for each application checked by someone other than
the equipment operator? ☐ ☐ A
By whom? ———

101–4. If data transmission is used, are controls adequate to determine that
transmission is correct and no messages are lost? ☐ ☐ B

   (a) Message counts ☐
   (b) Character counts ☐
   (c) Dual transmission ☐
   (d) Other ———.

101–5. Is input data adequately tested for
validity, correctness and sequence? ☐ ☐ B

Note: Questions may have to be
applied to each important data field
of the input being reviewed by the
auditor.

Fields Tested

(a) Validity tests:
    (1) Valid code ——————
    (2) Valid character ————
    (3) Valid field ——————
    (4) Valid transaction ———
    (5) Valid combinations ——
    (6) Missing data —————

(b) Sequence ————————

(c) Limit ——————————

(d) Reasonableness —————

(e) Other ——————————

                             Yes No

101–6. Is control over distribution of output adequate? Describe.   ☐ ☐ B

101–7. Describe the control function, if any, for evaluating quality of output.

102. *Programmed Control Over Processing (Chapter 6)*

102–1. Are control totals used to check for completeness of processing? These may include trailer file labels, run-to-run totals, etc.   ☐ ☐ B

102–2. Are programmed controls used to test processing of significant items?   ☐ ☐ B

                          Item applied to

(a) Limit and reasonableness test ——————————

(b) Crossfooting test —————

102–3. Does the program check for improper switch settings (if sense switches are used?)   ☐ ☐ C

103. *Control Over Handling of Errors*

103–1. Does the program provide an adequate console printout of control information (switch settings, control violations, operator intervention, etc.)? □ □ B

103–2. When a program is interrupted, are there adequate provisions for re-start? □ □ C

103–3. Are there adequate controls over the process of identifying, correcting and reprocessing data rejected by the program? □ □ B

103–4. Inquire into handling of unmatched transactions (no master record corresponding to transaction record). Is it adequate? □ □ A

    (a) Reject and note on error log □

    (b) Reject and write on suspense record □

    (c) Other _____

104. *Control Over Program and Data Files (Chapters 3 & 7)*

104–1. Is there adequate up-to-date documentation for the application (Chapter 3)? □ □ C

Yes No

    (a) Application summary □ □
    (b) Run manuals □ □
    (c) Operator instructions □ □

104–2. Is test data documented and kept up to date (Chapter 3)? □ □ C

104–3. Are controls over master file changes adequate (Chapter 3)? □ □ B

Yes No

    (a) Written request for change from outside data processing □ □

Yes No

(b) Register of all changes
reviewed by initiating
department   ☐ ☐

(c) Supervisory or other
review of changes   ☐ ☐

Yes No

104–4. Are there adequate provisions for periodically checking master file contents (Chapter 7)? ☐ ☐ B

Yes No

(a) Periodic printout and
review   ☐ ☐

(b) Periodic test against
physical count   ☐ ☐

(c) Other _____

104–5. Are the back-up and reconstruction provisions adequate (Chapter 7)? ☐ ☐ B
Describe _____

105. *Management or Audit Trail (Chapter 9)*

105–1. Do the records or references provide the means to adequately:

(a) Trace any transaction forward to a final total? ☐ ☐ A

(b) Trace any transaction back to the original source document or input? ☐ ☐ A

(c) Trace any final total back to the component transactions? ☐ ☐ A

105–2. When ledgers (general or subsidiary) are maintained on computer media, does the system of processing provide:

(a) An historical record of activity in the accounts? ☐ ☐ B

(b) A periodic trial balance of the accounts? ☐ ☐ B

105–3. Are source documents retained for an adequate period of time in a manner which allows identification with related output records and documents? ☐ ☐ C

INDEX

344

Printed by Lenz & Riecker, Inc.